PLAIN BUT WHOLESOME

Plain but Wholesome

FOODWAYS OF THE MORMON PIONEERS

Brock Cheney

The University of Utah Press | Salt Lake City

The Defiance House Man colophon is a registered trademark of
the University of Utah Press. It is based on a four-foot-tall Ancient
Puebloan pictograph (late PIII) near Glen Canyon, Utah.

16   15   14   13   12   1   2   3   4   5

Library of Congress Cataloging-in-Publication Data

Cheney, Brock, 1970–
Plain but wholesome : foodways of the Mormon pioneers/Brock Cheney.
        pages   cm
Includes bibliographical references and index.
ISBN 978-1-60781-208-1 (pbk. : alk. paper)
1. Mormon cooking.
2. Cooking, American.
3. Cooking—Utah.
I. Title.
TX715.C5215 2012
641.5′66—dc23   2012021495

Unless otherwise noted, images used by permission,
Utah State Historical Society, all rights reserved.

Printed and bound by Sheridan Books, Inc., Ann Arbor, Michigan.

for my girls

SHANNON

EMMA

SARAH

KATE

MARYANNE

JANE

and

RACHEL

CONTENTS

PREFACE

In the summer of 2003 I visited a living history museum near my home in Utah and watched a demonstration of pioneer foodways. After the museum docent wrapped up her spiel I asked about the historical research behind her activities. She replied that although her demonstration was generally accurate for American technology of the mid-nineteenth century, no research on Utah's unique culture and environment in the Mormon settlement era was available. Given that the pioneer ethos holds strong emotional sway for most modern Mormons, I was quite surprised.

I took up the challenge. In my earliest conceptions of this book I imagined a source book for museum docents and historical reenactors. The book would be composed primarily of historical recipes documented for the pioneer era (before 1870), with the clear sense that readers would try this at home, on the trail, or in a museum setting. Given the profound place of pioneers in Mormon culture, I imagined that I would find plenty of established research that only needed to be raked into a pile. But as my little project progressed I learned that this was virgin ground and that I would need to lay a considerable foundation to provide a context for the work.

The framework for this study combines history and folklore methods in an effort to come to terms with what might have been the physical reality of food for early Utah Mormon pioneers as well as the meaning that these foodways hold for modern generations. By necessity I saw fit to place some arbitrary boundaries on the study. The Nauvoo period is interesting, as are the foodways that come with the transcontinental railroad. Still, some limits are necessary, although they are broken from time to time. I chose to focus primarily on the time frame of 1846 to 1869. This encompasses the earliest trail experiences as Mormons made the exodus from Nauvoo, Illinois, to Winter Quarters. The trail experience has profound cultural meaning for Mormons in the West. The end date coincides with the arrival of the transcontinental railroad in Utah. This event ended the trail experience and also brought a vast array of new products and ingredients to Utah cooks and consumers. As with all arbitrary boundaries, I fudge the edges a bit; conditions in the southern settlements saw very little change as a result of the railroad in northern Utah.

I also chose to limit the scope of this study to Mormons in Utah within this time frame. Though Mormons established outposts around the globe in the nineteenth century, Utah Territory served as the Petri dish for Mormon culture. Non-Mormons also found a place in territorial Utah, and their foodways likewise deserve study. Their foodways echo those of their Mormon neighbors in many regards. Non-Mormon cooks in Colorado, Nevada, Idaho, and Montana used food items grown by and purchased from Mormon farmers but didn't participate in those elements of Mormon culture that dictated how foods were prepared or eaten.[1] Many Mormon settlers no doubt shared some recipes with their non-Mormon friends and neighbors. The perspective of both pious and irreverent Mormons lends considerable distinction to Mormon foodways, however, due to factors such as geographic and cultural isolation and multicultural interface with diverse European and Native American cultures. I leave the study of non-Mormon foodways to other scholars.

Historical approaches demand integrity of provenance for the original source. Ideally, I hoped to examine only recipe formulas that could be directly tied to a particular person, with a dated diary entry or newspaper article. Though food is all around us no matter where we look, however, it seems that we rarely write it down. The food elements of pioneer Utah are hard to find. A "recipe book" was an uncommon article in Brigham Young's Deseret, as most home cooks learned their craft by rote memorization. Many creations were more a matter of process than of formula or inspiration. Just as the modern Mormon wife uses no formulaic recipe to make her Sunday pot roast, neither did her historical equivalent need a recipe to make the morning cornmeal porridge.[2] As a result, we are left without many explicit recipes tied to pioneer-era Utah. Instead we often have terse diary entries that identify particular meals and dishes.

Contrariwise, I found a rich tradition of folk foodways passed orally from one generation to the next. Many families have a singular dish that defines their heritage and identity. These dishes are not prepared casually for incidental calorie consumption. They have evolved into ceremonial observances wherein deviation is not tolerated: to do so would shatter the veneration of ancestry.

In my family, cracked wheat mush falls in this category. Dating back to Swiss immigrants in the 1860s, the preparation calls for sifting the cereal through open fingers while stirring briskly to prevent lumping. The cereal is cooked thoroughly until it becomes rather stiff. It is served on a plate—not in a bowl—so it must be stiff enough to "stand alone," as Grandpa Stauffer used to say. These days the mush is served with cream and white sugar, though some say that brown sugar is also acceptable. Honey and maple syrup are never used. This tradition is "Stauffer Mush," named for Ulrich Stauffer. One story, which accords with his Swiss cultural heritage, says that he was meticulous and fussy about getting the perfect grind for the semicoarse meal required. Another story says that the semicoarse meal was the result of an accident by the miller, but Ulrich took the meal anyway and found that it made good mush. Ulrich did not write his formula down. It has distilled over five generations. In the Stauffer family, cooked wheat cereal has become a sacrament of heritage.[3] You probably have similar traditions in your own family.

Such traditions passed down orally carry on the same cookery patterns that emigrant settlers brought to Utah a century and a half ago. The food traditions of Scandinavia, Germany, Britain, and Appalachia were not carried to Utah in recipe books but were learned by rote from observation of older generations. Similarly, these cooks rarely set the recipe to paper, continuing to pass the formulas orally to the next generation. This folkloristic inheritance is the pride of many families but the bane of academic historians. As a folklorist and a historian, I often found myself alternately frustrated and overjoyed by the nature of the material I found.

We are not left entirely without written reference to the formulas, however. As Anglo settlers moved west, enterprising authors capitalized on a new boom in "emigrant literature." A highly literate Anglo populace demanded information with which to confront the challenges of the new frontier. William Clayton's *The Latter-Day Saints' Emigrants' Guide* is just one such publication in the genre. Other authors wrote cookbooks uniquely designed for the rough and rugged conditions expected by homesteaders. Angelina Maria Collins's *The Great Western Cookbook, or Table Receipts, Adapted to Western Housewifery* is a good example. Collins, hailing from the same New England tradition of sensibility that produced Brigham Young, provides many of the basic formulas for food items identified in Mormon diaries from Utah.

Though individual cooks rarely worked from written recipes, such material did exist in Utah. The Territorial Library catalogue for 1853 notes titles such as *Miss Leslie's Complete Cookery* (37th edition, about ten years old at the time), *Mrs. Beecher's Domestic Economy*, and *Mrs. Putnam's Receipt Book*.[4] Further, family histories cite other published works as having played a role in domestic cookery. Specifically, Esther Copley's *The Cook's Complete Guide* (1825) as well as *The Modern Cookbook* are said to have been in the territory during the settlement era.[5] These books reflect the popular food trends of the day, finding national audiences as well as Utah readers. Many Mormon pioneer recipes originated from such sources and found new expression when influenced by cultural and regional conditions. Such books also illustrate technology and cultural perceptions about food and food science endemic to the era. By combining information from a variety of primary sources we can shed new light on the daily activities of early Mormon settlers and pioneers.

Several years ago historian and folklorist William Montell faced a similar challenge in documenting the history of Coe Ridge, a black community in Tennessee that originated from the slave population of a former plantation. Many of the members of this community were illiterate, so the traditional tools of the historian (diaries, memoirs, and written/published family histories) were unavailable. Yet Montell wanted to give voice to the original members of the community rather than telling their story from an outsider's perspective. By using the still-circulating oral narratives and ballads of the community, he was able to create a cohesive narrative that extended back four generations. Cringing historians might be reassured to learn that the particular historical details of the oral narratives and ballads were reaffirmed by more traditional sources such as newspaper clippings, court records, and mentions in the published histories of neighboring white communities. Montell's study of Coe Ridge confirmed that oral folk traditions can have historical integrity.[6]

Here I use a similar approach. The diet of the Mormon pioneers and settlers fits a generalized pattern consisting primarily of flour and potatoes, supplemented with fruits and vegetables and garnished with small amounts of meat. Some modern Mormons might find shadows of religious observance in this diet.[7] British and Scandinavian emigrants assimilated many elements of American cookery, while still maintaining more symbolic dishes to preserve values for their heritage and ethnicity. Breads, cakes, puddings, and soups exhibit the greatest variations on particular themes, while meat, fruits, and vegetables involve less elaborate preparations. Within this framework, we find our context.

Not every claim to being a "seventh-generation recipe" can be accepted on the face of things. Some recipes show anachronistic ingredients, processes, or technology. Ingredients such as margarine, exotic spices, and modern brand-name food products indicate a recipe that has gone through "adaptation for the modern kitchen." Other modernized recipes are betrayed through comparison to cookery processes of the earlier era. The exact measurement of ingredients, for example, did not become commonplace until the last decade of the nineteenth century.[8] Most recipes calling for teaspoons, tablespoons, and cups are creations of later editing, as third- and fourth-generation descendants transcribed recipes that earlier generations had learned by rote.[9] For this reason I have endeavored to present food and food history with concrete ties to the pioneer era. When a recipe or source has a strong provenance in spite of modernized measurements, I have tried to include the supporting documentation while maintaining the source format. Still, I was forced to turn away from a great many recipes that hinted at a pioneer provenance but lacked documentation. Interested readers might follow up on the endnotes to discover generational evolutions of these foods, which are still around today.

Within the purview of the historian, some sources have been discredited over the years. The archival sources of the Daughters of Utah Pioneers (DUP) have often been dismissed from earnest examination due to the amateur approach that has characterized the curation of the collection. Often provenance is lacking, and many items exhibit a distinct editorial flavor. Yet the collection is a treasure trove of information and source material. I have used the DUP archival material extensively for this study. While published DUP materials often do not provide reference to the original sources, the provenance can be established in the DUP archives by cross-referencing membership applications, genealogical charts, and historical manuscripts, which I did for the references cited here. I am deeply grateful to the volunteer curatorial staff at the DUP Memorial Museum for their assistance and for their efforts to preserve this history. I encourage other historians working in other venues to consider this material.

When a recipe or process seems to fall within the contextual framework here but lacks a strong provenance, I appeal to contemporary published cookbooks from the eastern states. These frequently offer parallel patterns that support a historical context. For example, many Mormon pioneers report simmering peaches in molasses to make preserves. None gave a specific formula. Thankfully, the eastern cookbooks filled in the gap. Quite frankly, a biscuit is a biscuit, no matter where or when it was made (unless it comes from a British food tradition, in which case it is a cookie; see the recipe "Conversation Biscuit" in chapter 10 for an example).

Gourmet chefs and foodies view the recipe formula as the key to understanding the interpretation of an individual dish. Recipes are tangible. They present a possible formula for cookery success. Many of the recipes presented here offer a chance to re-create food items just for fun. From a larger scope, however, we view the recipe as merely a starting point for building context and discussion. As I look at pudding recipes, for example, I see an evolution of technology and technique that marks the pioneer era. Some early recipes call for using a large flat piece of cloth as a bag to hold the pudding as it boils. Later recipes call for steaming or baking the pudding in a tin. In each case the recipe illustrates a larger cultural context. When contrasted with the near disappearance of steamed puddings from our modern cuisine, these recipes serve as historical documents to open a new perspective for understanding pioneer food and culture.

In the midst of all this methodology, we confront a running current of folk belief regarding the Mormon pioneers. A note on the wall of the Brigham City tabernacle recalls the history of worship tradition there. Old-timers who had lived in Nauvoo before the Mormon exodus were given first rights for speaking from the pulpit. This regard for the pioneers flavors many facets of popular belief about the people who built Utah's first forts and towns. Ideas about deprivation, starvation, and hard times run as a theme throughout recollections of food traditions. These pioneers paid their dues through hunger. Yet a closer look at pioneer diaries reveals an often rich and sumptuous menu, including such exotic delicacies as blancmange, East Indian curry, and oysters on the half shell. In many cases food of the Mormon pioneers rivaled that of larger cities in the eastern states. Although some early settlers often experienced keen hunger, many meals also displayed incredible bounty.

Foodies will find plenty of recipes here; folklorists will find stories, audiences, and performances; academics will find notes with primary sources. Regardless of your own particular sensibility, I hope that this work contributes to a fresh look at the Mormon pioneer culture that continues to shape life (and food) in Utah today.

ACKNOWLEDGMENTS

This book would not have been possible without the assistance of many people. Special thanks to John Alley, who first showed interest in the project. I am also grateful to Peter DeLafosse and Reba Rauch, who believed in it; and to Gene Sessions and Kathryn MacKay at Weber State University for their collegial encouragement. Thanks to the kind, patient women at the Daughters of Utah Pioneers Memorial Museum in Salt Lake City for the gracious use of their archival materials. I'm grateful to friends and family who read numerous drafts and gave me feedback about my tone and voice. Most of all, thanks to Shannon for encouraging me in every moment along the way.

CHAPTER 1

From Soup

AN INTRODUCTION

The wilderness and the solitary place shall be glad for them;
and the desert shall rejoice, and blossom as the rose.
—Isaiah 35:1

Food as Celebration

July of 1849 was a scorcher in Salt Lake City, as it is every year. In the streets surrounding the old fort, delegations of men worked at erecting shade boweries. Brigham Young, the colonizing Mormon prophet and leader, assigned local bishops the job of preparing for a massive feast. Stacked end to end, the boweries housed long plank tables extending one after another for hundreds of feet. The citizens of this new Mormon agrarian community prepared to celebrate their triumph over the wilderness. Their feast would use food from the harvest to commemorate the moment.

July 24, 1849, marked two years since Brigham Young's entrance to the Great Salt Lake Valley. On that second anniversary Brigham is quoted as saying: "The reason we are celebrating the Twenty-fourth instead of the Fourth of July is that twenty more days were needed for some of our vegetables to mature. We waited so that we could have beets and cucumbers for our feast today."[1] Certainly Brigham's tongue is firmly in his cheek, glib with sarcasm turned against the patriotism that did the Mormons no good when they lived in the eastern states. At the same time, he makes direct note that the Mormons' survival in this arid new landscape depended on their skill as farmers working in harsh conditions. They not only conquered but feasted.

In 1848 the pioneers had feasted to celebrate their first season's harvest. Parley Pratt waxed eloquent in remembering the occasion:

> On the 10th of August we held a public feast under a bowery in the center of our fort. This was called a harvest feast; we partook freely of a rich variety of bread, beef, butter, cheese, cakes, pastry, green corn, melons and almost

every variety of vegetable. Large sheaves of wheat, rye, barley, oats, and other productions were hoisted up on poles for public exhibition.[2]

Andrew Jackson Allen, another early pioneer, also made mention of the diverse harvest, but with a greater sense of celebration. "We had a public feast and party," he reported, ". . . and we did have a day of rejoicing before the lord and feasted on that of saints got in early."[3] Still, that feast in 1848 was just a harvest celebration and not held on July 24, that most auspicious of dates.

The next year marked the first Pioneer Day, held on July 24, 1849. This celebration of the pioneers, their travails, their heroism, and their service in the army of God certainly trumped the celebration of the harvest. Of that first annual feast, Louisa Barnes Pratt observed: "The tables were spread with the choicest varieties of things produced from the richest soil, and by our own hands labor."[4] A party of Forty-niners headed to California stumbled upon the scene. Hailing from Boston, the group "appeared perfectly astonished to see the abundance and variety with which our tables were loaded, and said they did not believe that a greater variety could have been produced in that city."[5]

Only two years after arriving in the Great Salt Lake Valley, Mormon settlers shifted the focus of the celebration away from the harvest and instead established a highly ritualized commemoration of the pioneers. Their trials in the wilderness demanded recognition. Church doctrine forbade alcohol as a vehicle for festivities (at least in these formal settings),[6] so settlers observed the occasion with feasting. The hungry horde of pioneers gorged themselves elbow to elbow at lavishly spread tables. The feast served primarily as an occasion for reminding themselves of who they were: God's special people. But it was also a conscious effort at a conspicuous display to prove that the Mormon pioneers had forced the desert to blossom like a rose, as prophesied. Heavy platters bowing plank tables proved it so, and Mormon diarists have frequently made the metaphor explicit. Parley Pratt gives this example in his diary: "It was a great day with the people of these valleys, and long to be remembered . . . a first effort to redeem the interior deserts of America and to make her hitherto unknown solitudes 'blossom as the rose.'"[7]

Not surprisingly, other accounts of the same occasion paint a much different picture. William Morley Black entered the valley as a gold-seeking Forty-niner on that same date. He noted the large boweries but carried on until he came to the home of "Uncle Buck Smithson." Appealing to charity, he asked the Smithsons to feed him and his companions. Smithson replied: "I am fearful our simple supper would not please you gentlemen. We can give you a supper of milk, meat and pigweed greens, but bread we have none. You see the flour we brought with us a year ago has given out, we have not had bread for three weeks, and have no hopes of any until our harvest comes off."[8]

Black's experience appears to directly contradict the celebrations noted by Louisa Pratt on the same date. Could it be that some pioneers starved in isolation while others feasted in rich company? Such is the difficulty of discovering the truth of history. As the story unfolds, both are probably true. In the food history of Utah's Mormon pioneers, discrepancies of hunger and feasting are often seen side by side, based on

A community dinner circa 1900 in Salt Lake City, Utah, honoring the Old Folks. This tradition, more than 135 years old, continues in some Mormon communities.

how long the pioneers had been settled. Newcomers often went hungry until their crops proved themselves, while old settlers usually had plenty.

These two contrasting accounts demonstrate several themes in the food history of Mormon pioneers. Communal meals serve as the common setting for celebration. Privation and hardship are often emphasized and also embraced with joy. Bounty reflects God's blessing of the people. And food is used as the vehicle for this celebration.

Mormons today continue the tradition of joyful observance through feasting. The Pioneer Day feast on July 24 is just one case in point. On average this is the hottest day of the year, yet many Mormons still fill their antiquated Dutch ovens and celebrate the day over a bed of glowing charcoal briquettes. Throughout Mormon country, local festivals follow the seasonal harvests, with Cherry Days in North Ogden, Onion Days in Payson, Raspberry Days at Bear Lake, and Peach Days in Brigham City. Social events in other towns are contrived to use food as a social facilitator. A celebration more than a century old uses elaborate meals to celebrate the old-timers of the community of Koosharem.

Beginning in 1875, pioneer Charles Savage called for a formalized feast throughout Utah to honor the "old folks" of each community. These first settlers received royal treatment from their progeny each year, being taken out for picnics, entertainments, and dancing.[9] The tradition continues in some isolated communities today. Koosharem's Old Folks Day uses two elaborate meals on one day to call its citizens home for reunion. With a full dinner at noon and then a sumptuous supper in the evening,

Koosharem uses food as the vehicle for celebrating the place of its elders in the community. In Fountain Green, a traditionally Danish community, Lamb Day marks the beginning of spring, as the town turns out to eat pit-barbecued lamb. As a close-knit community built on a history of sheep ranchers, Fountain Green celebrates this agricultural heritage through a feast of its own local making. Though many American communities commemorate important dates with feasting, Mormon feasts verge on becoming a religious sacrament.[10]

The Providence Sauerkraut Dinner

Every autumn for as long as anyone can remember, the Mormons of Providence, Utah, have come together for a feast to commemorate their Swiss heritage and ancestors. A hundred and fifty years ago, Brigham Young ordered their forebears to explore the mountain valleys north of Salt Lake City and to build a settlement in Cache Valley. As was typical of early Mormon settlements, immigrants of various nationalities and ethnicity settled in enclaves, giving each town a distinctive identity. Swiss and German settlers built the little town of Providence on the south end of the valley and constructed traditional ethnic social institutions as its backbone. Children joined together in a Swiss choir. Newspaper editors published in the Old World language. Dramatic societies served as social outlets and cultural reinforcements. Likewise, church services in Swiss and German languages emphasized their heritage and culture.

Shortly after the settlement of Providence, its residents began an annual local harvest dinner, carrying on the same traditions that in other places evolved into Oktoberfest. The autumn harvest celebrations of those early days in Providence were marked by the traditional Swiss and German dishes that reminded the settlers of their homeland. Local records make reference to "roast beef" in these early years. This might have been sauerbraten, the tangy-sour roast beef of German tradition.[11] Although just reading the recipe is exhausting, we can see how a formal observance of the preparation might serve as an homage to the homeland.

Sauerbraten (Sour Beef)

For a sour roast take a good, fat piece from the round. In the Summer let it lay in vinegar 3–4 days and in the Winter 8–10 days. Then add bay leaves, cloves, allspice and perhaps a few juniper berries to the vinegar; put it on the stove and bring to a boil; the meat should first be freshened, then pour over it the boiling vinegar, which prevents the juices from being lost from the meat. If the vinegar is very sharp, mix with a little water. As onions harden in vinegar they should not be added until ready to cook. In the summer the meat should be kept uncovered in a refrigerator or other cool place, turning it frequently, being careful not to do this with the hands. Before cooking, lard the roast as follows, thereby making it juicier: Cut fat pork into strips the length of a finger, turn them in a mixture of salt, pepper and ground cloves, puncture the meat all over with a sharp knife and put in the lardoons; sprinkle some more salt over the meat, but not too much—over-salting makes the meat tough. Get plenty of good fat quite hot in an iron kettle, put in the meat and allow the broth which gathers to steam away rapidly, lightly browning the meat all around, being careful to often turn it in the fat. Then put a heaping tablespoonful of flour into the fat, also browning it, and immediately pour in from the side enough boiling water to cover the meat, covering the kettle at once so that none of the flavor may be lost. After a few minutes add a piece of meat weighing from 5 to 6 pounds, 2 small carrots, 3 to 4 large onions and a piece of rye bread crust, and if necessary some of the spiced vinegar in which the meat has laid; then cover the kettle tightly and cook slowly but uninterruptedly for about 2–2½ hours, turning the meat during this time and occasionally lifting it with a fork without piercing; add a little boiling water if necessary. A cupful of sweet cream put in during the last half hour of cooking greatly improves the gravy. When ready to serve put the meat on a warm dish and set it in the oven while the gravy is being prepared. If the latter should have become too thick during the cooking it can be thinned with water; if not thick enough, put in a little flour; if it should be too sour and the color brown enough, put in a cupful of milk, then pass it through a sieve and cook rapidly; part of the gravy is poured over the roast and the remainder served in a gravy boat.[12]

Farm wives produced egg noodles in huge volume in those early years. The day before the feast, local women cleared benches away to bare the board floors of the church house then swept and scrubbed them clean. Dozens and grosses of eggs went into huge bowls of flour to be kneaded and rolled out on clean bedsheets spread out on the floor of the church house. After cutting the sheets of rolled dough into noodle strips on the floor, the women hung them to dry on the backs of church pews. Mormon wives cooked some of these for the feast the next day, but most were packaged and sold at the bazaar that accompanied the feast. Proceeds supported the local congregation's budget as well as welfare projects for the women's auxiliary Relief Society.[13]

Egg Noodles

3 eggs, 1 pint flour, ¼ tsp salt. Mix. If a little more liquid is needed use water. Cut in portions and roll very thin, then let dry until they will not stick. Roll together and cut into thin noodles.   —Cecilia Ence Tobler[14]

Early Swiss settlers brought representative Swiss foods to the feast. That's what they knew how to cook. But as years passed, folks began including more generic and Americanized foods in the feast. The fried noodles and sauerkraut that were once daily staples became reserved only for this most symbolic occasion. Making sauerkraut became an annual meditation on Swiss ancestry instead of just being a way to preserve the crop.

As generations unfolded, many Mormon towns homogenized to a more ubiquitous form of Mormon culture, losing much of their unique character. In Providence, worship services in English replaced those once conducted in Swiss-German. The Swiss choir fizzled out, and the Swiss three-act plays ceased to be performed at the annual harvest bazaar. Ethnic clothing disappeared from everyday life and was seen only at annual folk festivals and parades. But Swiss and German food remained a part of contemporary culture, even throughout the twentieth century. Like most descendants of immigrants, Mormons are reluctant to give up their generational comfort foods, because they also symbolize the core of identity. We are what we eat.

A community group in Providence, Utah, circa 1960 assembled to shred cabbage for the annual Sauerkraut Dinner. Courtesy Providence City.

Modern Manifestations

Today the citizens of Providence still carry on with the harvest feast, which they call the Sauerkraut Dinner. The authentic feast is hosted by the Church of Jesus Christ of Latter-Day Saints (LDS) Providence 2nd Ward, largely organized by Ken Braegger and his friends. Ken raises his own cabbages and makes the kraut himself. Another sauerkraut dinner is hosted by the Providence city council. For the last few years, the municipal dinner has relied on a professional caterer for its sauerkraut and other items on the menu, due to legal and health code restrictions. "The stuff they sell in the stores doesn't taste like what I make," Ken confided. He tried the store-bought sauerkraut at the municipal feast: "It tasted okay."[15]

Ken knows a thing or two about sauerkraut. He is the third generation in Utah since his grandfather first came to the territory in 1865. His father learned to make sauerkraut from Ken's grandfather, Abraham Braegger Jr. of the first Swiss-American generation. Abraham settled in Willard, Utah, in 1865. Ken's sauerkraut is in that same Swiss tradition. As far as he's concerned, it is exactly the same as what his father and grandfather made, reaching back more than a century. Keeping a sauerkraut barrel in the cellar is part of Ken's genetic makeup. In those early years the barrels were made of oak and had to be soaked in the canal for a couple of days before using them. In his younger years Ken served as the Mormon bishop in Providence and presided over the annual sauerkraut dinners. He supervised the fermentation of thirteen barrels of sauerkraut: fifty-five gallons each, a hundred heads of cabbage to each barrel.[16]

Farmers in Providence, Utah, circa 1960 holding cabbages destined for the Sauerkraut Dinner. Courtesy Providence City.

Ken Braegger's celebration of his family and community heritage through food is not a singular instance in Utah food lore. Other families and communities also try to keep pioneer food elements alive, if not from day to day then at least for special occasions. Like the Braegger family, the descendants of Stephen Chipman continue to celebrate his contribution to Utah's food culture. As a pioneer of 1847 Chipman was instrumental in establishing modern Anglo agriculture in Utah. His family history records that he was one of the first to bring sheep herds to Utah Valley, but his family makes special note of his once famous "pink-eye beans." As early farmers tested varieties for hardiness to the region, Chipman found some success with the pink-eye bean, which subsequently became a reliable field crop for Utah farmers. For years the preparation of this bean constituted the "Chipman Dessert" used to commemorate their pioneer ancestry. Some Chipmans still living remember when the dish was served at family reunions. The famous beans seem to have faded from family lore in recent years, though one family member has vowed to resurrect this piece of the Chipman agrarian heritage.

Chipman Dessert

About 2 lbs. pink-eye beans, wash and cover with cold water. Add one or two ham hocks—salt to taste and simmer until beans are tender and the meat falls from the bones.   —Theodocia Chipman Shelley Melville, 1883–1974[17]

Just as the Braeggers have passed sauerkraut know-how down through generations and the Chipmans have continued their pink-eye bean tradition, the Bott descendants have carried on a baking tradition over the course of more than a century. Elizabeth Bott joined the wave of Mormon converts in migration from her childhood home in Staffordshire, England. When she was a child her mother taught her to make hot cross buns as an Easter-time tradition. She brought this tradition to Utah, where she continued to make the treats for her friends and neighbors in Randolph. When Elizabeth grew too old to continue, her granddaughters carried on the tradition for her.[18] Bott descendants today keep the recipe and tradition alive, as a celebration of their heritage. Still, as one great-great granddaughter confessed, "My daughter doesn't bake; she lives too close to Costco."

Hot Cross Buns

2 sieves flour

3 eggs

1 cup sugar

2 tsp. nutmeg

8 tsp. butter

pinch of salt

1 lb. raisins or currants

2 cups yeast or yeast foam

Let dough rise all night. In the morning roll out and cut. Let rise high. Bake. When you take them from the oven brush the tops with milk and sugar mixture to give a shiny look.   —Elizabeth Bott Brough, 1838–1921[19]

Note: As with many old formulas, the author assumes quite a bit of inherent knowledge on the part of the reader. A "sieve" is a flour sifter; in this recipe, assume that it holds about three cups. The "2 cups yeast" refers to home-cultured yeast. If you are using dry active yeast, use about one packet instead. The buns should be formed into balls, placed close together in a deep baking pan or Dutch oven, and allowed to rise in the pan. After baking, mark a cross on top of each bun using a thick icing or custard from a pastry bag.

Descendants of Mormon pioneers carry on these food traditions today, protecting, defining, and celebrating a cohesive body of culinary understanding and folk identity. Many families continue to incorporate ethnic food into their Christmas traditions. In Ephraim, Utah, the most concentrated center of Danish pioneer settlement, Memorial Day weekend is set aside for Danish celebrations of the town that calls itself "Little Denmark." In other corners of the state, Mormon and Native American families head for the hills in late summer to pick wild berries or gather pine nuts, just as their ancestors did a century ago. These pioneer food patterns seem to be slowly disappearing, but they continue to be practiced in many families and communities.

In the coming pages I hope to identify particular defining parameters for this body of cuisine that we might call "Mormon Pioneer Foodways." Although Mormon pioneers sold food to other settlers in the West, including miners, soldiers, Native American, and other non-Mormons, we will find that Mormon foodways stand as distinct from these other cultures. Mormon pioneers brought a religious sensibility to their diets. Their cuisine is infused with diversity from the European and

New England origins of the Mormon migration. These pioneers leaned heavily on wild game and wild plants throughout their early years. Seasonal harvests, both wild and domestic, dictated the rhythms of feasting. The Mormon pioneers brought a sophisticated understanding of food technology, which they used to preserve their abundant harvests. These foodways have found viability into the twenty-first century as a result of Mormon cultural values involving oral traditions and history.

Though non-Mormons and other outsiders have significantly impacted ethnic demographics in the inter-mountain West, Mormons continue to hold onto family recipes that illustrate their connection to the pioneer heritage. As I courted my soon-to-be wife, I was excited to learn that she shared Danish ancestry similar to mine. We immediately compared Danish family recipes. Our recipes, which had evolved from the same root origins, naturally showed minor variations on a theme. These same subtle changes manifest again and again in other families, through a plum pudding, a loaf of bread, or a cup of tea. Our common food traditions continue a dynamic evolution today.

Many of the physical elements of Mormon pioneer foodways have changed over time. Cooks these days use gas and electric ranges. They have no need to haul water in a bucket, let alone settle the silt from water hauled from the creek or ditch. We find reason to use the Dutch oven to celebrate on special occasions, but from day to day we use copper-bottomed stainless steel pans. Refrigerators and store-bought canned goods remove most of the need for preserved meat and produce. Rather than milking a cow twice daily, we store fresh milk for two weeks at a time. These physical considerations of the past contributed much of what defines Mormon pioneer foodways. As a result, the modern chef seeking to re-create an authentic "pioneer" dish must first re-create an authentic pioneer kitchen and pantry, with associated tools and ingredients.

Just as the physical tools of cookery have changed over time, so have the formulas, processes, and ingredients. Where the pioneer Mormon wife would have used saleratus (a naturally occurring chemical compound gathered from the wild), today's chef uses baking powder. Whereas the old pioneer recipe called for "butter the size of an egg," today's cookbook might ask for a fourth-cup of margarine. (I recommend that you stick with butter.) Boxed mixes have replaced scratch cooking from rote memory. Such changes certainly are not without impact. Butter and margarine have differing flavors, levels of viscosity, melting points, and chemical structures. While these nuances may be immaterial to the casual consumer of calories, they become imperative when food creations serve as a reflection of a connection to revered ancestors. Individual chefs might ponder such concerns with flavor and symbols in kitchens around the world. Here we also focus on larger historical themes.

What Does It Mean?

The study of food and food processes in the context of history and culture has been called "foodways." Folklorist Jay Anderson broke ground in this field during his study of Pilgrim food processes at Plimoth Plantation, Massachusetts, in the 1960s. His concise vernacular definition of foodways is "from seed to shit and everything in between."[20] In other words, we study the relationship between planting the garden and processing the harvest; between the preparation of a meal and its consumption; between the milking of the cow and her pile of manure and the garden upon which it is spread.

What we eat and how we eat it reveal volumes about who we are and how we think. Anthropologist Mary Douglass proposes that the foods a society eats might reveal a code. We could look at the Providence Sauerkraut Dinner as a secret message with meanings waiting to be decoded. Who makes the kraut? What does that say about the community? Why kraut instead of sausages or root beer? For Douglass, the answer to these questions reveals a message about politics and hierarchy of a society; who and what it includes or excludes; where its borders lie and how they are protected or violated.[21] In the case of the Providence Sauerkraut Dinner, we might see the former power structure of the ethnic Mormon congregations crumbling as a new cultural value—disconnected from the pioneer heritage—rises in its influence. A demographic influx of non-Mormon Hispanic families in southern Cache Valley might support this analysis. Yet many Mormon families continue their food traditions, alternately defying and reinforcing Douglass's paradigm.

Ken Braegger does not see himself as being engaged in a power struggle against new waves of outsiders assailing his sauerkraut tradition. Neither does he maintain any fantasies about bringing past history back to life or believe that he is somehow mystically or spiritually communing with the pioneers. Instead, he says, he is simply using his sauerkraut as an element in determining his character and culture in ways that feel familiar and comfortable. Likewise, he drives a Jeep 4x4. After serving in the U.S. Marines in World War II, he grew to like the Jeep. Like his sauerkraut, it has become an element of celebration in his self-chosen identity.[22]

As our story unfolds, we will find familiar themes from Utah history. Tales about the Mormon Battalion, massive global migration following the Irish potato famine, the Utah War, the transcontinental railroad, and Mormon-Indian relations both political and economic emerge from the diaries and recipes presented here. In fact, we might imagine that we could tell a convincing version of history through the daily meals of pioneers. And why not? In the agricultural communities that Mormons founded, the pursuit of food was their most common endeavor. We are about to sit down to a three-course meal: some food, some history, and some reflection on what it says about who we are.

Here I present a historical perspective on Mormon pioneer foodways. More than a cookbook, this study presents foodways processes and recipes as a populist reflection or social history of the Mormon pioneers who settled Utah in the second half of the nineteenth century. Diversity characterizes these people. Though most originated from Britain and northern Europe, others also show up: Yankees, American Indians, African Americans, and Southern planters. Originating from a hundred different places, the foodways of the "pioneers" are anything but homogeneous. Still, we can find common themes and threads among the foods they shared at communal meals as well as at home. I hope that an examination of their foods will bring insight into facets of life not explicitly documented in diaries.

Through the course of this study I discovered old recipes and new things to try. I also found cause to reexamine some of my views about who the pioneers really were and how their food reflected their cultural values. Likewise, I hope that you might try some of the foods presented here. I especially hope that you will find a new angle of reflection on the food you eat and the symbols it represents for you. Grab a spoon and let's dive in!

CHAPTER 2

Setting the Table

TOOLS AND ARTIFACTS

In furnishing a kitchen, there should be every thing likely to be
required, but not one article more than is wanted.
—Elizabeth Fries Ellet, *The Practical Housekeeper*, 1857

Food is temporary. Though much of our lives is devoted to pursuing it, food is fleeting. As soon as we have a little, it is gone without a trace except for a streak of gravy across a plate. The plate remains, however, often for centuries or millennia. Because our Mormon subjects consumed nearly all of the food we want to study, we are left with only plates to tell us about what it means. Fortunately, we have quite a few plates.

Hearth Culture

In a square, tidy pit on Antelope Island in the Great Salt Lake, archaeologist Kevin Jones carefully scrapes a centimeter of dirt from the Fremont-era (1,000 years ago) excavation. Dark charcoal stains streak across the grid-lined pit, and Jones identifies the feature as a hearth. A casual modern use of the term would imply domestic architecture—a hearth is part of a brick fireplace, which is part of a dwelling. But, Jones explains, "hearth" is just the archaeologist's term for a fire pit that was likely used for cooking purposes. A hearth could be as simple as a single reflector rock in front of a sprawling bed of coals on the ground. For 3,000 years, people have been building hearths near the wetlands and springs on Antelope Island.

Similar hearths are scattered over a thousand miles of the Mormon Pioneer Trail. The hearth is the center of the foodways experience. The little red square in the middle of a "log cabin" quilt block represents this hearth at the center of the home. William Clayton's *Latter-Day Saints' Emigrants' Guide* details campsites along the trail where water and fuel were available, at least in the early years. At each of these historic camping grounds, travelers established hearths from which they cooked and fed their families. As at the prehistoric Fremont hearth on Antelope Island, archaeological

Commemorative Nauvoo Temple plate, blue transfer stencil, circa 1846. The plate identifies the First Presidency and apostles of the LDS Church after the death of Joseph Smith.

investigation of campsites along the Mormon Pioneer Trail would reveal fascinating clues about what and how people ate. Abandoned spoons, broken bits of cast iron, and even the remains of butchered bones provide a record of the eating activities of Mormon travelers. Andrew Israelson, a Danish pioneer, remembered losing his silver spoon in the middle of a cattle stampede on the trail.[1] Such bits and pieces of lost food artifacts lay waiting to be found so that their stories can be told.

Archaeology and Food

Surprisingly, most of these pioneer artifacts still lie asleep in the ground. Although archaeologists have examined quite a few Mormon pioneer sites in the West, only a handful of archaeological studies dealing with the Mormon settlement period have been published. In part this may be due to continuous urban development on the same ground that earlier settlers called home. Another likely reason may be that Anasazi and Fremont Indian sites hold a more romantic interest for modern study.

In truth, prehistoric archaeology often trumps studies of historical sites in both funding and research interest.

Still, the physical record of archaeology presents solid evidence of what and how Mormon pioneers ate. Excavations and research relevant to the early Mormon settlement period include the excavation of the early pioneer cemetery at Salt Lake City;[2] the Social Hall excavation in Salt Lake City; and the excavation of the town of Goshen in Utah Valley.[3] In light of the recent dissolution of the Antiquities Division of Utah State History, it seems even more unlikely that Mormon pioneer historic sites will be given their archaeological due.

Mormon pioneers settled briefly at Goshen as an alternative to the fast-growing town of Santaquin. Adjacent water sources seemed to offer hope for farmers. Only after three years of fruitless effort did they realize that the soil was alkaline and barren. After abandoning the site, the stubborn Mormons moved their buildings intact two miles east to resettle a new Goshen.

Archaeologists found the footprints of numerous structures from the 1860s, largely undisturbed and with ample artifacts from the period. Archaeologist Dale Berge found evidence of cooking and food activities clustered around the main hearth in homes with a large central room as well as around hearths of outbuildings that might have served as summer kitchens.[4] In particular, Berge found lots and lots of peach pits strewn around the hearths. We might readily imagine these new settlers gorging on peaches brought from nearby orchard towns in Utah Valley. But it is

A summer kitchen in Centerville, Utah. Summer kitchens allowed a semienclosed work space, which kept the heat of the hearth out of the main house during summer months.

more likely that industrious housewives pitted and scalded peaches as they prepared to make fruit leather or peach preserves in a pot over the fire. This pattern reflects the same architectural plan and use noted by Clarissa Young at Brigham Young's Beehive House. Pearl Wonnacott recalled that her mother and grandmother (both pioneers of the 1860s) used peach pits as a fuel source. When a brisk, hot fire was wanted for heating irons and doing laundry, peach pits were just the thing.[5] This may account for the peach pits found near the hearth at Goshen.

Ceramics

In regard to the plates mentioned earlier, archaeologists found quite a few fragments at Goshen dating to the years of this study as well as other food-related artifacts. Assumptions about the Mormon pioneers were dispelled by the artifacts emerging from these archaeological investigations. We might imagine a spartan existence for this fledgling pioneer settlement three days from Salt Lake City: settlers making do with materials on hand for rough earthenware dishes. Artifacts found at Goshen seem to speak to the contrary. Liquor bottles and wine bottles were found along with cut-glass drinking tumblers. Fine ceramics from the eastern states in Blue Willow and other patterns graced these tables. The limitations of a frontier settlement clearly were not factors for these Mormons. Similar remains were found at the Salt Lake City Social Hall and also at the old pioneer fort in Salt Lake City, though from a later era.

The Salt Lake City museum of the Daughters of Utah Pioneers is another interesting source of physical artifacts relevant to our study of food culture. The museum, containing curiosities such as a stuffed two-headed lamb, also houses a diverse array of food-related artifacts from the era discussed here. Though a direct provenance is lacking for many pieces, others bear concrete identifications. Artifacts such as wooden bowls with their bottoms worn through, together with associated chopping tools, bring to mind the many apples, potatoes, and onions that went into puddings, pies, soups, and stuffing. Eggbeaters fashioned from willow twigs emphasize the self-sufficient economy. Loads and loads of Blue Willow dishes speak to the Mormon embrace of contemporary fashions. Passed down through generations, these tools and dishes were preserved as manifestations of a revered pioneer food tradition. Others were worn out, broken, forgotten, and left behind to wait as artifacts for archaeology.

Traveling with Brigham Young's vanguard company of 1847, William Clayton observed that the process of archaeology had already begun. In the spring of 1847 when passing through Nebraska territory, Clayton took note of abandoned farms along Plumb Creek: "Large lots of iron, old and new, several plows and a drag. All apparently left to rot. There are also two stoves, etc."[6] Our understanding of Mormon settlers and their approaches to cooking begins with these physical remains. Abandoned stoves marked the beginning of the frontier for Clayton. As he headed west with the vanguard company, Clayton's foodway patterns regressed from the civilization of cast-iron stoves and began a technological shift back to the open hearth and Dutch oven.

Not far from the Fremont archaeological site on Antelope Island, Fielding Garr built his own hearth in 1848. His long adobe ranch house still stands there today. It has two large common rooms, each with an open fireplace hearth. A rough granite

This cookstove, retrofitted into the hearth of earlier days, remained in Nauvoo, Illinois, after the Mormon exodus. Photographed by Susa Young Gates.

lintel carries the weight of the mantel, and wrought-iron pot hooks still hang from chains in the chimney. This hearth demonstrates the standard of cookery for that early era of Mormon settlement in the Salt Lake Valley. The tripods and irons used on the trail became eye-bolts and S-hooks set in mortar; sprawling beds of coals were contained within the dimensions of a stone hearth set into the floor.

Hearth cooking, whether on the trail or in an established home, required a set of tools adapted to the task. Because the cook worked directly above the coals, many pots required short feet to elevate the pot and keep it stable. The ubiquitous Dutch oven is our most common example, though settlers like Alice Langston Dalton called her deep pot simply a "bake oven." "All of the cooking was done in the fire place," she said. "We had what is known as bake ovens that we did the baking in. The live coals were pulled out of the fire place onto the hearth."[7] Frying pans required either a trivet or spider: devices with tall spindly legs to elevate a pan over a bed of live coals on the hearth. Other pots and kettles were suspended. Trail cooking required tripods or irons to hang the pots, while home hearths might have a crane or chains set into the mortar of the chimney. With the pot made stable, the cook manipulated the heat by shuffling greater or lesser volumes of hot coals under the pot. The cook also could swing the crane deeper into the chimney and fire for more heat. The accurate control of heat was the critical element that allowed a good cook to distinguish herself from amateurs.

The hearth at the Fielding Garr ranch house on Antelope Island. Original chains and iron mountings are used to suspend pots and kettles in the fire. Author's collection.

Hearth cooking also required a variety of specialized tools, including long-handled spoons, ladles, and spatulas. Accurate manipulation of heat under the pot demanded shovels and brooms for the messy coals. Most of the action happened at ground level, so a long-handled spoon saved considerable stooping and bending. Lid-lifters and pot hooks could do much of the work, but bending could not be eliminated altogether. Sometimes there was no substitute for a nose at pot level; poor eyesight in a dimly lit cabin necessitated bending to see what was happening in the pot. As with any task or chore, however, the right tool could make a significant difference. Like a modern kitchen with a cluttered drawer full of gadgets, the Mormon pioneer hearth would have a collection of long-handled tools. "A salamander," explains Sarah Josepha Buell Hale, "which is a flat iron with a long handle, is heated and placed over some articles, to brown them after they are dished. The kitchen fire-shovel, if made red hot, will answer the same purpose."[8]

Dutch Ovens Revered

All this is well and good, but it is the Dutch oven that has captured the hearts of Mormons everywhere. In a 1997 legislative move mocked by pundits, Utah lawmakers declared the Dutch oven to be the official cooking pot of Utah with House Bill 203. This legal maneuver reflects Utah's romance with cast iron. The headquarters of the International Dutch Oven Society are in Utah, which hosts its annual "world championship" Dutch oven competitions. Some Mormon families have enshrined their ancestral cast iron in realms of myth and legend. For others, the Dutch oven is revered as a symbol of patriarchal descent from noble lineage and is passed through inheritance from genera-tion to generation.[9] The Dutch oven is far more than just a black pot in Utah.

According to legend, Paul Revere invented the bake oven, as it was historically called. Like the true inventor of the lip-lidded, flat-bottomed, spike-footed pot, the origin of the name "Dutch oven" is lost to history. Some ascribe the moniker to early Dutch smelter technology in Europe. Dutch sand castings made advances in the 1600s beyond the primitive cast iron produced in Britain. Other theories give credit to the German settlers of Pennsylvania, who—taking advantage of native coal and iron resources—manufactured, used, and sold thousands of the pots in colo-nial America. As a central commodity within the Pennsylvania Dutch (German) economy, the term "Dutch oven" became common in regions of the South. Mormon pioneer folk culture, in contrast, originated primarily in the Yankee Northeast, where "bake ovens" and "camp kettles" are more frequently mentioned in diaries. As James Beard popularized regional cuisine in the 1970s, the revival of the Dutch oven came primarily from the South. The 1997 Utah legislation followed this popular trend.

Utah pioneers held their bake ovens in no less esteem than their modern descen-dants do. While en route from Nauvoo to Winter Quarters in 1846, Patty Sessions contracted something like the "ague" or malarial fever. Combined with the physical exhaustion of the trail, the illness made her retreat to bed. While languishing there, Patty began disposing of her possessions, with special attention to her kitchen items. Giving her ironware to a neighbor, she noted that she "let Jacob Hutchinson have the Pot and spider to carry on for the use of them if I want them to return them again when called for if not returned to be paid for."[10] Within a few days Patty recovered and promptly retrieved her kitchen essentials from her neighbor.

Emily Stewart Barnes, an early Kaysville settler, recalled the difference a Dutch oven made in her diet. "We did not have a stove to cook on—only one little black kettle and one frying pan. . . . Mother made a little bread cake, and put it in the fry-ing pan over some coals pulled from the fireplace; then she would tip the frying pan, holding it close to the fire, and that would cook the cake on top."[11] Like many early pioneers, Emily's family came to Utah with only the bare essentials. A frying pan could suffice for many basic needs. Her parents could prepare biscuits, pancakes, corn oysters, porridge, bacon, and more with this pan. With great relish Emily noted: "After a while . . . we got an iron bake kettle with a lid, so that we could put hot coals on top of the kettle as well as beneath it. Then we began to have big round loaves of bread."[12] It took time for the Barnes family to make this upgrade.

When these settlers speak of bake kettles and camp kettles we immediately imag-ine something akin to a Dutch oven made by Lodge or TexSport. The specimens housed in the Daughters of Utah Pioneers Memorial Museum in Salt Lake City defy these uniform modern creations. Some specimens come with a long fixed handle permanently attached, like a frying pan on legs. Others lack legs entirely. The ubiqui-tous pot of our understanding is a modern creation, while extant historical specimens exhibit a wide spectrum of diversity. The bake oven that liberated the Barnes family may have taken a variety of shapes.

Emily Barnes was living on the edge of a wild country as she grew up in the 1850s. Frontier conditions defined her world in relation to her ability to access refined foods and tools. The Mormon frontier shifted over time and place. While it had largely disappeared from Salt Lake City long before the coming of the railroad, the southern settlements continued to experience primitive conditions. The frontier extended into remote areas of Utah as new settlements broke new ground. Mormon settlement took hold only as agriculture claimed cultivated fields from rocky meadows and tons of equipment migrated outward from Salt Lake City. For Emily, this was the Kaysville frontier of the 1850s, only twenty miles from Salt Lake City.

In a different corner of Utah in 1872, Mercy Roundy was still cooking in the hearth in Kanaraville. Mrs. Jacob Gates, her neighbor in Pintura, had already abandoned the hearth and was turning out viands on a stove.[13] Transportation costs drove some decisions to switch from hearth to stove, but family cooking traditions also influenced these choices. Just as some authors today use computers and others insist on a typewriter or pen and paper, some cooks refused to give up their hearth-fired Dutch ovens.

Early chefs knew that their iron pots required ample grease to function properly. The nonsticking qualities of cast iron are the result of constantly burning oil into the pores of the pot. Osborne Russell, a fur trapper in the Rocky Mountains, once found himself stranded for several days, living on boiled roots. When his party finally was able to kill a bear, its most valued contribution was grease for the pot. Andrew Allen made a similar observation of early Mormon settlers boiling a wolf for grease. "It accured at the hird ground," he reported, "where a brother had cooked some of a large white wolf to get the oyl."[14] Keeping the pot greased allowed foods to be fried and baked without sticking.

Determining Temperature

Pioneer chefs worked with rough approximations of temperature: slow heat, medium, or quick. Their judgment of temperature was instinctual, based on experience and feel. This intuitive approach seems foreign to many modern cooks, who prefer to pin the ovens down to a specific temperature.

When cooking with cast iron on a fire, the key to success lies in controlling the level of heat under the pot. Some general rules of thumb are easily applied. If it is too uncomfortable for you to be near the pot, then the fire is too hot—your pot is probably more than 500°F. If you can stand near the pot only long enough to check its contents, it may be around 500°. If you can comfortably stir and taste what's in your pot, it is probably around 300°. The more air you allow to circulate under the pot, the hotter the coals.

Some modern chefs gauge temperature by a formula of compressed charcoal briquettes: ten briquettes under a twelve-inch pot and fifteen on the lid create an internal temperature of 350° long enough to bake a biscuit. If you use wood instead of charcoal, don't cook directly in the fire: remove the pot from the fire and shovel coals underneath it.

Most mistakes are made with too much heat. Although bread and biscuits like a quick oven of 450°, it is easy to put too much heat on the pot and turn out a biscuit black on the outside and doughy in the middle. Similarly, frying bacon on too hot a fire quickly causes a grease fire in the pan.

Masonry Ovens

Some industrious settlers built semipermanent ovens as they established their new farms and settlements. Rosina Mueller Beacham remembered her early childhood in Santa Clara and the domed baking oven made from stone belonging to her father (John Henry Mueller). As an immigrant from Switzerland, John Mueller came to Utah with a group of other Swiss immigrants in 1860. Most of the Swiss emigration that year came in response to Brigham Young's effort to recruit skilled wine makers for the new Dixie settlement.

John Mueller would have been familiar with the fine artisan breads of Europe. On the frontier of Utah's Dixie he built his own bread oven from stone. "He would get up early and build a fire in [the oven]," Rosina wrote. "When it had burned down he would push the coals to the back and put the bread in. Then shut the door. He would turn the bread around once. The heat of the coals and the hot rocks would bake the bread."[15]

Rosina is probably mistaken in some of her details. If the oven door was closed, the fire would go out for lack of oxygen and coat the loaves with acrid smoke. The practice of sealing the oven with live coals is somewhat suspect. The more typical practice was to sweep the live coals out and then (having loaded the loaves) close the oven up to retain heat, which radiated from the thermal mass of stone.

John Mueller's bake oven was not a singular rarity. In fact, the Social Hall on Salt Lake City's State Street boasted two bake ovens as well as an open hearth in its basement, used as a community recreation center. With such an elaborate kitchen, the facility found use by Brigham Young's large family of plural wives for their annual Christmas parties. Capable of turning out dozens of loaves of bread as well as

Archaeological remains of the hearth and ovens from the Social Hall in Salt Lake City may still be seen at the Social Hall Heritage Museum, 43 South State Street. Author's collection.

numerous hot dishes, the Social Hall ovens and hearth fed thousands over the years.[16] The Social Hall kitchen can be seen today as part of an archaeological museum exhibit on the site (43 South State Street in Salt Lake City).

The Transition from Hearth to Cookstove

Soon after arriving in the Great Salt Lake Valley, retailers offered settlers cast-iron cookstoves as an alternative to the hearth and Dutch oven. When immigrant Clarissa Wilhelm pulled into Salt Lake City in 1851, her first purchase was a down payment on a "step-stove" bought on contract from Halliday and Spencer, her employers.[17] At least as early as 1856 C. J. Whitehouse's Tin Store and Stove Depot advertised a variety of cast-iron and sheet-steel stoves for sale.[18] "Stoves! Stoves!" cried R. C. Sharkey in 1862, informing "the public that he has just brought from the East a good Assortment of New Era, Charter Oak, and Premium Cooking-Stoves."[19] Home chefs had as many options as they could afford.

In this early era of retail shopping in Zion, availability and price directly reflected the difficulties of freighting overland by mule train. Thus sheet-steel stoves weighed less and were more affordable than cast iron. In the 1860s diversified dry-goods retailers such as W. S. Godbe offered competing lines of stoves. And by 1869 (with the coming of the transcontinental railroad), Charter Oak stove dealers tried to outspend their rivals, Buck and Wright, with competing advertisements in the *Deseret News*.[20] Such technological marvels came later to Utah's outlying settlements. Lorena Washburn's neighbors in Manti were still cooking in the hearth circa 1868.[21] Rosina Beacham's family in Santa Clara got their first stove in 1874. "It was called a step stove," she said, because of its two-tiered design.[22] Technological upgrades came slowly over time and distance.

An early photograph of Main Street in Salt Lake City shows shops selling ironware, tinware, and cookstoves as well as other hardware used by chefs in territorial Utah.

Cookstoves elevated most of the backbreaking chores of cooking to eliminate crouching, kneeling, and stooping. But this change for the better also required a completely different set of tools. Dutch ovens with their spiked legs were unsuitable for a solid stove top; the huge cast-iron kettle was left to rust in the yard, used only for large-scale tasks such as rendering lard. Inside, the kettle was replaced by an oblong, flat-bottomed copper boiler on the stove top for the constant heating of water. Cast-iron pots lost their legs, and lightweight copper kettles found greater use. The long-handled lid lifters, ladles, and spoons from the hearth became obsolete with the cookstove. The upgrade from hearth to stove required a monetary outlay far beyond the stove itself, including a completely different set of pots and tools.

Often the switch to a stove also brought a change of fuel from wood to coal. The manipulation of heat through the cavernous bowels of the stove was more mysterious than the straightforward "more fire or less" approach of the hearth. An assortment of confusing dampers controlled the flow of air through the stove and regulated heat. In the face of this expense for new tools and intimidating learning curve, many cooks no doubt stubbornly stuck with their hearth traditions for years.

Coopered Vessels

Beyond the tools and apparatus directly tied to the fire, pioneer food traditions were bound by a hundred other artifacts. When we think of all of the utility served by Tupperware and Rubbermaid today, we might find quick parallels to wooden, clay, glass, and pewter items in the pioneer pantry. Patty Sessions made note of having her pickle tub coopered again.[23] Emily Barnes remembered her mother's wooden tub, exclusively used for cheese making.[24]

These barrels and buckets were made by the cooper, an artisan who fitted wooden staves together using bands and the natural tendency of the wood to swell. Before the advent of affordable galvanized steel, wooden containers filled many functions. The cooper bound dozens of small slats or staves together with hoops of wood or iron to create buckets. Coopered items such as tubs, kegs, buckets, and piggins found broad application in dairying, brewing, pickling, and even laundry chores. Because of their wooden composition, these vessels required constant use to keep from drying and shrinking. A barrel or bucket that dried out soon shrank and leaked. Repeated drying, shrinking, and swelling tended to crush fibers in the wooden staves to a point where they would not swell again. These coopered containers required much more maintenance than a Tupperware bowl.

Brewing, pickling, and vinegar making relied heavily on coopered kegs, but these containers also offered hazards. The enclosed containers allowed a nearly air-tight protection from airborne contaminants, but their wooden surface was not easily cleaned. By the mid-nineteenth century most dairies had realized the dangers of using wooden buckets that would harbor the "milk fever," though they had no understanding of bacteria. Brewers likewise knew that a keg that had held vinegar would spoil any wine or beer put in it. Some proposed methods akin to alchemy as a way to treat barrels that had been spoiled, but even this was a gamble. Still, some understanding is evident in Patty Sessions's specialized use of a pickle tub and the Barnes family's specialized tub used only for cheese making. When laundry day came, Emily's family borrowed a laundry tub from neighbors rather than use the cheese tub. Though microbiology was a mystery to early settlers, this specialized use of coopered vessels suggests that pioneers had a working knowledge of best practices for success. This common understanding is reflected in Elizabeth Ellet's advice in *The Practical Housekeeper*: "If any substance has fermented or become putrid in a wooden cask or tub, it is sure to taint the vessel so as to produce a similar effect upon any thing that may be put into it in future."[25] Louis Pasteur and others had just begun to discover the secrets of microbiology in Europe, but the perils of wooden containers were well understood in pioneer Utah.

Coopered containers came into play for specific modes of food production and storage. The open pores of the wooden vessels facilitated ongoing cultures for cheese making. Coopered barrels also proved durable enough for transportation of liquids like molasses, vinegar, or wine. The settlements in Santa Clara shipped thousands of barrels of wine by wagon to the Salt Lake City markets. Early settlers used wooden containers for these specific needs.

Earthenware

Ceramic and pottery containers served other culinary needs. Having a more durable and easily cleaned surface, ceramic pottery readily served for pantry storage. Soon after arriving in the Salt Lake valley, settlers established potteries to manufacture the broad range of containers needed for pantry preserves. With fruit farming as a priority, Mormon farmers and housewives required ceramic containers of all sizes for pickles, jams, jellies, and brandied peaches. With seals made variously of grape leaves, lard, candle wax, olive oil, or a dried bladder, these ceramic containers served the same functions as a mason jar. Five- and ten-gallon crocks were also used for fermenting sauerkraut and pickles and for brining hams. Regina Erickson wrote: "I remember crockery jars, all sizes. The larger ones were used for pickles, and the smaller ones for jam flavored with whole cinnamon sticks."[26]

Utah's early settlers found crockery jars readily available. As early as 1851 potters set up shop to supply the demand. Ephraim Thompson boasted a wide variety of home-manufactured earthenware items for sale, including "jars, butter boxes, milk pans, bowls, plates, &c."[27]

Mormon missionaries in England made thousands of converts, among them skilled artisans from Staffordshire. Home of the famed pottery houses, Staffordshire was the center of ceramics production for the British Empire. These skilled potters abandoned the kilns of their homeland and set up shop in Utah. Likewise, potters from Denmark's Jutland peninsula joined the migration and soon turned out new utilitarian pieces to serve the needs of Utah settlers.[28]

Danish and English potters supplied a variety of goods to the Utah market. Chimney flue tiles and flowerpots represented a small share of local production, but containers for food dominated ten to one in the industry. Each fall Utah's potters ramped up production of crocks to supply housewives with vessels for the burgeoning fruit harvest. Like modern grocery stores with pallets of mason jars, Utah's potters supplied replacements for all of the crocks that had been broken, lost, or loaned in the past year.[29] Potters offered their goods for sale through general merchandise and dry goods stores. "Croxall, Cartwright & Co. have on hand a GENERAL

ASSORTMENT of POTTERYWARE of a very superior quality, for domestic and other purposes. Call and examine yourselves at the POTTERY, 4 blocks South of Godbe's Exchange Buildings."[30]

Local antiques collectors have a high regard for these locally produced earthenware containers. We might be led to believe that Mormon settlers ate most meals on locally produced earthenware. Yet the fragments found in the archaeological record tell a different story. Archaeologists found quite a few fragments at Goshen dating to the years considered here as well as other food-related artifacts.

Given the wide lip service paid to the economic self-sufficiency of Mormon pioneers, we might expect the Goshen plates to be primarily rough, locally produced earthenware. Indeed, archaeologists found quite a few sherds and fragments of plates and vessels made from local red clay and finished in a variety of glazes, including salt glaze, lead glaze, and clear glaze. These were likely produced in the territory. But far outnumbering these rough local pieces were the whiteware plates and bowls, a fine pottery not produced locally. Many of these were decorated with blue transfer stencils, particularly the famous Blue Willow design.[31] In fact, artifacts throughout the site indicated that Mormon pioneers participated in many elements of material culture common to the popular culture of the eastern states.

Measuring Units

Cookery in the early pioneer era often relied on rote memorization of formulas. Many recipes exhibit their own unique set of nonstandardized measurements. Chefs utilized individualized methods for finding success. Standardized measurements of ingredients were not known until the scientific approach to cooking became popularized in the work of Mary Lincoln and Fannie Farmer at the Boston Cooking school.

Still, Mormon chefs in the pioneer settlements had to measure their ingredients somehow. The pinch of salt may have varied from chef to chef, but we can tie some measurements to more concrete containers. The teacup of flour was likely a specific teacup used for every measurement. In other cases recipes relied on relative proportions. Sarah Annie Clark Hale's recipe for English plum pudding (see chapter 10) calls for "bowls" of ingredients. Though she likely used the same bowl each time in making the pudding, "bowl" could just as easily be read "part," as in "two parts flour, one part suet."

Other recipes call for measures by weight (see the recipe for bride's cake in chapter 9). The measurements "two pounds of sifted flour, two pounds of sifted loaf-sugar, two pounds of fresh butter" call for a scale. The DUP Memorial Museum in Salt Lake City displays many large and small examples of portable balance beam scales and weights used for such calculations. In addition to measuring volumes for cooking, these scales measured weights for exchanges between neighbors, for the marketing of produce, for payment of tithing, and even for newborn babies. Though guesstimates would suffice for some things, bride's cakes and babies demanded a more careful reckoning.

Food on the Landscape

The physical artifacts associated with pioneer food do not end with the kitchen. Mormon settlers were cultural agrarians. The growing of food defined their lives. While

Pear trees. *Left:* a pear tree, 150 years old or more, on the site of Brown's Fort (now called Fort Buenaventura, a Weber County Park property) in Ogden, Utah; *right:* a young pear tree grafted from the tree on the left at Fort Buenaventura. Author's collection.

some histories of Utah focus on politics, the economy, mining, or industry, Mormon settlers were primarily farmers. Remains of food-related efforts lie everywhere on the landscape, both as artifacts and as alterations of the land. A shallow linear depression in the ground in many communities might represent a ditch that once irrigated a crop. On Antelope Island, piles of rocks culled before the plow identify a long fallow wheat field, with sagebrush creeping back slowly. Craters and sunken hollows lined with rocks indicate where a cellar, now collapsed, once harbored apples, cider, or potatoes. Fremont Indian artifacts on the same landscape give even greater context to food activities over millennia. We continue to record our meals with artifacts in the ground. Landfills today burst with plastic packaging, representing meals that we've consumed.

Not all of this history is dead and decaying. In a recent bit of research, Brigham Young University professor Mark Thomas identified fruit trees in the urban business districts of Salt Lake City dating back more than a hundred years.[32] A pear tree in Ogden is a century and a half old. These heirloom fruit trees are truly antiques. Modern markets move increasingly toward such mutant hybrid creations as the pluot: a modern cross between a plum and apricot.

The material objects used by Mormon settlers in their daily lives serve to inform us about details that were not recorded in diaries. These antiques tell us about the lives of their owners and the values they held. Handcart pioneer Mary Ann Jones remembered one of her fellow English travelers carrying a tea colander tied to her apron string as they walked across the continent. Many other personal possessions were left behind, but tea was an important cultural marker. The colander became essential in preserving the English cultural identity in the New World. Though some new cultural dimensions were adopted, pioneers preserved others through the artifacts they brought with them.

The physical artifacts from pioneer cookery reflect a world of values and techniques at odds with our modern kitchen. These antiques often illustrate stories from the lives of early Mormon settlers. A crock, a cabbage shredder, and a Dutch oven all serve as a tangible connection to the past. Ken Braegger, our sauerkraut-making friend in Cache Valley, recalled that for years he felt a special fondness for his cabbage shredder, thinking that it had come from Europe a century earlier with his grandfather. But upon examining it one day he found a small inked stamp that read "Made in Ohio" and was forced to revise his family history.[33]

These stories reflect a social value for community, for delayed gratification, for shared intimate moments. A cheese-maker's tub tells a story about a woman and her cow and the patiently interwoven fabric of neighbors who share tools and food items. These stories are the opposite of a teenager sitting alone in front of a computer with a plastic bag of artificially flavored Cheetos. When we use these artifacts to re-create pioneer food items, we can internalize these stories and lives in a way not possible by simply reading about them. In a sense, we become a literal part of that story, just as an apple scion is grafted to new root stock.

CHAPTER 3

Pasture, Garden, Pantry, and Cellar

INGREDIENTS

One for the squirrel, one for the crow, one to rot, and one to grow on.
—Iowa corn-planting proverb

On a chilly Sunday in October 1854, Patty Sessions sat down to dinner with her husband. The table reflected the relative wealth she had come to know in her seven years in the Salt Lake Valley. As a member of the vanguard company in 1847, Patty had worked with gusto to improve her lot. Her table showed it. In her diary for October 29, 1854, she recorded an opulent menu for her Sunday dinner: cabbage, beets, carrots, and pork.[1] Some of her neighbors were still eating pigweed at this time, but Patty's gardening skills and years of investment brought three different vegetable dishes and a meat course to the table. Her menu reflects a seasonal diet composed of fall-harvested garden produce; autumn is also the season to butcher hogs. Cabbage, beets, carrots, and pork might sound more like a shopping list than a menu to a modern reader. Though we may not have her notes on the preparation of these items, we can learn a thing or two about the ingredients themselves.

With a Dutch oven and fire in the hearth standing ready, I turn now to a discussion of the ingredients of Mormon cookery. Food begins with agriculture. Cream for coffee and milk for gravy, flour for bread and the yeast to raise it, and the fruit for a pie or pudding begin with a cow, a wheat field, an orchard, and an irrigation ditch. When we fail to understand Mormon pioneer foodways, it is often because we have a can of fruit pie filling but no ditch or orchard to give it context. These common ingredients—cream, flour, fruit—show up frequently when we look at the diet of the Mormon pioneer. We recognize that these ingredients are part of our modern diet as well. "I know what flour is," you say. "It comes from wheat." Even so, we are about to discover how foreign this diet might be.

Horses pull a plow to prepare for planting. Early settlers would likely have used oxen for this task. Horses became more common after settlements were established.

The basic food ingredients that composed meals like the Sessions' dinner stand as antiquities in the world of agriculture. In the 150 years since Patty Sessions recorded her meals agriculture has shifted from seeds and animals that bred in the fashion of birds and bees to a brave new world composed of hybrid strains, genetically modified organisms, and artificial insemination. The crops and livestock of the Mormon pioneer reproduced naturally of their own accord; today's crops reproduce when triggered by a human hand. To differentiate the old-fashioned ingredients from new-fangled inventions of genetic manipulation, we call the pioneer types "heirloom." This name simply means that the genetic material reproduces in a natural fashion without human interventions and reproduces true to type so that each generation closely resembles the previous one. Strangely, this natural reproduction constitutes just a fraction of a percentage of the total of agricultural produce in the United States today.

Upon arriving in the Salt Lake Valley, members of the vanguard company of 1847 immediately put their plows to the earth and planted potatoes. The seeds they brought with them from the eastern states represented a cultural heritage. Within a week of arriving in the valley William Clayton reported that nearly fifty acres had been planted in buckwheat, corn, oats, potatoes, turnips, beans, and miscellaneous garden seed. Brigham Young ordered further plantings of peach pits and apple seeds.[2]

Desiring to keep some of their ethnic heritage alive as they put down new roots in a foreign land, some settlers brought seeds from the Old World with them. Mary Ann Hafen was one of these who brought seeds from Switzerland to plant in the desert of southern Utah.[3] Similarly, Daniel Tyler, a veteran of the Mexican War, brought seeds from California with him back to Utah:

Different members of our company brought various kinds of garden and fruit seeds, as well as grains from California, which were found very useful in this inland Valley, situated a thousand miles from any source of supply, as the mass had little or none of them, though a few may have been reasonably supplied. Lt. James Pace introduced the club-head wheat. The author and perhaps some others, the California pea, now so general and prolific as the field pea of Utah.[4]

Such importations of culture gave rise to new dishes. Potatoes, not tomatoes, figured prominently in the diet of Yankees from New England, the homeland of many Mormon pioneers. But when Benjamin Morgan Roberts returned from his stint in the army with the Mormon Battalion in 1847, he brought with him a new soup, "St. Jacob's," which blended the bacon and potatoes of traditional New England chowder with the tomatoes of the Southwest. For the Roberts family, the dish came to represent this essential chapter in their family history, akin to the "Chipman Dessert" of pink-eye beans.

St. Jacob's Soup

¼ pound salt pork
2 good sized potatoes, diced
2 onions, sliced
4 fresh tomatoes

Cut pork or bacon into small pieces and cook until brown, but not crisp. Cook potatoes and onions in boiling water until tender; add pork with some of drippings, also tomatoes, and simmer for 10 minutes. Serve with hard bread which has been toasted and cut into cubes. Seasoning should be added to taste.

—Benjamin Morgan Roberts, 1827–1891

The contributor notes that Benjamin's son, "Isaac Bullock Roberts, could prepare this soup better than anyone. The secret—learned from careful watching—was that he neglected to wash the potatoes before or after peeling."[5]

Some might say, "Ah! My ancestors came from New England, so they must have had foods familiar to me." The past is *still* a foreign place, even for those who might consider themselves locals. The carrots, potatoes, apples, and peaches familiar to us today are a world apart from the same fruits and vegetables grown by our farming ancestors. More than 98 percent of today's corn crop in North America is either hybridized or genetically modified. Neither of these technologies was available to pioneering Mormon farmers. The U.S. Department of Agriculture (USDA) keeps seed stock for some of these old heirloom varieties. In Geneva, New York, the Plant Genetics Resource Center maintains a collection of 2,500 apple tree varieties (who knew there were so many!). Phil Forsline, curator of the collection, observed that despite such diversity today's commercial apple crop still originates from just five of those: Red Delicious, Golden Delicious, Jonathan, Macintosh, and Cox's Orange

Pippin. Gala and Fuji share parentage from these.[6] In contrast, Mormon pioneer orchardists in the nineteenth century worked with dozens of different apple varieties.

In the spring of 1857 Wilford Woodruff proudly took note of the varieties in his orchard: Winter Pearmain, Yellow Newton Pippin, Rhode Island Greening, Alexander, Virginia Greening, Golden Russet, Fall Beauty, Milam Peaks Pleasant, Early June, Early Harvest, Baldwin, Tolpoy Hockien, Winesap (which he also renamed "20 ounce" for its huge fruits), Winter Queen, Newark King, June Eating, Esop Spitzenburgh, Mother Portor, Red June, Williams Early Red, Summer Pearmain, Red Astrocan, Golden Sweet, Rainbo (or Seek No Further), and Fall Pippin.[7] In 1856 Charles Oliphant reported further apple varieties as Sweet Mountain Home, Mountain Chief, Fall Spice, Lake, Hamilton Tart, Hamilton Sweet, Green Winter, Big Red, Geninton, and Yellow Bell Flower.[8] Of these, a modern Mormon cook might be lucky to find the Baldwin at the grocery store. The infamous, ubiquitous Red and Golden Delicious didn't arrive on the scene until the turn of the century. Our theoretical modern Mormon chef is more likely to find apple varieties that have been selected for their ability to grow on other continents in opposite seasons and then survive the shipping process to reach the markets of North America. Through the course of industrial agriculture, we have lost hundreds of varieties of fruits, vegetables, and grains and extirpated dozens of breeds of cattle, sheep, pigs, chickens, and goats that once made meat pies, roasts, and sausages. Because of these losses, we can never truly know the diverse bounty that Mormon settlers experienced in their harvests.

Apples provided a sugary treat when sugar was hard to come by.

Prize Strawberry Plants. Plants of the Wilson's Albany and Vicomtesse Strawberries which received the first prize in 1861 will be sold at $5 for 100 or $30 per 1000 this spring. These are the best. Also, Hovey's Seedling and Scarlet Magnate, at $1 per 100. Also, Blackberry, English Red White, Long Bunched Currant and Gooseberry Plants, exceedingly good and cheap.[9]   —*Deseret News*, 1856

In regard to the plantings of the vanguard company of 1847, William Clayton noted that potatoes were among the first crops planted. This company carried seed potatoes that would not last till the next spring—they had to be planted immediately. Potatoes planted in this manner involve a direct propagation of flesh from flesh. Farmers pruned flesh from the potato crop of 1846 to plant as seed for the crop of 1847. In this way we might trace some portion of each potato back hundreds of years.

A not-uncommon circumstance soon brought a need for a new potato breed. Through the first half of the nineteenth century European and American agriculture leaned heavily on Irish potato varieties, particularly one called the Lumper. Irish farmers knew little of the need for strengthening their breeding stock against blights and disease. Overplanting weakened the gene pool for this variety, which eventually fell victim to blight in 1844. Potato crops across the globe rotted in the ground. As a result, millions of Irish faced famine. Thousands of Irish families fled to America, looking for a more stable existence.

In 1850 Chauncey Goodrich received some potato samples through a friend stationed in the American embassy in Panama. Using one sample called the Rough Purple Chili, Goodrich selected and crossed varieties. In 1853 he introduced the Garnet Chili, a large, round red potato with white flesh. Chile's mountain regions, the ancestral home to all potatoes, hold hundreds of yet-undiscovered potato varieties. This new variety proved resistant to various blights, and the potato farmers of Europe and America quickly embraced it as the antidote to the Irish potato famine. The Garnet Chili proved its value as a genetic contributor to what eventually became the Russet potato. Today the Russet and its progeny account for more than 90 percent of the potato crop in America. Although the Garnet Chili was among the most common varieties of potatoes in America 150 years ago, it is believed to be extinct today. Its second-generation descendant, the Early Rose, is still available from USDA inventories (and some gardening networks) but is not grown commercially.[10]

Compared to modern potato varieties, the Early Rose is truly an antique. Many generations have passed since this old spud made its debut in the United States. Its story is not an uncommon one. We might find similar tales about King Philip corn or Red Fife wheat. Once the staple cash crop of farmers across the nation, these venerable breeds now stand on the brink of extinction. The Feejee tomato appeared on the 1864 seed list of Mormon seedsman Joseph Ellis Johnson.[11] A forerunner of most modern American tomato varieties, the Feejee tomato is now thought to be entirely extinct. These heirlooms are source varieties that contributed the foundations of the modern hybrids on which American agriculture stands. Yet they are also just one bad season from extinction, as their genetic base erodes with each year they are not planted.

A familiar chore: peeling potatoes for dinner.

In the agricultural venues of the twenty-first century these older vegetable breeds are often called "heirloom" varieties. The title is a contrast primarily with hybrid varieties. Heirloom plants breed through open pollination, freely exchanging DNA through natural propagation (facilitated by birds, bees, and wind). Heirloom plants propagate kind for kind: seeds from Brandywine tomatoes naturally yield successive generations of Brandywine tomato plants. The "heirloom" title connotes a sort of antiquity, particularly when contrasted with modern agriculture. Most modern crops are not heirloom but hybrid.

Hybrid plants are an artificial cross-breeding of two different varieties. Rather than being propagated by birds or bees, they are bred by human intervention. Hybrid seed-corn farmers place a bag over the tassels of corn plants, preventing the pollen (male seed) from reaching the silk (female flower). Instead the farmers go down the rows with pollen gathered from a different variety and inseminate the silks by hand. From this unnatural union the first generation yields an increased vigor and bounty, but seeds from subsequent generations fail to produce true to type and are often sterile. These seed-corn producers aim for sterility, which compels farmers to buy more seed each year rather than saving seed from their crop. For genetically modified corn crops (engineered to withstand Roundup pesticide applications) saving seed is prohibited by contract.

Not all heirlooms and open-pollinated varieties are historic, however. Agronomists and backyard plant breeders have selectively invented many new varieties in recent years. Broccoli and zucchini are both twentieth-century inventions unknown to the first Mormon settlers. Distinct historic varieties evolved as science and farming became ever more closely married. The further back into history we go, the more limited and rudimentary these historic vegetables and varieties become.

Garden Seeds for Sale. 100 lbs sugar beet; also rutabaga or Swedish turnip, carrot, parsnip, onion, radish, lettuce, early June peas, cucumber, melon, cabbage, with a variety of other garden seeds.[12]   —*Deseret News*, 1853

Planting an heirloom garden can be one way to make a more direct connection with the foodways of Mormon pioneers. Resources abound for the modern heirloom gardener. Seed Savers Exchange offers heirloom seeds for sale as well as a network directory of other gardeners who safeguard heirloom seeds of a thousand varieties. Some varieties are easier for beginning gardeners. Corn, beans, squash, and carrots yield easily. Other varieties such as tomatoes, potatoes, and melons take a more practiced hand. But any endeavor in your own garden plot will enrich the study of historical food far beyond what might be possible with canned food from the grocery store.

Curiously, garlic does not show up in Mormon diaries or menus. Though many Mormons today embrace the aromatic herb, it appears that this acceptance has only occurred in the last fifty years. Immigrants from England and Scandinavia would not have found use for garlic, which is generally cultivated only in warmer climates. Mormon missionaries brought only a few converts from Italy, Greece, and France. As a result, Mormon chefs were slow to find a use for garlic, though its cousin the onion was widely employed.

Mormon chefs used nutmeg as their go-to seasoning. When recipes called for additional spice, that spice was usually nutmeg. Pioneer Patience Loader noted that

A woman moves a chicken through the process of becoming food. Her nice clothing indicates a posed photograph from the turn of the century.

her new husband allowed a pound of nutmeg when he provided a pantry for their new home.[13] These would have been whole nuts, grated as needed. Other dry whole spices such as cardamom, cinnamon, cloves, and pepper were also available but used less widely.

Fruit varieties hold a particular place of interest for the student of Mormon pioneer food. Anxious to fulfill the prophecy that "the desert shall blossom as the rose," farmers such as Wilford Woodruff devoted extensive energy to developing apples, peaches, and pears suited to the Utah climate. Starting from traditional stocks common in the eastern states, farmers selected and altered stocks and renamed them after local personalities. The Winesap apple became known in Utah as the Pound apple, due to its large fruits.[14] Even so, Utah orchards today are dominated by Red Delicious apples. The Pound is nearly entirely gone, with only a few study specimens remaining. The renaming of varieties creates consternation for agricultural historians.

We might tell a similar story in relation to animal breeds. Early breeds often served multiple functions. The oxen that pulled Mormon wagons over the Rocky Mountains, red and white Shorthorn cattle, provided beef and milk in addition to their draft power. The sheep of the Navajo Indians, the Spanish Churro, became the sheep of the intermountain Mormon kingdom, providing both wool and mutton. Emily Barnes remembered that her neighbor John Hooper "brought with him what they called cochin China chickens. They were large red chickens. Everyone tried to get a start so would go and buy or borrow a few."[15] These birds provided eggs and meat.

Yet by the turn of the century these fundamental breeds had lost ground to new-comers. The introduction of Barred Plymouth Rock chickens in 1869, with their uniform plumage and vertical single comb, made the old rose-combed Dominique breed obsolete nearly overnight. Fine-wooled Spanish Merino sheep from Europe prompted a craze for downy softness that made the old Churro wool seem so coarse as to be undesirable. By 1960 the breed tottered on the edge of extinction. Holstein cattle dominated over Shorthorns by the sheer volume of milk that they produced. Specialized agriculture split beef and dairy breeds so that Angus and Herefords displaced the smaller Shorthorn steers.

Fruits, vegetables, and livestock make a fairly smooth transition from the field or barnyard to the pot or table. Other crops require more intense levels of refining before we might call them "ingredients." Milk could be used directly for cheese or skimmed for cream. Cream could be poured straight into coffee, churned to butter, or clabbered on the stove before being served as a dessert. A cut of meat could be cooked without any other preparation or might be cured or ground before using. But the most obvious example of intensive refining is wheat.

Wheat, like most grain crops, has a fairly intense cycle of production, harvest, and milling before it is ready to eat. With some varieties (called "winter wheat") that are planted in the fall and harvested in late spring, it might seem even more complex. Once sown, wheat only requires irrigation. The thickly planted fields choke out most weeds so that further cultivation is unnecessary. Mormon pioneer farmers would have harvested their winter wheat in June, while it still looked green in the field. When the individual wheat berries no longer exuded a milky juice when crushed, it would be ready to cut. For years most of this work was done by hand with a sickle or scythe. Often it was a family or community effort. Men would cut the green wheat and lay it down in orderly rows. Women would come behind and bind the wheat into shocks, using a few lengths of wheat straw. Children would follow last and stack the shocks in standing bunches to let it dry. If the wheat was cut after the heads had dried, the force of the cutting blow would burst the seeds and lose the crop. Gleaners cleaned up what was left, often gathering dozens of bushels.

Once the wheat was dry, farmers took the bundles to the threshing barn. In the early days before fanning mills and threshing machines Emily Barnes described how her family processed their wheat crop. "We would take the sheaves of wheat and lay them on a sheet; then beat them with a stick till all the wheat was out. Then we would pour the wheat out of a bucket and let the wind clean it."[16] In her early years Emily's family lived on the lower end of the economy, without the benefit of mechanization in the harvest. Many Utah farmers adopted mechanized processes for the harvest long before the coming of the railroad. The Deseret Manufacturing and Agricultural Society offered a premium or prize to any farmer who might invent a superior reaper or threshing machine. More prosperous farmers accomplished these chores with machinery. Brigham Young and Ezra Benson hired out their threshing machine and fanning mill (likely powered by horses on a treadmill) to those who could afford it in 1851.[17]

With a wagon full of clean wheat (grist), the farmers could sell it at the market or have it processed into flour. The Chase Mill at Liberty Park in Salt Lake City was one

Wheat harvest, circa 1870. The whole community comes together for this critical work party celebrating the efforts of a season.

of the earliest grist mills in the territory. Water from Red Butte Creek flowed into a mill pond where Isaac Chase could regulate its flow to his machinery. Before gasoline and steam engines, such water power drove most industrial operations. When channeled through ditches and over a waterwheel, the moving mass of water turned grindstones that cut the tiny seeds to pieces, revealing the germ and endosperm inside.

This flour was composed of the entire wheat berry—the outer bran, the germ, and the endosperm. It was whole wheat flour. Chase's mill, however, was sophisticated enough to sift these parts separately once again. Wheat germ, though high in nutritive value, is also laden with oils, which turn rancid if not refrigerated. Bran contributes dietary fiber but makes a poor cake. John Neff's grist mill (built in 1848 near the mouth of Mill Creek Canyon near Salt Lake City) sifted out variations of grist and flour from whole wheat to graham, shorts, and middlings and fine white baker's flour.[18] Still other flour variations came from blending different kinds of grain, such as rye with wheat or corn with rye. Cornmeal (also known as Indian meal or bannock) required similar refinements.

In many early settlements, like those of southern Utah in the 1860s, wheat was a long time in coming. Alice Langston Dalton grew up in Rockville in the 1860s. She wrote: "We made quite a lot of corn bread as there was no wheat grown here until I was six or eight years of age [in the 1870s]. My father, in order to get flower [*sic*] would take his molasses and dried fruits and vegetables north and trade for flour, machinery and other things to use."[19]

As Dalton noted, corn is often the staple grain of new settlements. Corn can be grown in small patches grubbed out between rocks and irrigated by bucket as

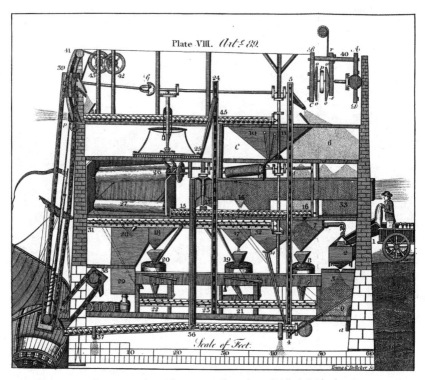

A plate from Oliver Evans's 1795 classic *The Young Mill-wright and Miller's Guide*, showing a cross section of the interior of a flour mill. Evans's designs were likely the basis for early flour mills in Utah. Courtesy Clark Cheney.

necessary. Wheat requires larger fields, well cultivated and without stones. It demands a dense planting over a large area in order to find support against the wind. In these larger fields, wheat can't be irrigated by bucket. For these and other reasons, early settlers leaned on corn.

As the staple grain of outlying settlements, corn carried many of the same processing concerns as wheat. Like wheat, corn has an oily germ just waiting to go rancid. Cornmeal is bound to spoil if not used quickly. Corn, like wheat, has a hull that is difficult to digest. But unlike wheat, the germ and the hull cannot be removed through milling. Instead early settlers removed the hull through a home-based process involving lye. Twice while on the trail from Winter Quarters to Utah in 1847 Patty Sessions worked through this process to hull her corn.[20] The end product is hominy.

Traditionally we perceive hominy as a food item from the Old South, associated with share cropping and African American foodways. This association highlights the connection of corn culture with rural and marginal food patterns. There is some truth here, but hominy held a considerable place in the foodways of many Mormon pioneers. During the Utah War of 1857, Henry Ballard took part in the defense of Echo Canyon as the Mormon settlements awaited the arrival of the U.S. Army. He wrote that he survived on a diet of hominy and beef while pulling picket duty in Echo

Canyon.[22] But hominy also found a place at more formal settings. The Territorial Ball of 1860 (a rather high-class affair) featured hominy as part of the vegetable course. Hominy ran through all levels of Mormon cuisine.

Hominy

I use the proportion of a tablespoon of powdered lye* to one quart of water. When the water is boiling I turn in the corn and stir it constantly to prevent burning. Boil it until the outer skins and little black specs [*sic*] at the end of the grain come loose, which will be in about twenty minutes. Then take the hominy from the fire, drain and turn water on it. Rub it gently to loosen the husks and turn dipper after dipper of cold water on it until you have washed it out in the cold water four or five times. Put back on the fire and boil again in fresh water, and when it just comes to a boil, drain it off and repeat until all the husks are gone and the hominy has become firm, white and tender. It will keep a long time, although we do not allow it to keep long at our house.

—Isabella Rogers, 1858–1951[23]

* Powdered lye shows Isabella's modern adaptation. In her younger days, she would have used liquid lye manufactured at home by leeching water through hardwood ashes.

Shocked corn stands drying in the field. Before combine tractors farmers would bundle shocks of corn to dry the ears. The ears were then husked and stored whole in corncribs until they were needed as feed for livestock.

Corn helped settlers hang on while their farms took root. But as soon as Mormon farmers could plow larger acreage, wheat and wheat flour took center stage as the base of the settlers' diet. Stories abound of neighbors sharing their last cup of flour in desperate times or of trail-bound emigrants marching for days on one cup of flour. Though other wild ingredients surrounded them in the wilderness, they yearned for wheat and flour. On its own flour can be quite palatable when baked as bread. With a little sweetness added (as in a cake), it can become delightful. Before sugar refining technology became practical near the end of the nineteenth century, Mormon settlers experimented widely with different approaches for sweetening their diet. Molasses proved to be the most readily available solution.

The earliest settlers tried all manner of sources for sweetening: sap from the box elder tree was hailed as producing sugar comparable to eastern sugar maples. Some boiled parsnips or watermelons to render a bit of syrup. By the mid-1850s industrial-minded entrepreneurs mounted a sugaring enterprise. Although it never found success, locals used the sugar beet and sorghum cane crops individually to produce their own molasses. A few excerpts from the diary of Wilford Woodruff illustrate:

> 10-31-57: I spent the fore part of the day grinding sugar cane. I got 30 gallons of juice from a small wagon box of cane.
> 11-2-57: I spent most of the day at home preparing to make beet molasses.
> 11-14-57: I spent the day & night making beet molasses. We made 24 gallons during the day and night which closed up our molasses making for this year. We made 110 gallans [sic] of Beet Molasses & 15 gallons of Chinees [sic] sugar cane Molasses.[23]

An active member of the Deseret Agricultural and Manufacturing Society, Wilford followed a rigorous empirical approach to finding best agricultural practices. In particular the society was interested in making the leap from molasses to crystallized sugar. In earlier efforts the society experimented with imphee cane.[24] It crystallized quickly and yielded one gallon of syrup from five gallons of juice. By 1866 sorghum had become the preferred cane. Its syrup readily crystallized to sugar, with more efficiency than the imphee cane.

To Make Molasses

First, take the cane when the seed turns brown strip the blades off and all the boot that comes easy, do not let the cane freeze or dry in the sun any longer than you can conveniently get it up, then crush it as soon as possible, soon after the juice is pressed out, put it in a hogshead or barrel, and let it stand overnight.

Second, take pinion pine and burn it into charcoal, take half a bushel and beat it up as fine as grains of wheat, put it up into a hopper on coarse straw or hay, then put upon that half a bushel of your coarsest coal, then pour your sugar water upon that and let it run through slowly, after it runs through that, then take a coarse piece of cloth and strain well, then put it into a copper or brass boiler and boil it slowly until the juice turns red, then add one pound of sugar to every twenty gallons of juice, and continue to boil slowly till thick enough to string off the dipper while hot, then put it in stoneware and let it remain six days without moving, then drain the syrup from the surface and dry the sugar in the open air.

This method rendered five pounds of sugar for every gallon of syrup.[25]

A modern consumer might have difficulty reckoning such a volume of sweetening, when we might only purchase fifty pounds of granulated sugar annually. Much of the sugar we use today is included in our food products before we purchase them. Soft drinks, for example, contain ten teaspoons of sugar in each serving. Jellies and jams are likewise loaded with sugar. Settlers like Woodruff had to procure all of this sweetening on the front end and then use it in producing fruit preserves at home. With Woodruff's polygamous marriages, even more sweetening was needed for multiple homesteads. In addition, sweetening was frequently used as a medium of exchange. In this light Woodruff's 1858 production, which exceeded 250 gallons, seems hardly enough.

Home-based efforts like those of Woodruff supplied the bulk of sweetening used by Utah settlers. Capitalists tried a variety of industrial milling efforts to produce granular sugar (most notably the sugar mill that gave its name to the Sugar House neighborhood southeast of downtown Salt Lake City), but all failed. As former LDS church historian Leonard Arrington noted, "Molasses remained the principal source of sweet in the territory until the successful establishment of the beet sugar factory at Lehi in the 1890s."[26]

Sweets like molasses also produce vinegar for flavoring and food preservation. Molasses and vinegar opened up worlds of possibility for food preservation. Used

The sugar factory or mill was first built in 1853. A similarly modeled building serves as the visitor center at the This Is the Place Monument in the foothills above Salt Lake City.

in volume, either could suffice to deter bacterial growth. Molasses took considerable effort to procure, but vinegar often came without asking.

All vinegar begins as alcohol.[27] Alcohol begins as sugar. Working from a base of something sweet, the pioneers introduced yeast (sometimes unwittingly) to the sweetness and started fermentation. With barley malt, the fermentation yielded beer; with apples, cider; with grapes, wine. Some frugal settlers used sugar-laden pea shells (still carrying their dusty coating of yeast) as fuel for fermentation.[28] Once the fermentation of the original sugars was completed, vinegar makers exposed the new alcohol to air. Levi Savage, a Mormon wine maker in Toquerville, left this terse diary entry regarding his vinegar-making process: "I repared [sic] some barrels & put water on the pummys [pommace] to make vinegar."[29] After the first run of wine production, he added water again to the pommace (crushed grapes, skins, and stems) to extract the last lingering sugars. In the absence of a strong yeast fermentation, the open vats attracted the vinegar bacteria instead. Alcohol production works best in absence of oxygen exposure. The vinegar bacteria *Acetebater*, however, thrives with lots of fresh air. Once the culture was established, repeated feeding resulted in a constant supply of vinegar.

Vinegar
To Make in Three Weeks.—Molasses 1 qt.; yeast 1 pt.; warm rain water 3 gals. Put all into a jug or keg, and tie a piece of gauze over the bung to keep out flies and let in air. In hot weather set it in the sun; in cold weather set it by the stove or in the chimney corner, and in three weeks you will have good vinegar. When this is getting low, pour out some for use, and fill up the jug in the same proportion as at first, and you will never have trouble for want of good vinegar.[30]

Note: because airborne vinegar bacteria proliferate readily, many brewers and vintners advise against making beer, wine, or cider if you've recently made vinegar in the same kitchen; the risk of cross-contamination is high.   —*Dr. Chase's Recipes*, 1864

Beyond the specific food items in a recipe, Mormon settlers defined their diet by the seasons. Church leaders often opined on dietary habits from the pulpit. George Q. Cannon objected to eating "flesh" in the summer time, advocating fish and eggs instead. Swine, he thought, should be reserved for winter consumption. Brigham Young advised, "Kill your cattle when they are fat, and salt down the meat, that you may have meat to eat in the winter."[31] Some might point to this as a prophetic revelation for the needs of a peculiar people. We see it simply as a reflection of a seasonal diet common throughout the country, combining food consumption with preservation technology. Hogs weaned in June become fat and ready to butcher in December, as Patty Sessions showed with her diary entries in December 1854.

Similarly, Patty showed her keen awareness of the absence of fresh vegetables in her diet during the trek from Nauvoo to Winter Quarters. She noted in September 1846: "P G brought home a watter mellon [sic] and some apples came into camp I bought a 14 dozen gave a cent a piece the first vegatable I have tasted this year it was good."[32] Her diary entries for December of each year invariably describe butchering hogs. Both meat and vegetable defined the seasonality of the nineteenth-century diet.

Gardens opened each spring with peas and radishes. Settlers also gathered sego bulbs from the hills in late spring, before the desert sun withered the delicate lily. Lettuce dipped in salted vinegar water, the standby salad of refinement, merged spring into summer. Beans and corn came on in midsummer. Tomatoes, cabbages, potatoes, and carrots rounded out the fall. John D. Lee noted his donation of "peas, beans, beets, cucumbers, green corn, melons, etc." to the July 24 feast in 1859.[33] Fresh vegetables graced tables in the warm seasons, and preserved fruits carried settlers through harsh winters. Barrels of apple cider bubbled away in cellars, carefully aging through the winter for spring consumption.

Some dishes also reflect seasonality in their composition. Steamed bread puddings, a hallmark of cuisine from a bygone era, separate into summer puddings and winter puddings. Summer puddings have a lighter, savory character, often being served with gravy (think of a traditional Yorkshire pudding). Winter puddings are sweeter and spicier, with more lard, fruit, and nuts.[34] As an example, Elizabeth Kane shared a plum pudding with Brigham Young in December 1872. Winter puddings often came with a sweet sauce. The increased use of fats and sugars marks the transition to a winter diet for Mormon pioneers. Though many of the old pioneer ingredients are gone, we still see their shadows in our food patterns from time to time.

The raw food items that stocked the pioneer pantry, smokehouse, and root cellar are worlds apart from what you might find at the supermarket. Though some of the old breeds and seeds can still be obtained today, the raw ingredients we would most likely use to re-create Mormon pioneer food come from industrial agriculture fueled by hybrids, genetically modified sources, and petroleum-based pesticides and fertilizers. We might reach for something akin to the pioneer diet, but some elements are likely so far removed as to be out of reach. Were we to sit down to a Sunday dinner in Patty Sessions's home in 1854, we would experience food as foreign to our palate as any cuisine from China or India.

Resources for Heirloom Gardeners

Seed Savers Exchange: a nonprofit network organization to facilitate the preservation and exchange of open pollinated seeds. A retail catalog offers seeds to gardeners who don't have seeds to trade; a seed inventory identifies other gardeners who do have seeds to trade (www.seedsavers.org).

Native Seeds/SEARCH: A nonprofit organization selling seeds for crops traditionally grown by Native Americans in the American Southwest (www.nativeseeds.org).

Resources for Heirloom Livestock Breeders

The American Livestock Breeds Conservancy (ALBC) is a nonprofit membership organization working to protect over 150 breeds of livestock and poultry from extinction. Similar to Seed Savers Exchange, the ALBC publishes a listing of specific breeds and breeders to facilitate exchange and strengthen the breeds (www.albc-usa.org).

CHAPTER 4

Four Ounces of Flour

FOOD ON THE TRAIL

For some must push and some must pull
As we go marching up the hill;
So merrily on our way we go
Until we reach the Valley-o.
— "The Handcart Song," 1856

In a glass museum display case three brown feathers pierce a yellowed card. The accompanying note attributes the feathers to Harriet Amelia Folsom. Upon waking one morning in 1846, she found herself part of the Mormon exodus from Nauvoo. She tied her apron around her waist and went to gather breakfast. Her father appointed this chore; it was an easy task for an eight-year-old girl to scoop up the quail that ran heedlessly through the camp on the west side of the Mississippi. As the Mormon pioneers made their exodus from Nauvoo, they believed that these flocks of quail were a miraculous demonstration of God's love for his chosen people. Years later, after marrying Brigham Young, Amelia often recounted this memory of her apron filled with clucking quail.[1] In the minds of trail-bound Mormons, they subsisted on a diet of miracles.

Much of what we revere about the pioneer myth is found in the seminal experience of crossing the plains. Parallels to the journeys of Moses in the wilderness evoke metaphors linking pioneers and the camp of Israel. Just as manna and quail defined the Israelites' journey, we see the food and meals prepared on the pioneer trail as critical to understanding our pioneer ancestors. The trail experience of the Mormon pioneer has been called a crucible and serves as a metaphor for the Mormon pioneer experience as a whole. In later years status as a pioneer who had crossed the plains gave an individual a particular place of honor in the community. Today we see the food element of this trail experience as a vital medium through which the experience can be interpreted.

Historian Wil Bagley recently wrote a brief criticism regarding popular perceptions of the trail experience. Noting particularly the Martin and Willie company handcart disasters, he observed that these key points in history have come to represent the epitome of the pioneer experience to devout modern Mormons.[2] Mormon handcart reenactments eclipse the wagon experience; many young people seem to believe that all Mormon pioneers came by handcart and that all starved. In fact, the Martin and Willie company disasters represent only a tiny fraction of the pioneer trail experience. Similarly, historians for the National Park Service observed that the trail experience was a grand adventure for the overwhelming majority of pioneers, largely void of tragedy.[3] Still, many pioneers did experience keen hunger, both as part of the trail experience and also after settling in Utah.

Death from starvation, illness, and exposure runs as a recurrent theme through many Mormon trail narratives. We often focus on these hardships because they carry pathos and emotive weight. Many scholars, however, have voiced their dissent from this focus. John Unruh, historian of the overland migration, concluded that death rates during the trail experience ranged between 3 and 4 percent. Melvin Bashore, a senior librarian with the LDS Church History Library, focused on the Mormon trail experience and estimated an overall trail death rate of 3 percent. This figure is skewed by the anomaly of the Martin and Willie companies, however. While 250 immigrant companies followed the Mormon trail (each company representing hundreds of people), 7 of those companies account for 47 percent of all Mormon trail deaths. Of those companies, 80 experienced no deaths whatsoever. The 3 percent mortality rate gains context in a 1939 study estimating that the Mormons might have expected a 2.5 percent mortality rate in the eastern states if they had stayed home and not experienced the trail.[4]

Discussion of food on the trail begins with provisions from the wagon. Brigham Young issued his directives for supplies, as did dozens of other authors of "Emigrants' Guides." After weeks of threatening to pack up and leave Nauvoo following the assassination of Joseph Smith, Brigham Young published a list of requisite provisions for the trail. The *Nauvoo Neighbor*, one of the official newspapers of the LDS Church, listed the following essential foodstuffs for each family:

1000 lbs. of flour or other bread or bread stuffs in good sack	½ lb. cloves
	25 lbs. salt
2 or more milk cows	5 lbs. saleratus
1 or more good beeves	10 lbs. dried apples
1 lb. tea	½ bushel of beans
5 lbs. coffee	A few lbs. of dried beef or bacon
100 lbs. sugar	5 lbs. dried peaches
1 lb. cayenne pepper	20 lbs. dried pumpkin
2 lbs. black pepper	25 lb. seed grain
½ lb. mustard	1 gal. alcohol
1 doz. nutmegs	Cooking utensils to consist of a
10 lbs. rice for each family	bake kettle, frying pan, coffee
1 lb. cinnamon	pot, and tea kettle.[5]

These provisioning lists were ideals. Heber C. Kimball, prosperous farmer that he was, left Nauvoo well outfitted for the journey. His provisions exceeded many of the

THE PIONEERS.

An illustration of pioneers on the plains from T. B. H. Stenhouse's exposé *The Rocky Mountain Saints* (New York: D. Appleton and Company, 1873).

standard recommended allowances for flour, bacon, beans, and salt. Divided among six wagons, Kimball's supplies were measured in tons.[6]

Caroline Hopkins Clark (1831–1900), a middle-class English pioneer of 1866, advised her friends:

> Be sure when you come to bring plenty of flour, suet, lard, currants, raisins, a little tartaric acid, bicarbonate of soda, baking powder. . . . Be sure to bring some onions and potatoes. If you cook your meat one day and have some left, it makes nice potatoe pies. You must bring flour. Then the fat of the meat makes a nice crust.[7]

Caroline's letter comes from experience, after she had made it to Utah. She seems not to have been terribly put out by the conditions on the trail, in spite of the death of her year-old baby en route and of another child once settled, with a third baby born soon after.

Handcart trekkers were each allowed between 17 and 50 pounds of bedding, clothing, and personal items.[8] Beyond these limited personal items, handcarts were loaded primarily with flour, with a total load of 500 pounds. Additional flour as well as small staples (bacon, coffee, dried apples) followed the train in one or two support wagons drawn by oxen. Cattle to be butchered on the trail carried their own weight as they were driven along behind the wagons. In dire circumstances, wagon companies butchered oxen that were unfit to carry on.

These provisions lists form the first incarnation of the Mormon emigrants' trail diet. Like infantry soldiers who were expected to forage for food in addition to their rations, wagon companies might have experienced various levels of affluence or preparedness; the "daily ration" certainly was not universal for either group. Adult handcart trekkers with the Willie Company and Martin Company were initially issued a daily ration of "1 lb wheat flour, 2½ ounces pork, 2 ounces sugar, 2 ounces dried apples, ¼ lb coffee, ½ ounce tea, soda, and soap."[9] This daily ration amounts to about 2,230 calories per day. Travelers could occasionally purchase additional luxury items such as beef, butter, or bacon at forts and towns along the trail.[10]

Andrew Jenson, a Danish emigrant of the 1860s, remembered a more comfortable daily ration, which "consisted of 1½ pounds of flour and one pound of bacon each day for each adult besides sugar, molasses, dried fruit and other eatables."[11] Jenson's allotment likely came from a standard established by the Perpetual Emigration Fund (PEF). These immigrants received passage through charitable donations by Mormons already in Utah. The dietary allowance for each ten people included 1,000 lbs. flour, 50 lbs. bacon, 50 lbs. rice, 30 lbs. beans, 20 lbs. dried apples, and 50 lbs. sugar.[12] Certainly Heber Kimball's personal wealth would have allowed an almost opulent table on the trail compared to the handcart trekkers who followed ten years after him.

These supply lists stand in direct relation to the daily calories burned on the trail as well as in anticipation of what might lie at the end of the trail. Though pioneers generally put in less than an eight-hour day, the level of activity was intense. Walking up and down hills over uneven ground in shoes that could never be called orthopedic, immigrants burned a minimum of 200 calories an hour. Rest stops at lunch gave some respite, but the miles had to be covered. Daily mileage varied, depending on the mode of travel. The first handcart company of 1856 (Ellsworth Company) completed a journey of 1,400 miles in nine weeks, averaging 23 miles a day.[13] Another English handcart trekker reported daily mileage varying between 5 and 32 miles, depending on trail conditions and the condition of the pioneers themselves.[14] The open prairies of Nebraska rolled by much more quickly than the rugged trails through the Rocky Mountains. Wagon companies powered by oxen moved more slowly and may have averaged 10 miles a day, making the 1,000-mile journey in roughly 100 days, not counting Sabbath rest days.

Most pioneers walked every step of the way. For handcart emigrants (a minority of all pioneers), the exercise of pulling the cart increased the expenditure of energy. Men and boys (and some women, like Mary Fielding Smith) drove oxen, walking beside them with a switch or goad to direct them. Beef and dairy cattle required herding on foot as well. Herding cows is an exercise in two steps forward and one step back. Walking was more comfortable than riding in these crowded wagons without springs or air-cushioned suspension. Once in camp for the evening, women kept on working, preparing meals and cleaning up dishes. This labor involved hauling gallons of water in cast-iron and wooden containers. Men cared for cattle and milked cows. Pioneers burned calories every waking minute.

In the face of this inventory of labor, it appears that the daily caloric expenditure easily exceeded 3,000 calories. The daily rations for PEF and handcart immigrants (as described above), however, only afforded 2,200 calories, if the ration was fully available. Though some pioneers were able to purchase extra supplies or gather wild foods along the trail, the calories burned often exceeded the calories consumed. This is especially true for handcart emigrants, who served as their own beasts of burden.

The emigrants could become ravenous. When they were well supplied, suppers composed of fatty meat and potatoes along with biscuits and beans provided a steady supply of calories. Still, hunger gnawed at emigrants every day as a result of the gauntlet of the trail. One traveler remembered:

> Near Fort Laramie one of the emigrants, after having eaten his supper one night took a stroll through the camp of one of the wagon companies near by, where an acquaintance and friend kindly asked him to have some supper. With "thanks" he thought he would. So he sat down with the wagon people and did full justice to some fried beef and bacon, with biscuit, which he thought was as savory dish as he had tasted in many a day. After [waiting] as long as he could put on a face to do so, he finished his second supper, but without feeling much more satisfied than when he first sat down. If anybody else had kindly extended to him another invitation to supper that night, I have no doubt he would have accepted gladly, and done full justice to the supper.[15]

A Typical Daily Trail Menu

Based on the sources cited here, we can piece together what might be a typical day's fuel from food. This menu assumes an adequate supply of staple ingredients, as was the common experience, rather than the spectacular deprivations that make tragic headlines.

Breakfast—rusk served with butter and molasses, fried salt pork, bacon, or ham, coffee with cream, perhaps some dried fruit or berries in cream.
Dinner (or "lunch" in modern parlance)—biscuit with molasses and fresh milk.
Supper—stewed beef or beef steak fried in bacon fat, sautéed onions, biscuits, and coffee; perhaps a molasses cake for a special occasion.

John Fairbanks's trail diary notes an almost religious observance of breakfast each morning but provides no specifics for the menu.[16] Breakfasts might have been cornmeal mush or hasty pudding, lumpy dick (flour gruel), biscuits, or scrapple. Wilford Woodruff recorded the hasty breakfast of another party they surprised on the trail: "In clearing up their breakfast they strewed their meal, salt, bacon, Short Cake, Jonney cake [corn bread] Beans & other things upon the ground through their encampment."[17]

Woodruff might like us to believe that all was order and cleanliness in the Mormon trail camp. John Jaques told a different story. After crossing a long dry stretch of prairie he watched as the cattle bolted for what was to be the camp watering hole that evening. The cattle waded in and made a mucky mess of it. "But it was all the water available and so it was used to cooking purposes—making coffee, tea, bread

Mormon immigrants making camp on the Elk Horn River, 1848. It is not certain whether such squalor was typical.

and porridge or hasty pudding, which when made was quite black, but was eaten and drunk nevertheless."[18]

Flour Hasty Pudding

Tie together half a dozen peach-leaves, put them into a quart of milk, and set it on the fire to boil. When it has come to a hard boil, take out the leaves, but let the pot remain boiling on the fire. Then with a large wooden spoon in one hand, and some wheat flour in the other, thicken and stir it till it is about the consistency of a boiled custard. Afterwards throw in, one at a time, a dozen small bits of butter rolled in a thick coat of flour. You may enrich it by stirring in a beaten egg or two, a few minutes before you take it from the fire. When done, pour it into a deep dish, and strew brown sugar thickly over the top. Eat it warm.

—*Directions for Cookery*, 1853[19]

Note: This dish may also be made of cornmeal. The peach leaves contribute acids and pectin to set the milk curd.

Add a small pinch of dirt, sand, or ash to each serving to simulate trail conditions.

According to Lorenzo Young, the Mormon companies approached breakfast with more order and civility. He made particular note of one joyful breakfast. After getting up early to pick wild strawberries, Lorenzo returned to find a spread of biscuits with butter, coffee, strawberries with sweetening, and a bit of pickled pork. With such "luxuries of life" the trail didn't seem quite so bad.[20] Such opulence may have been less than common. Handcart trekkers often made breakfast with a thin gruel of flour in water or a biscuit with molasses.[21] Though trail conditions didn't often allow for luxury, neither was the wolf constantly at the door.

In order to make the recommended daily mileage, lunch might be eaten on the road from a pocket store of bread spread with butter, lard, or molasses. Annie Taylor Dee, whose family brought two freshened cows on the trail, remembered innumerable lunches of bread and fresh milk, with no fire for cooking.[22] The wagons and carts would stop for an hour or two to "bait" the animals. At dinner the company could butcher a steer to provide fresh beef for the whole camp. Travelers frequently noted stewed beef or soup from a beef bone as they wrote about their evening meals. Creative emigrants devised ways to make pies from apples dried for the trail.

A Family Stew of Beef.—Take any piece of beef good for stewing, cut it into small pieces, slice 2 or 3 large onions, and put them into the stew pan with 2 ounces of butter or good beef-dripping. When melted, dredge in some flour, add the meat also dredged with flour, and enough water to keep it from burning. When the gravy has drawn, fill up with boiling water, let it come to a boil gently, skim the pot well, then add a spoonful of mixed spices, and a bay-leaf or two; set the pan by the side of the fire to stew slowly for a couple of hours. 6 lbs. of meat will take 3 hours. This dish may be thickened like Irish stew, with potatoes, or it may be served with the addition of chopped vegetables of all kinds, previously fried.

—*The Ladies' New Book of Cookery*, 1852[23]

The fundamental dietary staple that emerges from this list of provisions and menus is the biscuit. Travelers would have much preferred yeast-leavened bread, but the rigors of the trail often prevented bread making. Bread requires yeast cultivation in warm temperatures over an extended period and in a restful environment. Though some pioneers solved the dilemma with sourdough, most travelers could rarely afford all three factors, as they traveled twenty miles daily over rough ground. Instead, they often made soda biscuits to round out the necessary carbohydrates to fuel their journey. Soda biscuits rise quickly in the oven through chemical leavenings that can be managed with much more convenience than yeast. Indeed, the advent of baking soda (as opposed to earlier and less reliable alternatives such as pearlash or artificial saleratus) may be seen as one of the primary facilitators of the great westward movement.

Some travelers found mineral deposits along the way to use as a substitute for baking soda. Although naturally occurring saleratus ("alkali of soda" or potassium bicarbonate) exhibits most of the same chemical properties as baking soda (sodium bicarbonate), pioneers often reported that saleratus carried off-flavors, lacked reliable strength, or was dirty in its natural form. Mormon pioneer diarist Patty Sessions was one of these who gathered saleratus, both on the trail and after she settled in Utah territory. Willie Company handcart emigrants gathered large quantities of the stuff near Independence Rock, just days prior to becoming snowbound.[24] Gathering saleratus was a fundamental foodways activity for the Mormon pioneer, similar to salt expeditions for frontier colonial settlers.

Chemical leavening required an acid element in the bread to activate the leavening. Some pioneer emigrants carried their own stores of cream of tartar to use in activating saleratus or soda.[25] Others kept a fresh dairy cow and could have used buttermilk or soured cream to spark the acid reaction. Sourdough, vinegar, or other acidic foods can also activate soda.

Prospecting for Saleratus

You can find saleratus in naturally occurring deposits in many of the same places discovered by the pioneers. Take a small bottle of vinegar with you (as well as a container to store your harvest) and look for crusty white crystalline patches on the ground. If you pour a bit of vinegar on the patch and it dissolves into a foam, it's probably saleratus. Search in the following locations for possible deposits.

- In Rich County, Utah: Saleratus Creek, 41.3050N 111.0714W
- In Emery County, Utah: 38.98111N 110.15139W
- Near Crescent Junction, Utah: 38.92778N 109.48222W
- Manti Meadows Wildlife Management Area, 3 miles southwest of Manti, Utah
- In Wyoming: Saleratus Lake, 1.6 miles northeast of Independence Rock
- In Idaho, in and around the town of Soda Springs.

Some sites may lie on private land; some deposits may be designated as historic sites or landmarks and off-limits for prospecting. Get permission from private land owners before trespassing or gathering.

Once you find some saleratus, store it in a dry environment. When you are ready to use it, dissolve it in the water you use to mix your dough. Let any silt or dirt settle out of suspension and use the water to mix your dough. Happy prospecting!

Caroline Clark made a variety of breads on the trail. She sometimes used chemical leavens and at other times employed bacterial cultures. In writing to her friends in England, she described her bread for the trail in detail: "We bought a skillet to bake our bread in. Sometimes we make pancakes for a change. We also make cakes in the pan and often bran dumplings with baking powder. We use cream of tarter [*sic*] and soda to make our bread, and sometimes sour dough. It makes very good bread."[26]

Cream of Tartar Biscuit

Take a quart of flour, mix into it two tea-spoonsful of cream of tartar, two tea-spoonsful of salt, a table-spoonful of lard; then take a pint of warm water and a tea-spoonful of soda, knead it into the flour, and work it well. Roll it out about half an inch thick, and cut the biscuit with a round cutter, or into square pieces.

—*The Great Western Cookbook,* 1857[27]

Not all bread on the trail was chemically leavened, however. A sourdough start could keep a yeast culture alive until the camp took rest for a day of baking and laundry. Other baking practices have been nearly lost from the modern food lexicon. Our modern palate might prefer donuts and muffins to the baked goods of ancestors. Mormon pioneers used leftover scraps of yeast-leavened dough and dribblings of flour to create a twice-leavened, twice-baked pastry called rusk, somewhat akin to zwieback. Patty Sessions baked rusk while camped at Winter Quarters. Eliza Partridge described baking rusk on the trail before reaching Florence.[28]

Rusk

Melt four ounces of butter in half a pint of new milk; then add to this seven eggs, well beaten, a quarter of a pint of yeast, and three ounces of sugar; put this mixture, by degrees, into as much flour as will make an extremely light paste, more like batter, and set it to rise before the fire for half an hour; then add more flour to make it rather stiffer, but not stiff. Work it well, and divide it into small loaves or cakes, about five or six inches wide, and flatten them. When baked and cold, slice them the thickness of rusks, and brown them a little in the oven.   —*The Practical Housekeeper,* 1857[29]

Flour for the trail took several forms. We think of refined bleached white flour, but this is an invention of the twentieth century. Flour available at Omaha or Florence was rather coarse and "unbolted"—the typical whole wheat flour. Millers also offered a more affordable alternative primarily consisting of bran and germ, with just enough endosperm to make it look like flour. Sold as "shorts" or "middlings," this flour stands in stark contrast to the bolted "superfine," which millers achieved by sifting through silk fabric between grindings. While superfine might have been used by the better bakers in bigger cities, pioneers short of cash on the edge of the frontier often bought shorts.[30]

A variation on flour for the road was "self-rising flour." Chemist and entrepreneur Henry Jones claimed a U.S. patent in 1852, but cooks in Britain had been using the stuff for several years. Still available today in much the same form, self-rising flour is simply premixed with the proper proportion of chemical leavenings such as baking soda and tartaric acid. This meant that emigrants would not be dependent upon scavenging saleratus from naturally occurring deposits near the Sweetwater River or Soda Springs.

Sometimes good flour was also available in these frontier outposts. Upon leaving Nauvoo in 1846, Louisa Pratt counted her blessings when she was able to buy "flour best quality, $1.25 per hundred [pounds]" in Bonaparte, Iowa. When the party got a few miles down the road, the available flour for purchase was more expensive and of lesser quality. Some wives insisted that their husbands return to Bonaparte to stock up.[31]

Before the days of U.S. Food and Drug Administration (FDA) inspection, unscrupulous merchants adulterated flour with chalk or gypsum. Mrs. Hale noted that flour was sometimes "mixed with other substances, to swell its bulk and weight. *Whiting, ground stones, and bones, and plaster of Paris,* are the ingredients chiefly used. To be sure, none of these things are absolutely poisonous; but they are injurious, and no one wants them in bread. In our country we think such deceptions are seldom attempted, still it may be well to know how to detect the least bad matter in flour."[32] She advised those purchasing flour to squeeze a fistful to see if it would hold shape. Good flour would show the lines of the hand when squeezed tightly. This simple test measured the oil found in the germ and endosperm and also detected adulteration. Unsuspecting travelers found themselves miles down the road before they discovered the deceit.

In this regard the flour available 150 years ago is nearly the opposite of our flour today, which is all endosperm and no germ or bran. Germ from wheat or corn flour contains natural oils. When these oils go rancid, the flour spoils. It seems odd that pioneers would have provisioned for their journey with flour that (though higher in nutritive value) was only waiting to spoil. By carrying only enough flour to feed the train from one supply station to the next, pioneers limited their exposure to spoilage or the more common disaster of flour getting wet during a river crossing or downpour. With such a disparity between our flour and theirs, any bread we endeavor to re-create will often fall short.

Pioneers sometimes safeguarded their flour for the trek by baking it into crackers before undertaking the journey. Others bought crackers by the barrel in addition to buying flour. Called ship's bread, sea biscuits, or hard tack, these heavy, dense crackers stored indefinitely (if weevils aren't considered spoilage). Before Andrew Jenson became the first church historian, he came to Utah as a Danish emigrant at the age of sixteen. He remembered eating sea biscuits made of rye, wheat, and oatmeal during his sea journey.[33] The rye flour reflects Jenson's Danish heritage. English emigrants would have had a plain wheat flour sea biscuit. The California Bakery (established in 1851) in Salt Lake City offered crackers and hard bread for resupply, specifically targeting California-bound miners and emigrants.[34] Incidentally, it also sold fresh yeast. One Oregon-bound pioneer left this description of making hard bread for the trail:

> Father fixed up a place to mix up a lot of dough and knead it with a lever fastened to the wall. He would put a pile of dough into a kind of trough and would have us boys spend the evening kneading the dough thoroughly, then roll it out and cut it into cracker shape about four inches square and then bake them hard and fill them into seamless grain sacks. There would be no lard or butter used, as there would be danger of them spoiling.[35]

Sea Biscuits or Hard Tack

Sift together four cups of flour and a teaspoon of salt. Mix well. Add a cup of water to make a very stiff dough. Knead for two minutes, then roll or pound the dough out in a sheet ½ inch thick. Fold the dough up again into several layers, and then pound and roll out again. Continue, folding and rolling out for 30 minutes until dough is very smooth and elastic. Roll out again and cut into 4 inch squares. Prick with a toothpick or fork to make cracker shapes. Bake on ungreased cookie sheets at 325° for one hour. Serves 5,000.

To eat these hard-as-rocks wafers, pioneers could soak them in water or milk and dissolve them to thicken soups and stews. If broken and pounded to crumbs, they might be used to augment a pudding. Crackers could also be eaten without much additional cooking in inclement weather. Anna Rowley, once stranded with the Willie Company, remembered finding

> two hard sea biscuits that were still in my trunk. They had been left over from the sea voyage, they were not large, and were so hard, they couldn't be broken. Surely that was not enough to feed 8 people, but 5 loaves and 2 fishes were not enough to feed 5000 people either, but through a miracle, Jesus had

MORMONS CROSSING THE PLAINS.

An engraving from *Harper's Weekly* in 1865 depicting the handcart migration. Note the assorted cooking pots hanging below the axle.

done it. So, with God's help, nothing is impossible. I found the biscuits and put them in a dutch oven and covered them with water and asked for God's blessing, then I put the lid on the pan and set it on the coals. When I took off the lid a little later, I found the pan filled with food.[36]

Notions of pioneer trail food often focus on privation. Certainly the trail experience was less than comfortable for most. In this regard, the flour gruel or "lumpy dick" on which stranded handcart trekkers subsisted is the pièce de résistance of pioneer cuisine. Handcart survivor Alice Strong remembered: "During these times we had only a little thin flour gruel 2 or 3 times a day and this was meager nourishment for a mother with a nursing baby." Patience Loader made a thin gruel to feed her dying father, shortly before reaching Martin's Cove. John Jaques remembered the wisdom his mother showed in making biscuits from the flour, which were more portable, palatable, and nourishing than the gruel other families ate.[37] Nick Wilson, a pioneer boy growing up near Grantsville, Utah, in the 1850s, remembered his diet of "greens and lumpy dick" as a primary motivation for running away to live with Washakie's Shoshone Indian band.[38]

Lumpy Dick

At its simplest, the gruel is simply flour sifted into water and then boiled until the flour thickens. Though there are certainly a thousand better ways to use flour, I include these examples as an homage to the spirit of Mormon privation.

Heat Milk scalding hot—in a bowl beat an egg with a fork a few moments then add some sugar, pinch of salt & grated nutmeg, flour enough to use up the egg—

rub between your hands till about like rice, then stir into the hot milk. Cook a few moments and serve with milk or cream.   —Johanna N. Lindholm, 1836–1909[39]

A slightly more elevated version comes to us from Hannah Wells, of southern Utah. "Bring one quart of milk to boiling point in a skillet and sprinkle white flour a little at a time slowly, not stirring but gradually 'poking' and mixing so it will not get slick and smooth, but ever so slightly lumpy. Keep at high heat but do not boil hard for about 15 minutes. It should take enough flour to be a fairly thick (like cereal) consistency and be served warm with very thick cream. Used as pudding you add butter, sugar and cinnamon or nutmeg. Used as a morning breakfast, it was served with butter and salt."[40]

This dish is meant to be lumpy, not smooth like gravy. Garnish with butter, sugar, cinnamon, nutmeg, cream, or just salt. I recommend as many garnishments as your pantry can muster, though lumpy dick on the trail would be austere.

In contrast, I much prefer the appetizing memories related by John Bond, a child with the Hodgett wagon company that followed the Martin and Willie companies. John lingered at his family's wagon while other members of the company attended a prayer meeting because he "saw sister Scott cooking a nice pot of dumplings just before the bugle sounded. She hid the dumplings under the wagon, being a zealous woman, and went to prayer meeting, but I did not go this time. I stood back and looked for the dumplings, found them and being so hungry I could not resist the temptations, sat down and ate them all. I admit that those dumplings did me more good than all the prayers that could have been offered."[41] Anna Rowley witnessed the miraculous increase of her Dutch oven full of hard tack. Sister Scott was left to witness the mysterious disappearance of her dumplings. In fact, such thieving of food was not uncommon among hard-pressed pioneer companies.

Hard Dumplings

Mix flour and water, with a bit of salt, to the consistency of dough. Make it into dumplings, and boil them half an hour. Serve them with butter and salt.

—*The Complete Cook*, 1864[42]

Or:

Norfolk Dumplings

Make a stiff pancake batter; drop this batter by small spoonful into quick boiling water; let them boil from 2 to 3 minutes, when they will be enough done: drain, and lay a piece of fresh butter over each.   —*The Ladies' New Book of Cookery*, 1852[43]

Not everything was made of flour, though. Wild game and gathered fruits figure prominently in filling out the pioneer trail diet. In describing her trail experience from Nauvoo to Winter Quarters, diarist Eliza Partridge frequently noted wild ingredients that supplemented her meals. In March 1846 she records eating rabbit three times, prairie hens twice, ducks twice, and squirrels twice. In April her husband went out to hunt turkeys and stayed out all night before finding success with a tom for the table.[44] Caroline Clark noted in her diary: "At times Roland goes to the river and

catches us fish and sometimes John shoots birds. We get wild currants and gooseberries to make puddings. So, altogether we get along very well."[45]

Patty Sessions often augmented her cuisine with wild game. At other times she
leaned heavily on wild berries and currants to fill her pastries. In July 1846 she noted
gathering gooseberries and chokecherries after making camp for the night. A prolific
baker of pies, Patty continued to use wild berries and fruits even after settling in Utah.

Gooseberry Pie
Observations.—Gooseberries, currants, cherries, raspberries plums of many kinds,
cranberries, and damsons, are used for making large pies. Cherries are mixed with
currants or raspberries, or both; and currants with raspberries. The usual proportion of
sugar is one pound to a quart of fruit, or not quite so much to very ripe fruit. Lay the
fruit in the dish, highest in the middle, with the sugar between it, add a little water;
wet the edge of the dish with water, cover with paste about half an inch thick; close it,
pare it, make a hole in the middle, and bake in a moderate oven.
—*The Ladies' New Book of Cookery*, 1852[46]

Traveling immigrants often had access to freshly butchered domestic beef and
pork, from which they made roasts, stews, and even mince pies. Much of the land in
what is now Illinois, Iowa, and Nebraska was populated by small family farms. By the
1860s Mormon emigrants had access to domestic farm produce from homesteads and
resupply stations along the trail. Rarely did these later travelers feel the full isolation
of the wilderness: they were always just a day or two from another outpost, fort, or
settlement. Many Oregon-bound travelers (and some Mormons as well) saw the fer-
tility of the Nebraska plains and abandoned their ambitions for farms in California
and Oregon for a more immediate opportunity in the Midwest. As a result, Mormon
emigrants could count on resupplying en route to Utah, if they could pay the prices
demanded by enterprising farmers.

John Jaques provides an example of this pattern of resupply. At Fort Laramie, he
purchased "20 lb biscuit at 15 cents, twelve pounds of bacon at 15 cents and 3 pounds
of rice at 17 cents and so on."[47] Once settled in Utah, Mormon farmers also employed
this same approach in charging higher prices to California-bound travelers. During
the Utah War of 1857 Danish pioneer Hans Jensen Hals gleefully wrote: "We ben-
efited much from the soldiers when they bought our vegetables, butter eggs and pork
and other things we charged them high prices."[48]

Other Mormon travelers relied more exclusively on wild game. As the vanguard
company of 1847 traveled across the plains, hunters supplied much of the fresh meat.
At one point Brigham Young felt compelled to reprimand the hunters for killing excessive numbers of deer and buffalo, which were wasted and not eaten. This may have
been a response to the hunting expedition of Perrigrine Sessions in July. After finding no success for several days, Perrigrine and his hunting companions killed several
buffalo and sent back to camp for a wagon. That evening they hauled 1,800 pounds of
buffalo meat into camp.[49] Brigham Young's reprimand may also have been caused by
a stingy concern for wasting lead and powder in the face of an unknown future in the
Rocky Mountains.

Frederick Piercy's celestial depiction of Fort Laramie in 1853 published by Ackerman Lithograph. Westward travelers resupplied here, at a cost.

Of buffalo meat on the trail, Emily Stewart Barnes recalled: "Some of the company killed one, and what a feasting we had! Everyone had some, and what we could not eat while good we fixed as we would jerked beef, that is, in small strips about one pound in a piece or strip and hung it up in the top of the wagon bows to dry."[50]

Jerked Beef

Certainly we may dry meat in the sun as Emily's father did, risking contamination from flies. Here's a more domestic option.

Slice two pounds of very lean meat (fatty meat will go rancid) thinly, cutting with the grain. Salt the meat well (some also like a bit of coarse ground black pepper) and pound well with a tenderizing mallet. Thread one end of the strips onto skewers and hang them in the oven. I like to hang one strip between each rod of the wire oven rack, with the skewer resting on the rack. The strips should not touch each other. Using your oven's lowest setting, dry the meat overnight with the door propped open to allow moisture to escape. The meat should be thoroughly dry. Moist and tender jerky will spoil quickly unless a curing agent such as saltpeter (sodium or potassium nitrate) is used. When stored in a dry, well ventilated place, this jerky can keep for several months.[51]

Some pioneer diaries record an almost exclusive reliance on wild game. William James, a handcart pioneer from England, included a shotgun in his seventeen pounds of personal items. Other members of the Martin Company to which he belonged remembered him as being a reliable hunter, often feeding his family with rabbits and sage hens. As he lay freezing to death at Martin's Cove, his only concern was for the safety of this shotgun, which had fed his family.[52]

Mormon immigrants hunted buffalo in this manner on the Great Plains. This scene comes from propaganda targeting Mormon immigrants: Frederick Piercy, *Route from Liverpool to Great Salt Lake Valley* (1855).

Rabbits

Rabbits being rather dry meat, are much improved by larding. Should the process be deemed too troublesome upon common occasions, a good effect may be produced by lining the inside of the rabbit with slices of fat bacon previously to putting in the stuffing. This is a very easy method of improvement, and ought never to be neglected. . . .

Rabbit, with Herbs

Cut either of the two into pieces, put it into a stew-pan with butter, salt, pepper, parsley, sorrel, and young onions chopped. When sufficiently done, add the juice of a lemon. The legs may be broiled and laid on the top.

—*The Ladies' New Book of Cookery*, 1852[53]

Rescuers of the Martin and Willie handcart companies also relied on wild game. Ephraim Hanks secured his place as a hero to the company when he parceled out fresh buffalo meat to every kettle in camp. Notable in his narrative is the attention he gave to providing a fat cow. The beef cattle in the camp had been worn down from being overworked in the cold weather with insufficient fodder. As a result, when the lean beef was fried, it proved disgusting to every cook in camp.[54] The buffalo provided by Hanks, in contrast, carried fat that facilitated cooking as well as providing critical fat calories to fuel the cold-weather journey. Hanks butchered his buffalo into long thin strips of meat. While some might have fried it in the usual manner, it sounds as if Hanks might have been following an earlier pattern set by the old trappers, who roasted long strips of meat on sticks held over the fire.[55]

Andrew Allen described using a similar technique for cooking his biscuits while on a picket detail during the Utah War. Stationed in Echo Canyon awaiting the invasion of federal troops, he wrapped strips of dough around a stick and then roasted it over his campfire.[56] Modern Boy Scouts and Girl Scouts continue to use this age-old method.

After the Martin/Willie disaster, some rescuers stayed in the mountains of Wyoming that winter to guard freight and baggage left behind. Wild game came to figure prominently in their trail experience as well. Initially, the small fort at Devil's Gate commanded by Daniel Jones was outfitted with supplies left from the rescue effort. Jones counted on having potatoes, onions, flour, beef, and coffee sufficient to last through five months of Wyoming winter. By late February, however, men with appetites increased by hard labor in cold weather had consumed the stores. At one point they were reduced to eating rawhide.

Even after his elaborate preparation of the rawhide, Jones and his company were saved by a miracle. Knowing that the rawhide offered no sustenance and might even injure them, Jones asked God to bless not the rawhide but the stomachs of those who ate it. Their prayers were apparently answered: no one who stayed with Jones that winter died.

Devil's Gate, a geological formation on the Sweetwater River in Wyoming, near the site where the Martin and Willie handcart companies met disaster in 1856. From Piercy, *Route from Liverpool to Great Salt Lake Valley* (1855).

An immigrant train stopped in Echo Canyon, 1866. Note the oxen in the yoke rather than horses, even after the Civil War flooded eastern markets with mules and horses.

Boiled Rawhide

Daniel Jones kindly left us this recommendation: "Scorch and scrape hair off; this had a tendency to kill and purify the taste that scalding gave it. After scraping, boil one hour in plenty of water, throwing the water away that had extracted all the glue, then wash and scrape the hide thoroughly, washing in cold water, then boil to a jelly and let it get cold, and then eat with a little sugar sprinkled on it."[57]

Why, those fellers were lucky! When I was a boy we didn't have sugar to sprinkle on our rawhide.

When a large party of Shoshone Indians showed up at Devil's Gate expecting tribute, Jones had nothing to feed them but "weak soup and strong coffee." Relations warmed after he gave them their fill, however. The Shoshones invited Jones to return to the Indian camp, where they fed him fresh antelope. In these lean months of winter, stores in the Shoshone camp were also thin. In the days that followed, the Shoshones tracked and killed a lone lean buffalo, which they gave to the Mormon guard out of pity and friendship. This kind gift carried the outpost through until supply wagons came the next spring.[58]

When rescuers arrived in the early spring, they commented on how pitiful the men were in their starved condition. With indignant pride Jones replied that any one of his winter-starved men could whip any one of the corn-fed boys from the valley. Such goading continued, and eventually a match was arranged. In the end the rawhide survivors proved their mettle and prevailed in the wrestling contest, much to the embarrassment of the corn-fed boys.[59]

The stories and experiences of the Mormon pioneer trail carry immense emotional weight in contemporary Mormon culture. These legends establish particular food experiences as metaphors for the pioneer experience as a whole. Quail descended on the camp of Israel, heightening the metaphor of Brigham Young as Moses and the providence of God. Still, some pioneers experienced keen hunger and even starvation. Patience Loader, a handcarter with the Martin Company, remembered one man so crazed with hunger that he resorted to gnawing on the fingers of a sleeping girl.[60] The biscuit or hard tack, representing the pain and sacrifices of the trail, might be seen as an incarnation of the Eucharist wafer and gruel as sacramental wine. We are fortunate to be able to share a small part of this experience in re-creating such simple foods, though we may choose not to re-create pioneer hunger. As we attempt to connect with pioneer ancestors, the layers of meaning that we find are limited only by the irreverence of the unbeliever.

We have many other examples of pioneers who traveled easily, ate well, and arrived in Salt Lake City with nothing unusual to report. Food on the trail could be opulent, as reported by Caroline Clark, Lorenzo Young, and others. With the wilderness as a veritable Garden of Eden, some early travelers harvested a bounty of wild meat, fruits, and vegetables that for many years excelled that of their own farms. Even so, we often prefer to focus our attention on privation, which suits our notions of the mythical pioneer. Perhaps we need to believe that pioneers made a sacrifice so that we might live in comfort. Comfortable living does little to inspire us, but privation and hardship prompt us to reflect on the possibilities of what might have been.

CHAPTER 5

The Staff of Life

BREAD AND LEAVEN

In the sweat of thy face shalt thou eat bread, till thou return unto the ground;
for out of it wast thou taken: for dust thou *art*, and unto dust shalt thou return.
—Genesis 3:19

Nancy O'Neal Rich died in October 1849, just a year after arriving in the Great Salt Lake Valley. Her husband, Joseph, laid her to rest in a cemetery just outside the old fort wall, confident that she would rise again in the not too distant resurrection. Her grave was soon forgotten as the settlement of Salt Lake City quickly expanded, and a new cemetery was established up on the hill. When Nancy's slumber was next disturbed, however, it was not by Gabriel's horn. New housing construction in 1986 tore open the forgotten and unmarked graves.[1]

Scholars quickly jumped at the opportunity to study an isolated population through forensic anthropology and archaeology. Remains of twenty-six bodies presented a perfect case study for the pioneer diet and mortality. When archaeologists compared these remains with a parallel graveyard population of cowboys drawn from Wyoming in the 1860s, they made a remarkable discovery: the cowboy remains featured healthy sound teeth, while the teeth of pioneers showed significant decay. Rather than attributing the decay to poor hygiene (since brushing their teeth was not a habit for either population), archaeologists determined the cause to be dietary. The not-so-startling conclusion: the cowboys ate more meat, while Mormon pioneer farmers ate more wheat, potatoes, and starch. Enzymes in their saliva easily converted these starches to sugars, resulting in decayed teeth.[2]

All of this comes to us as no surprise. With more than half of Mormon migration from Europe originating in the British Isles,[3] we expect to find a traditionally starchy English diet. Furthermore, as Mormon farmers forced the desert to "blossom as the rose" against its will, they had starches and sugary fruits in mind. In 1848 LDS Church leaders apportioned lots and acreage for farming, divvying out more than 5,000 acres.

Wheat stands in shocks to dry after harvest on the Christian Christiansen farm, circa 1880. Bread begins here.

In 1849 the claims for acreage surpassed 11,000, as settlements expanded beyond the waterways of what is now downtown Salt Lake City to include settlements to the north. That fall 200 people left the Great Salt Lake Valley and established farms on the Sanpete River to the south. By 1850 Mormon farmers claimed tens of thousands of acres under cultivation, primarily in grain crops. These settlers lived on bread.[4]

Emigration records also back up this cultural conclusion. As Brigham Young prepared to outfit thousands of pioneers for their westward trek, he mandated lists of provisions to fill out the wagons. Staples such as sugar, salt, coffee, and bacon certainly showed up on his lists. But the greatest weight on the wagons and handcarts was made up of wheat flour. Handcart pioneers, however, were not capable of carrying adequate flour for the entire journey. For them, Young appointed agents on the trail to ensure that resupply stations would have flour waiting at Florence in Nebraska or Fort Laramie and Fort Bridger in Wyoming. Such complex carbohydrates fueled the daily calorie consumption of the Mormon migration. Theirs was a diet of flour.

Chemical Leavens

Though cultures around the world make a variety of unleavened breads from flour, Mormon pioneers insisted on leavening theirs. Chemical leavenings such as saleratus, "yeast powder," and other versions of baking soda raised bread for emigrants on the trail.[5] Saleratus, a naturally occurring mineral with properties similar to baking soda, was often dirty and had unpredictable levels of concentration or purity. Soda, in contrast, was manufactured commercially with more careful tolerances.

Patty Sessions frequently described using saleratus on the Mormon trail, both for cooking and as a barter item. Hubert Howe Bancroft's *History of Utah* suggests that pioneers like Patty relied exclusively on saleratus gathered in Wyoming for the first five years after settlement in the Great Salt Lake Valley. Annual excursions to Saleratus Lake near Independence Rock sustained bread makers in Utah for several years.[6]

Pioneers in the Utah settlements also identified local deposits of saleratus. One such entrepreneur, Livy Olsen, crossed the plains by handcart as an infant. His parents settled on the Sanpete River. As a young boy, he gathered wagonloads of saleratus from deposits near the river. His father then shipped saleratus to Salt Lake City for sale, credit, or barter.[7] William Stewart, who set up shop as a shoemaker in Kaysville, also relied on natural leavens gathered near the Great Salt Lake. His daughter Emily Stewart Barnes recalled the birth of her brother Hyrum in those early days. As her mother lay in bed, Emily noted: "Father got our breakfast, and we had beautiful yellow biscuits which were made with soda gathered near the [Great Salt] lake just south of Payne's."[8]

Yeast

Once settled in Utah territory these pioneers had more reliable access to baker's and brewer's yeast. After all, Angelina Maria Collins observed, "One thing is certain: good bread can never be made without sweet yeast."[9] As early as 1853 Salt Lake City's California Bakery offered yeast for sale to home bakers. The bakery had been in operation for two years and likely sold yeast even earlier. In 1859 the Hand in Hand Bakery advised its patrons to "dispense with your salt-rising and saleratus biscuits" in favor of its yeast-leavened bread.[10] The task of bread making begins first and foremost as a pursuit of yeast.

A bakery operated from a tent in the railroad boomtown of Corinne, Utah, circa 1869.

In the days before Louis Pasteur's scientific experiments with bacteria and micro-organisms, bakers and chefs understood very little about yeast. Certainly they knew that yeast would leaven bread and that yeast had a limited window of viability. But that yeast was a living thing that required nourishment and a friendly environment was a mystery. Popular understanding of the time suggested that yeast actually did its work while decaying rather than as part of a life cycle of propagation.[11] Indeed, Sarah Hale wrote in her influential 1852 cookbook, "The substances essential to vinous fermentation are—*sugar, vegetable extract, the tartaric or malic acids, and water.* Sugar is the most essential of these, as from its decomposition alcohol is derived."[12]

Cookbooks of the mid-1800s suggest that small amounts of yeast could be multiplied into larger amounts by creating a particular environment. Contextual clues lead us to understand that pioneers believed yeast increased by adulterating the starch medium rather than through cell reproduction. This brief instruction from *The Great Western Cook Book* illustrates the idea:

> Boil a handful of hops half an hour, in two quarts of water. Take ten boiled potatoes and mash them very fine, and strain the water from the hops on them as soon as it has boiled. Mix into it a pint of flour, and two tablespoonsful of salt. When it is lukewarm, add a pint of good brewer's yeast, and let it stand six hours to rise. Strain it through a cullender [*sic*], and put it into a close stone vessel. It will keep a week in summer, and longer in winter.[13]

Utah settlers employed this same cultural understanding of yeast. The editors of the *Deseret News* demonstrated the Utah grasp on popular kitchen science when they published a similar concept in 1854:

> To Make Yeast: Hop yeast may be most conveniently made in the following manner: Boil a double handful of hops in a gallon of pure soft water for fifteen or twenty minutes; strain off the liquor while scalding hot; stir in wheat meal or flour till a thick batter is formed; let it stand till it becomes blood warm; add a pint of good lively fresh yeast, and stir it well; then let it stand at a place where it will keep at a temperature of about 70 degrees Fahrenheit, till it becomes perfectly light. This yeast will keep from one to two weeks, if corked tight in a clean earthen jug, and kept in a cool cellar.[14]

This was likely the procedure followed by Regina Erickson's mother. Regina remembered a stoneware jar "used to keep a start of live yeast, set on top of the coal stove warming oven near the back where the temperature was right. I remember licking off the bubbles of yeast as the jar overflowed, and it tasted good."[15] Regina is clearly referring to feeding a culture of sweet yeast, not a sourdough start. In these examples the goal seems to be finding a medium to host the yeast, which can be stored over a short time span. Most similar directions for "making yeast" indicate that the yeast can be stored a week or two in a cool dark cellar. The modern chef realizes that this is generally the lifespan of fresh yeast in a cool environment, no matter what medium hosts the yeast.

Each of these examples assumes that the baker has a little bit of fresh yeast to work with. Hence the household cook must make a constant effort to multiply fresh yeast in order to bake bread. The various volumes on domestic economy from this era emphasize that bakery-bought bread is less wholesome. Commercial bakers, their methods, and ingredients were not to be trusted. At the same time, most cookbooks of the era acknowledge that fresh yeast from a commercial bakery or brewery is stronger and more reliable. When we see that many do-it-yourself yeast prescriptions call for embedding yeast in a host starch, we understand why a recipe might call for a tablespoon of fresh brewer's yeast or a pint of homemade yeast.

Many Utah settlers relied on a designated proprietor for home-grown yeast within their community. Nellie Child remembered her grandmother Eleanor Huntington Parry as such a proprietor. Neighbors would come for fresh yeast on baking day, and Eleanor would ladle it out from a crock. Customers would pay for their yeast with a small quantity of flour or sugar—food items used to feed the living yeast colony. With potato water, flour, sugar, and hops, Eleanor would feed the yeast crock again to replenish it.[16]

Beyond those resourceful settlers who grew their own yeast cultures, home chefs also purchased fresh yeast from retail suppliers. The *Deseret News* contains advertisements for the California Bakery offering fresh yeast for sale as early as 1853. W. H. Hockings, proprietor of the City Brewery, advertised that home brewers and bakers could buy his fresh yeast on Tuesdays and Fridays.[17] Though many settlers did use saleratus during the early lean years, they certainly produced no French *pain au levain* (leavened bread) from saleratus. While it is probable that Mormon settlers initially subsisted on chemically leavened bread, many settlers also purchased or grew their own live yeast cultures.

A view of Main Street in Salt Lake City, circa 1850, showing the Golden Gate Bakery. Some settlers bought bread here, while others bought yeast to make their own bread.

Emigrants from New England, where Mormonism was born, would have been familiar with cider production as a part of the farm economy. Cider making also requires yeast. Though it was unknown to these farmers, the dusty film on the skins of apples (as well as other items such as grapes, pears, and pea shells) indicated that wild airborne yeasts had already found the natural sugars in the fruits. In this pioneering era many refused to believe that airborne microscopic particles even existed. In spite of this denial, yeasts found their sweets. After crushing the apples, cider makers allowed the pommace to stand exposed to the air overnight. This process attracted even more airborne yeast, unbeknownst to the cider maker. When the cider maker pressed the pulp the following day, the yeast-rich must (juice to be fermented) quickly began a natural fermentation. Through the course of fermentation, the yeasts multiplied again and again as they fed on the sugars of the apple juice. After the cycle was completed, the cider maker collected a thick cake of yeast that settled from suspension to rest on the bottom of the fermentation barrel. This yeast could then be used for baking or fermenting.

Danish emigrant Georgien Dorcas taught Mormon pioneers a similar method in 1853, using brewer's wort made from barley. As with the apple pommace, wild airborne yeast cells found the exposed sweet barley malt soup attractive and invaded the friendly medium to begin multiplying. After fermentation had run its course, dormant yeasts settled out of suspension to form sludge on the bottom of the kettle. Dorcas combined this sludge with a salt-rising sponge to begin feeding and multiplying the yeast.[18] Settlers then used this fresh yeast directly in baking or for growing a sustainable yeast culture.

Mrs. Esther Howland recommended a similar method for attracting airborne yeasts to a liquid culture using wheat flour and sugar. Working from the popular belief of the day that sweet liquid spontaneously generated yeast, Howland's procedure uses no yeast to begin the culture. It relies exclusively on attracting airborne yeast.

Gathering Yeast

Boil one pound of good flour, a quarter of a pound of brown sugar, add a little salt, in two gallons of water, for one hour. When milk-warm, bottle it and cork it close, and it will be fit for use in twenty-four hours. One pint of the yeast will make eighteen lbs. of bread.   —*The New England Economical Housekeeper*, 1845[19]

This process is the basis of the Belgian brewing style, which uses open vats of sugary barley wort to attract yeast. Over time breweries and bakeries developed their own latent localized cultures of yeasts, which become especially adapted to the local climate and nutrient sources. A modern instructional manual on baking tells the story of a wooden bowl handed down in one family through generations of bakers. The bowl was used particularly for mixing dough for a sourdough rye bread: the cook had only to mix rye flour and water in the bowl and then leave it to stand overnight. Generations and even a century of baking had impregnated the bowl with yeasts and bacteria such that by morning the dough would have risen.[20]

This same process happens in larger scale in kitchens modern and historical. Over time the porous surfaces of kitchens—the wooden spoon, the wooden cabinetry, the wall behind the refrigerator—all become hosts for the airborne yeasts that thrive in the very particularly unique environment of a kitchen. Thus the bread you bake will inevitably take on unique characteristics, different from the bread of your mother, who lives only a mile away.

Sourdough

The bakers who supplied San Francisco Forty-niners with bread utilized this same process in creating their sourdough, mixing a start with flour and water. These artisan bakers allowed yeasts to settle on the exposed paste. When the mix began to bubble and swell, they knew that wild yeasts had begun their work. The bakers then fed this mother dough with more flour and water each day for several days, allowing it to rise and fall again each day. The mother dough took on a sour, acidic character and became the basis for the famed sourdough breads of the frontier.[21]

The San Francisco sourdough is unique among other sourdoughs around the world. The particular environmental conditions there gave rise to a symbiotic relationship between specific strains of bacteria and wild yeast. The resulting culture produces bread with a distinctive flavor and tang. Containing its own self-sufficient culture, the mother dough can leaven itself for breads. Its acid character also activates soda and saleratus to be used in making biscuits, pancakes, and quick breads.

The Boudin Bakery is San Francisco's oldest bakery. Descended from generations of bakers in the French tradition, the current owners claim that their mother dough is the original intact culture started more than 150 years ago. During the earthquake and subsequent fire of 1906, Louise Boudin is said to have rushed back into the burning building to save the mother dough. The family then set up temporary baking operations in the city park until a new bakery could be built on the present site.[22]

Mormon pioneers carried sourdough across the plains to leaven their bread. Their sourdoughs would not have contained the identical bacteria as the San Francisco sourdough but would have begun from whatever wild strains may have been common at Winter Quarters. Pioneer settler Mary Lois Walker Morris noted that while crossing the plains she made bread by mixing "a small piece of dough or leaven" with flour and water and letting it rise all day as she traveled. Sometimes, she noted, it turned sour and made sour bread. At other times it made good bread.[23] From these notes it appears that Mary was using a sourdough culture. The variable sour or sweet tones that Mary experienced are a result of the relative moisture content of the leaven and the temperature of the dough during fermentation. A more liquid leaven makes a sweeter dough; a solid leaven is sourer. A note in *The Complete Cook* explains this leaven more explicitly:

> Originally what is called leaven was uniformly employed, and it is now sometimes used as a substitute for yeast. Those who use it keep a pound or more of dough from baking to baking. It is kept in a wooden barrel, or bowl, covered with flour. Before it is fit to use, it must be both stale and sour. Bread made in this way is said to be more digestible, but it is not so pleasant to the taste.[24]

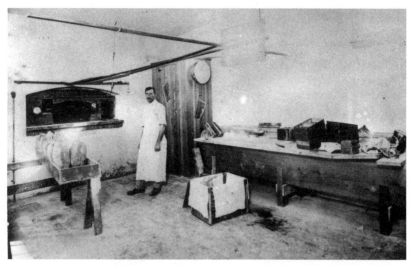

Interior view of a bakery in Helper, Utah. Though the scene is near the turn of the century, details appear not to have changed much. The oven in the wall is fired directly. Loaves are free formed rather than using metal bread pans. The long wooden trough on the right side is used for fermenting large masses of dough. Long-handled peels (used to remove bread from the oven) hang from the ceiling.

Many a gourmand would disagree with this assessment of sourdough and French *pain au levain,* but Mary concurred.

Lydia Arnold Titus gave a more explicit account of her sourdough: "When we camped I made rising and set it on the warm ground. It would be up about midnight. I'd get up and put it to sponge and in the morning first thing I would mix the dough and put it in the reflector oven. With good hot coals the bread or cakes for a hardy breakfast were ready by the time the men rounded up all the teams."[25]

Lydia's diary gives several contextual clues that emphasize the trail conditions in which she worked. The "rising" is clearly a sourdough culture, allowing her to renew her leaven day after a day on the trail. The reflector oven made of tinned sheets allowed a collapsible compact utility, also important for the trail. The logistical details and division of labor echo other pioneer accounts of trail life.

Another Mormon settler, Mary Clayton, recorded her sourdough process in her diary. The original diary appears to have been lost; this fragment comes to us by way of a Mormon Relief Society cookbook published for a sesquicentennial celebration. Like Lydia Titus, Mary Clayton left several contextual clues that affirm the territorial time frame of her sourdough method. As with many early yeast concoctions, Mary used potatoes to attract wild yeasts and then fed them with starches. In her era before standardized measurements in recipes, her unit of measure was her teacup. Rather than storing her starter in the refrigerator or ice box, she recommends "a cool place." These are the hallmarks of cooking in an era before Fannie Farmer and the Boston Cooking School.

> **Sourdough Starter**
> Boil one good-sized potato until mealy. Mash about ¼ of the potato real fine and add
> to approximately two teacups of the water in which potato was cooked. Add one
> teaspoon sugar to lukewarm potato water. Add enough flour [about two cups] to
> make a sponge and put it in a warm place and let it work. Let it stand for 5 days. For
> pancakes pour off what you would like for breakfast and leave a starter of the sponge.
> Store starter in a cool place.   —Mary Clayton[26]

From these sources it appears that Mormon pioneers were familiar with the sourdough process. Probably due to the pampering that a sourdough start requires, many myths and legends have grown up around its culture. The culture or start often comes with a pedigree and affidavit of authenticity, verifying its age at over a century. Families carefully pass the start from one heir to the next. The age of the mother dough is purported to account directly for the flavor of the bread.

Most of this is pure ego fed by poppycock for marketing purposes. The character of a sourdough is directly due to the organisms that compose it. The symbiotic relationship between the bacteria *Lactobacillus sanfrancisco* and the wild yeast classified as *Candida humilis* produces a consistent result: San Francisco sourdough. Other specific bacteria/yeast combinations found in other localities produce different results. The temperature at which the culture is fermented increases or decreases acidity accordingly. The liquid or dry character of the culture likewise has an effect on the organisms that multiply there. Any of these variables can be manipulated to change the flavor of the sourdough. But the age of the culture is largely irrelevant.

The tangy character of sourdough is most directly a result of the temperature at fermentation and the relative moisture content of the loaf rather than the age of the start. Even a week-old sourdough can be made to shrivel your tongue and pucker your lips simply by letting it ferment in a drier state at a higher temperature. Still, we find a yearning to connect with the past in a tangible manner. Just as we might imagine that at this very moment I am breathing in an oxygen molecule that once passed through the lungs of Brigham Young, we could also imagine that bacteria from the pioneer era might flavor my sourdough. Assertions about the antiquity of a sourdough start are directed toward this end: "I am eating the very same yeast my ancestor ate." The flavor and character of the bread come more from the process than from the generational provenance of the start. Yet we indulge in nostalgia as we eat. It isn't all about calories or taste.

> **Make Your Own Sourdough Starter**
> ¾ cup flour
> ½ cup water
> just a pinch of dry yeast
> Combine all ingredients and mix well. On this first day it will have the consistency
> of dough. Put the mixture in a tall glass or plastic container (1–2 quarts) with a tight
> fitting lid. Leave the lid off or place a thin layer of cheesecloth over the jar, but let the
> air reach the culture. Scrape the sides of the jar down. Let stand at room temperature
> for 24 hours.

On the second day the mixture should have grown noticeably in volume, beginning to show some bubbles in a more liquid state. Add ¾ cup of flour and ½ cup water to this mixture. Stir well and scrape down the sides of the container. Replace the lid and let stand at room temperature for 24 hours.

On the third day the start will have grown again, perhaps nearly doubling in volume. With a consistency of pancake batter, the mixture will give a definite sour odor and have a sour yeasty flavor. Add ¾ cup flour and ½ cup water. Stir well and scrape down the sides of the container. Replace the lid and let sit at room temperature.

Once the starter has risen again, it is ready to use. It can be left on the counter for two or three days after a feeding but should be refrigerated if not used daily. Some bread recipes require two or three cups of starter. If you want to maintain a constant start you might need to feed and multiply the starter to a larger volume, so there will be some left once you have taken what the recipe requires. At a minimum you should remove one cup of the starter every week and replace it with ¾ cup flour and ½ cup water. If fed regularly and refrigerated when not used, this starter can be maintained indefinitely. If the starter sits out too long without feeding, it will show pink colors on the surface and black streaks when stirred. If this happens, throw it out and make a new starter.

This same process can be used to make a sourdough starter from rye flour. Rye flour differs from wheat flour in one important regard: its hull is more difficult to break down. Therefore rye bread works best with a sourdough method that helps to break down the hull. In order to facilitate this, use a more liquid environment. A daily feeding ratio of ½ cup water and ⅔ cup rye flour serves this need.

Salt-Rising Bread

Another misunderstood option for leavening is the oft-maligned and misnomered salt-rising bread. Using neither yeast nor acid, salt-rising bread depended on creating a culture of the bacteria *Clostridium perfringens* (yes, it doubles as a cheese culture) in an environment consisting of potatoes, cornmeal, water, and salt. Like yeast cells, this bacteria also produces a gas as it multiplies. When captured in bread dough the gas can cause bread to rise. Of course, pioneers didn't have any idea about the microbiology they were nurturing. They only knew it had to be kept stable at a warm temperature until the magic took place.

Sour though it may be, sourdough bread evokes the familiar smells of yeast and baking. Some pioneer bakers relied on an altogether different culture that came with a different set of aromas. "Salt-rising" bread and its associated bacteria create a cheesy smell that some find nostalgic and others find offensive. Bakers advertising in the *Deseret News* in 1864 tried to convince housewives that their yeast-risen bread was superior. They argued that their hop-cultured yeast was "far preferable to stinking salt-rising bread."[27] Thus we learn that home bakers were persisting with the salt-rising bread tradition even though fresh yeast had been available for purchase from the bakery for at least ten years. Some old-timers today still wax nostalgic about that stinking salt-rising bread. At any rate, territorial baking contests offered premiums for this bread, making it the prize of careful bakers because it was no small feat to create. I've warned you; you should warn your family before you begin working this dough.

To Make Excellent Bread without Yeast

Scald about two handfuls of Indian meal; into which put a little salt, and as much cold water as will make it rather warmer than new milk; then stir in wheat flour, till it is as thick as a family pudding, and set it down by the fire to rise. In about half an hour it generally grows thin; you may sprinkle a little fresh flour on the top, and mind to turn the pot round, that it may not bake at the side of it. In three or four hours, if you mind the above directions, it will rise and ferment as if you had set it with hop yeast; when it does, make it up in soft dough, flour a pan, put in your bread, set it before the fire, covered up, turn it round to make it equally warm, and in about half an hour it will be light enough to bake. It suits best to bake it in a Dutch oven, as it should be put into the oven as soon as it is light.   —*The Practical Housekeeper*, 1857[28]

Modern Adaptation: Salt-Rising Bread

Add two cups of water to 1¾ cup cornmeal and ¼ cup flour. Mix well and set in a very warm place to rise overnight. To make salt-rising bread, the most critical element is to maintain a constant temperature of 115°F. Just as baker's yeast thrives at 75°F, the bacterium responsible for this leaven thrives at 115°F. Our historical documents suggest setting a bowl by the fire or wrapping a warm bowl in towels or blankets to insulate against temperature loss. The easiest way to accomplish this in the modern day is with a yogurt maker. Yogurt also uses this same thermophilic environment, but yogurt makers can be rather expensive. Other options include leaving the culture start in the oven with the incandescent oven light turned on or leaving the oven's gas pilot light on with the oven door slightly ajar. I've had success by using a small incandescent bulb inside a Styrofoam cooler. A dimmer switch helps to regulate temperature.

When your start has risen in the morning (don't even bother trying if it hasn't risen in a dramatic fashion), melt 1 tablespoon of shortening into one pint of scalded milk that has been cooled to lukewarm. To this, add 1 teaspoon of salt, 1 tablespoon of sugar, and enough flour (about 6–7 cups) to make a soft dough that can be handled easily. Mix this all into the start and knead it briefly on a wooden surface; tile will cool the dough.

Don't knead the dough too long, because kneading might cause it to lose temperature. Divide the dough into loaves and set it directly into pans. If you're using a baking stone, form your loaves and let them rise ready for the oven. Again, because of the unique bacteria leavening used, it must rise at 115°. This bread will only rise once before the culture is exhausted. When the dough is well risen and doubled in size, put it into the oven. Bake at 400° for 45 minutes or until the loaves give a hollow sound when thumped on the bottom. Watch out for the cheesy smell. This recipe makes two large loaves, but it may be doubled.

Early settlers in Utah used these wild bacterial cultures to leaven their bread. From the clues that we find in the *Deseret News*, however, it would appear that the preferred bread method was more consistent with the English baking tradition. Fresh sweet yeast and sweet fresh dough are mentioned in dozens of recipes. The terms "French bread" and "levain" are nonexistent, though pioneer Caroline Hopkins Clark did tell her friends: "We use cream of tarter [*sic*] and soda to make our bread [on the trail], and sometimes sour dough. It makes very good bread."[29] Occasionally we see references to the "sponge method," but these are eclipsed by calls for sweet fresh yeast. While Mormon bakers certainly had access to the French baking methods, their cultural inheritance came primarily from the English brewing and baking traditions.

The *Deseret News* published recipes for settlers in the 1850s, reflecting this cultural background. Often these recipes came into the *News* office over the telegraph from other newspapers in the East. Here is one suggestion offered to Mormon settlers.

Infallible Recipe for Making Bread

In the first place, there are three indispensable requisites for making good bread, *viz.*:—Good flour, good yeast, and a careful hand. From three quarts of sifted flour, take one half pint of it in a separate vessel, and scald it with boiling water; let the paste cool to blood heat, and then add one egg, one tea-spoonful of sugar, one table-spoonful of salt, one cup of new milk, one cup of well risen yeast. Whip the whole well with a spoon, and then pour it into the midst of the three quarts of flour; knead it well, with as much warm water as will make it into a moderately stiff dough; let your bread rise till at least twice its size; then, after kneading a great deal, mould out your loaves or rolls into smooth, regular forms, wet them over with cold water, to prevent cracking, and set them to raise again under a clean cloth, till by touching on one side, they will quiver on the opposite side, then wet again with cold water, and bake immediately. If fermentation has not arrived at this point, the bread will not be sufficiently light—if the bread is suffered to go beyond this point, it will lose its sweetness.[30]

Such recipes follow a certain baking tradition that relies on lots of yeast and a few adjunct ingredients to raise bread in a short time. Using egg, sugar, and milk lends a distinct texture to the dough and crumb and also supplies nutrients for a fast rise. Utah's bakers would likely have used an alternative locally produced sweetener such as molasses. Sugar was a pricy imported commodity. Many modern bakers continue to use similar formulas with a heavy infusion of yeast and a shortened rise.

More traditional baking methods allow only four ingredients for a proper loaf of bread: flour, water, yeast, and salt. Utah bakers who reserved their use of sweetening for cakes and morning coffee would have used recipes more akin to a traditional sponge method.

Clearly there are a few differences between original recipes and modern adaptations. The originals do not specify much about the second rising or the baking method. The modern adaptation uses dry yeast where the original uses live moist yeast. The original uses no salt, but salt is quite traditional in other recipes. (In fact, bread without salt is almost disgusting.) The original calls for mixing the poolish in a larger body of flour. The use of loaf pans was unheard of before the late nineteenth century. Although many modern bread formulas might follow this general approach, the historical differences are primarily found in the heat source and hearth design and the measurement of ingredients.

Bread

Put a quartern of flour into a large basin, or small pan, with two tea-spoonfuls of salt; make a hole in the middle, then put in a basin four table-spoonfuls of good yeast,* stir in a pint of milk lukewarm; put it in the hole of the flour, stir just to make it of a thin batter, and then strew a little flour over the top; then set it on one side of the fire, cover it over with a cloth, let it stand till the next morning; add half a pint more of warm milk, and make it into dough, knead it for ten minutes, then set it in a warm place by the fire for one hour and a half, then knead it again, and it is ready for either loaves or bricks.   —*The Complete Cook*, 1864[31]

> * This relatively smaller volume would indicate pure, fresh brewer's yeast. The "quartern"
> is a flexible measurement, usually indicating a fourth part of a larger volume, such as
> a fourth of a pound or fourth of a gallon. In this case I believe that six cups of flour
> (about two pounds) is appropriate for the volumes of yeast, salt, and liquid.

Modern Adaptation

First make a sponge (*poolish* in French baking tradition) by combining ½ cup milk at room temperature with ½ teaspoon dry active yeast. Let the yeast rehydrate for a min-ute then add ¾ cup flour. Stir the flour into the milk until a stiff batter comes together, then stir briskly for 100 strokes more. Cover with a damp cloth or plastic wrap and set it to rest in a draft-free place with a steady 75° temperature. After two hours this sponge will become soupy and bubbly, with a strong wheaty, yeasty aroma. You can use it at this point or let it continue to ferment for as much as eight hours. The longer you let it ferment, the better the bread. Slow and steady development of the sponge makes more yeast and a better crumb texture in the final bread. Bread that calls for fast-acting yeast with a finished loaf in three hours does not allow the yeast to come to full strength. Such bread will have a lifeless crust and a weak crumb showing small holes and short cell fibers.

Once your sponge is ready, stir the sponge into 2½ cups milk at room tempera-ture. Break up the sponge completely with a wooden spoon, until the mix becomes slightly frothy. Add another ½ teaspoon dry active yeast. Also add a tablespoon of salt at this point. When it is mixed, work in about 5 cups of flour until the dough becomes difficult to stir with a wooden spoon. Turn it out on a floured board and knead in as much as 2 cups more of flour. Knead for fifteen minutes at a minimum. After the dough is finished, it will have a smooth satin texture, not sticky. When well kneaded, the dough will hold a ball shape without sagging. When a pinch is pulled away from the ball, the dough will spring quickly back to shape. If it doesn't do this, add a little more flour and keep kneading. Many old cooks noted that the bread was harder to make on a cloudy day, as relative humidity kept the dough too sticky.

When the dough is finished, grease a large bowl with butter or lard and set the dough ball in the bowl. Cover with a damp cloth or plastic wrap and set the bowl in a warm, draft-free place to rise. It should nearly double in size in less than two hours. When it has risen, set the dough on a well-floured board and cut it into two halves. Flatten each half into a disc, pressing all of the trapped gas out of the dough with the heel of your hand. Bring the edges of the disc back into a ball and set it to rise with the seamed side up, smooth side down. The individual loaves should be set on a well-floured lint-free cloth, in a bowl eight inches across by three inches deep. Cover with a well-floured cloth, and let rise 1½ to 2 hours. As a modern alternative you might instead set it to rise in bread pans, with the smooth side up.

Half an hour before baking, heat your oven or hearth. If you want to bake in a Dutch oven, heat one oven for each loaf. If you are using a baking stone in your oven, heat it to 450°. You might cast a little coarse cornmeal on the stone as well to keep the loaves from sticking. When the loaves are ready, gently turn them onto the stone or Dutch oven, easing the loaf onto the stone with your other hand. The dough is very fragile and will lose its rising if not treated gently. Once the dough is on the hearth, score the top of the loaf immediately with a razor or very sharp, finely serrated knife. Just before closing the oven up, toss a few ice cubes directly on the floor of the oven and shut the door to make steam. This steam makes the crust on the bread. Bake for 40 minutes and cool on wire racks when done.

Quick Breads

Much debate has raged over the issue of quick breads in nineteenth-century American cookery. Defined as breads leavened by chemicals rather than yeast, quick breads evoked opposition from those who were suspicious of the relatively new advent of chemical leavenings in a society where science had not yet found a strong footing. Even so (as noted above), Utah pioneers leaned heavily on soda and saleratus, especially during the first five years in Utah territory.

Whole Wheat Bread

1 egg
3 Tbs. Molasses
½ cup raisins
2 c. whole wheat flour
1 tsp soda
⅓ cup brown sugar
2 c. buttermilk
½ cup nuts, if desired
1 tsp salt
1½ Tbs. melted butter

Mix all ingredients together, bake in a loaf pan in a moderate oven for about one hour.
—Phoebe Hale, circa 1850[32]

Wheat bread in the English baking tradition is not the whole story. With more than 20 percent of Mormon foreign migration originating from Denmark and Scandinavia, the rustic darker breads of northern Europe also play a part in the story. Andrew Jenson, an early Mormon church historian, recalled his immigration from

Copenhagen, Denmark, in 1866. Once aboard ship, he and his shipmates arose at 6 A.M. for prayers. "Then we ate breakfast which consisted of tea and rye bread in the beginning, but after all the bread had been consumed we feasted on sea biscuits, which were made of rye, wheat and oatmeal."[33] Food historians are ever grateful to such detail-oriented diarists.

> **Rye Bread—Barley Bread**—and bread made of equal parts of rye flour and wheat flour, or of equal parts of barley flour, rye flour, and wheat flour—are made in the same way as already described. Milk,* or milk and water, is preferred, in making rye bread, to pure water.   —*The Complete Confectioner, Pastry-Cook, and Baker*, 1864[34]
>
> * I've had better success using water rather than milk.

A keen observer might note many similarities among the various bread recipes offered here. The preceding recipe for rye bread makes grand assumptions of preexisting knowledge on the part of the baker and gives no formula for how much water or salt should be used. The baker should fill in the gaps. In truth, such similarities exist between variant recipes of all genres. A biscuit is much the same as a coffee cake but stiffer and with less sugar. A pancake is much the same as a coffee cake, but the batter is thinner, so we fry instead of bake it. When we begin to observe these common lines, we realize that it is not the recipes that define these people and their food but rather their larger dietary trends.

The *Deseret News* editors unwittingly acknowledged the intuitive nature of baking when they published this recipe in 1859:

The Brigham City flour mill, built in 1856, supplied flour to northern Utah. In later years it was purchased by John Bott, a stonecutter who used the building as his workshop in making monuments and headstones.

Take flour made of good wheat, ground down without bolting; use good yeast only for raising; make up and bake as every good bread maker does with fine flour. It is better to bake in a moderate heat and rather longer than required for fine flour. By adding a tablespoonful of good molasses (when kneading) for every ordinary sized loaf, the bread will retain its moisture and softness till several days or a week old.[35]

No measurements or methods are given. In other words, every good bread maker knew the standard formula for how to make bread with good flour. Many bread recipes encountered in this study simply give variations of ingredients without specifying how much of each or a method for mixing, kneading, or baking. The distinction of the preceding example is that it accommodates bread made from whole wheat flour or of coarser grindings like shorts and middlings. We might imagine that the editors of the *Deseret News* understood the rough state of milling in the territory and included this recipe for the benefit of bakers who routinely worked with coarser cuts of flour. In any case, bread making is not best done from formulaic recipes but rather from a dynamic understanding of flour and yeast in a variety of conditions. I believe that pioneers would look at our modern approach to recipe formulas and just shake their heads at what we don't know.

The real story here is not the recipe but the relentless pursuit of yeast and leavens that allowed rugged pioneers to create the illusion of a civilized society. These early settlers depended on bread to provide the bulk of carbohydrates that fueled their daily endeavors. Therefore the pursuit of bread meant the pursuit of yeast and chemical leavenings. Though they could have eaten unleavened hard biscuits, dumplings, tortillas, or even gruel without using a leaven, they insisted on yeast. For many, bread was the primary source of calories from day to day, with little other food for variety. Others baked bread with exquisite skill. For these, bread became just one element in a diverse menu. With a primitive and unstable environment, limited understanding of chemistry and microbiology, and coarse ingredients to work with, this pursuit seemed doomed to fail. Yet those who recorded eating this bread spoke of its delights.

The Israelites on their exodus from Egypt leaned on manna to make their bread, and it became a symbol of their identity. It is no surprise that Jesus used bread as a symbol of divinity as he instituted a new religion. Likewise, bread is the defining element of the Mormon pioneer diet. We might eat it for nourishment. We might bake it as an homage to pioneering ancestors. Andrew Jenson ate rye bread because he was Danish and Danes grew a lot of rye. I keep a sourdough culture to remind me of my connection to my ancestors and their world that I imagine myself to be a part of. Today we don't need to fuel a transcontinental trek. Instead we feel the need to fuel our dreams and fantasies about pioneer ancestors, and we can do so with bread.

CHAPTER 6

Berries, Bulbs, and Beasts

WILD-GATHERED FOOD

Simon Peter went up, and drew the net to land full of
great fishes, an hundred and fifty and three.
—John 21:11

Emily Stewart needed a new dress. In May 1860 she turned fifteen years old and began to notice increased attention from bachelors and eligible polygamists alike. Emily was of an age for courtship. Her father, a shoemaker, had advanced his station in life and could provide adequate groceries for his family, but extra money for dresses didn't come easily. If Emily was to have the yards of fabric she needed, she would have to earn the money herself.

As she found her way through adolescence, Emily began to receive more attention from boys and men. She had previously dismissed their flirtations, but the time was fast approaching for her to think more seriously about courtship and marriage. John Barnes, a friend of the family and well-to-do businessman in town (and already married to two wives), had shown definite interest. Poor as her family was, Emily needed an income to pay for the yards of fabric necessary for a suitable courtship costume.

Each summer Emily spent a good deal of time in the mountain canyons east of her Kaysville home. She knew the seasons of each berry and where to find them. The previous season her mother had shown her a new plant in the wilderness garden—wild hops. This bushy vining plant grew feathery bulbous flowers. Grocers in Salt Lake City were paying fifty cents per pound for the light-as-air flowers. The making of beer and yeast demanded this herb, with its bitter astringent to drive off harmful wild bacteria. Herbal doctors also recommended hops for making tea. With this recollection, the shoemaker's daughter headed barefoot to the canyon to earn her new fabric.[1]

Emily's project with the hops illustrates three different ways in which Mormon pioneers often used the wild plants and animals that surrounded their nascent farms. Particularly in the early years of settlement (which shifted as new settlements sprouted up farther from the Salt Lake City nucleus), pioneers used wild native plants for subsistence until their own crops took hold. Often they learned of these subsistence foods from their Goshute and Shoshone neighbors. Even after settlements were established, pioneers harvested wild sources to diversify their menu beyond what they could produce domestically.

Once established on their farms along the Wasatch mountains, Mormon settlers continued to rely on wild food sources anytime it was convenient or when it was cheaper than buying something retail. It would be inefficient to devote time to cultivating berries in the back garden when they grew with no attention at all up the canyon. When travels to other settlements took them out into the wilderness, pioneers could pack lighter, knowing that they could forage as they journeyed. Mormon settlers conveniently ate the wild animals, fish, and plants that they found in the course of their travels.

Pioneers also turned to wild foods for sheer pleasure. Domestic food sources had to be coaxed along in the desert climate, with stingy harvests as the norm. Many wild sources offered an abundance that could fuel hedonistic abandon, allowing feasters to gorge themselves in Roman style. Subsistence, convenience, and recreation defined the pioneers' relationship as consumers with their local ecosystem.

Indian Instruction

The first seasons in the Great Salt Lake Valley were particularly lean. Before 1847 came to a close, nearly 2,000 pilgrims had come to call the valley home. Yet they had no crop to harvest that fall. Settlers had to save their wheat for planting the next spring rather than grinding it to flour. The thronging thousands had only what they had carried from the eastern states. To provide for his flock, Brigham Young sent Porter Rockwell and others on an expedition to San Bernardino, California, in hopes of buying beef cattle. The expedition didn't return until February 1848, and the cattle they brought were worn from the trail.[2]

In the fall of 1847 people were getting hungry. Newman Buckley turned to watch with curiosity as local Goshute women went out into the sagebrush plains each day with empty baskets and came back in the evening with a heavy load of edibles. When he went to investigate, he learned that they were harvesting sego bulbs and thistle roots to store for the winter.[3] George Washington Brown also noted exchanges of Anglo and Indian food items in 1847.[4] The pattern of Mormon settlers borrowing foodways from the indigenous populace was established that first season.

Through the coming years political relations between Mormons and Indians would take varied paths. Inevitably, the Indian people would suffer again and again in this power-brokered relationship. Mormon settlers depended on their Indian neighbors for survival in the early years of settlement. The climate of the Rocky Mountains was entirely foreign to the newcomers, as were the flora and fauna of the area. Local Indians provided the knowledge to unlock the secrets to survival in this arid region. In this singular early instance the Indian people held power for a moment, in the form of ecological knowledge. Once the Mormons established a foothold, however, their politics took a dramatic change.

Paiute Indians first welcomed Mormon settlers to Utah but were not always treated fairly. Note the variety of food-processing tools.

As Mormon settlements fanned out along every waterway and riparian zone in Utah's dry environment, Mormons began competing for natural resources formerly utilized only by Indians. The limits of the desert ecology were much more finite than early settlers imagined. Mormon settlers put a strain on the food systems of their Indian neighbors as cattle and sheep impacted the graze and browse available to deer and elk, the Indians' meat sources. Eventually skirmishes between the two cultures broke out, sometimes ending in bloodshed on both sides.

As death tallies mounted, Mormon militias fought to displace Shoshone and Ute people in a permanent fashion. Brigham Young grouped all Indians in the same category as wolves and magpies and called for their selective extermination. The extermination order of Governor Lilburn Boggs against Mormons in Missouri seems to have been quickly forgotten once power dynamics had changed. Indian tribes fought back vigorously and caused a temporary withdrawal of Mormon settlements in outlying areas. Eventually Brigham Young saw the economic impact of his policies and adopted a new approach: it was cheaper to feed the Indians than to fight them.[5] Food was, and continues to be, a political issue.

This policy of appeasement sounds more familiar for many Mormons today. We prefer to imagine Brigham Young as a pragmatic patriarch who limited hostilities out of economic considerations, even if not for humanitarian reasons. This policy came only after severe conflict and losses for both sides. Even so, armed conflict continued for more than a decade after this policy was adopted, ending only after the Utes were forced to the reservation.

Still, the exchange of food processes and technology continued in spite of political tension. Heber McBride, a pioneer of 1856, learned some of his food patterns from the local Indians. He wrote: "As the weather was quite warm we had to jerk our meet [*sic*] so it would not spoil and I happened to be all the one that knew how it was done as I had watched the Indians jerk their meat." Dried and salted beef was already an element of the Anglo food system before the pioneers migrated west. McBride

Utah's Indians taught Mormon settlers basic food technologies. Here meat dries on a rack for jerky.

blended the Indian method of jerking and smoking with his Anglo mode of salting beef. By first dipping the strips of meat into boiling salted water before smoking them on green willows, he obtained a more stable product.[6]

Native Weeds

It was a long wait until the harvest of 1848 came in. Andrew Allen arrived with the last of the 1847 emigrants. Like most of the company, he had no understanding of the new climate and its late frosts. Andrew and many of his neighbors planted their crops too early that spring and were horrified to watch a late frost cut down the young plants. He wrote: "When vegetation sprang up the people many of them had to go to the prairies to seek roots to eat, such as wild onions and thistles roots those were not pleasant but hunger made them good."[7]

Andrew was not alone in eating such wild plants. For many settlers, it was years before good harvests became common enough to lean exclusively on domesticated foods. Recurring droughts and plagues of crickets decimated crops year after year. Emily Barnes's family seemed to turn to wild foods quite frequently in these times. She recalled the hard winter of 1856, which followed a poor harvest. By spring food supplies were thin throughout the Mormon settlements. In these times her family and many others relied on wild foods. She explained:

> We did the best we could to not starve to death. . . . We had to go early in the morning to gather nettles to eat. . . . We also gathered some sego roots and pulled some wild onions to eat. There were two kinds of pigweeds; one light colored, which Aunt called "fat hen" and the other was red.[8]

Emily was likely referring to lamb's quarter as the light-colored fat hen. Pigweed is easily identified by its red stalks. Mary Ann Hafen, a handcart pioneer of 1860, settled in Utah's Dixie. Her mother had carefully carried seeds from Europe to plant in their new settlement; but until they took root, Mary Ann remembered, "pigweed with a small portion of bread was our menu, day in and day out."[9]

Most settlers were not entirely without resources, however. Many kept a milk cow, but milk alone was not adequate. These Yankee and English emigrants were used to bread as their source for carbohydrates. Many combined the wild roots and berries with milk to create new dishes. William Greenwood helped to establish the new Mormon settlements at Parowan in 1856. His daughter Mary remembered that the family cow provided an abundance of milk and butter, but they had no bread for the butter. She wrote that "to make their milk seem more foodable they gathered bullberries and boild [sic] them in it; the acid in the berries curdled the milk which gave them something to chew."[10] Mary seems to echo a common strain in Mormon pioneer foodways: milk was perceived not so much as a beverage but as a food item.

Diverse Diets

Priddy Meeks, another hardy pioneer, recorded a diet with a little more diversity during those first years. His diet included "crows, hawks, wild rose hips, wolf meat, sego bulbs, thistle roots."[11] He also recorded several elk-hunting expeditions into the mountains. It appears that in these efforts acquiring fat was as important as finding meat.

Meeks made a detailed record of a hunting expedition in the fall of 1847. His family was seized in the throes of famine, and an elk would be his solution. By divine providence, he was able to kill an elk. But as he was packing it out of the mountains, he met another party of starving hunters whose similar plan had failed. Not having been blessed by stumbling upon an elk, the starving hunters boiled weeds in water for sustenance. Meeks quickly built a fire and shared broiled elk ribs with them.[12] Our modern sensibility might wonder why he shared ribs instead of a thick steak or roast. The ribs and their accompanying marrow offered the most immediate source of high-value fat and calories.

In the absence of butter and lard, Catherine Ellen Camp Greer made particular note of her efforts to obtain marrow from buffalo bones:

> After we had cut the meat off the bones, they would build a big log fire and put the bones in and scrape the coals all over them and cover them with ashes until they were roasted. . . . You have no idea how much marrow would be contained in the larger leg bones; sometimes almost a pint, and we used this for butter.[13]

Marrow Bones

They must be sawn into convenient sizes; cover the ends with a little dough made of flour and water, and tie them in a floured cloth, boil them an hour and a half, serve on a napkin with dry toast. —*The Complete Cook*, 1864[14]

Andrew Allen made note of the effort to procure grease for cooking as he observed two hunters who managed to trap a wolf. With horror, he noted that hunger pressed some to eat what would normally be forbidden.

> It accured at the hird ground where a brother had cooked some of a large white wolf (He had caught in a trap) to get the oyl and at night the brethren that ware getting wood there came to the camp at night to stop over and thay eat all the meat he had cooked, I sea that my self.[15]

Andrew's friends were seeking cooking oil. In using a cast-iron Dutch oven or frying pan, oil is essential to keeping food from sticking to the bottom of the pan and burning. The pursuit of fat from a wolf might be excused on these grounds, but those who ate wolves or saw it done seemed to look on this as an act entirely contrary to civilization. Daniel Jones noted his refusal to eat the wolves that nosed around their starvation quarters at Devil's Gate during the winter of 1856–57. They ate boiled rawhide instead.

Dog for Dinner

Among Indian cultures, however, eating canines seems to have been more common. Anson Call traveled west with the companies of 1847 after waiting out the snows at

Winter Quarters. A local Pawnee chief invited Anson and other Mormon leaders to visit their settlement nearby. Anson noted that the chief "made a feast for us and had killed his best dog, and after we had eat it he then wanted to commence the talk."[16] Here it seems that eating such meat was part of a rather ritualized social custom. When politics and food supply were not issues in play, Mormon pioneers seem to have readily embraced distinctive Indian foodways. In fact, the sharing of food has always been an act of cultural exchange.

In the previous decade Rocky Mountain fur trappers and mountain men assimilated Indian food patterns and ate such dishes with relish. Not too far from Winter Quarters in place or time, an earlier traveler noted: "If a Pawnee honours you with a feast, you must expect to be regaled on dog meat as a matter of course, besides you must eat out of the same ladle with all the other guests—taking a mouthful of meat and a drink of broth, and then passing it around on the same principle as the pipe. Dog soup is the favorite dish of the Pawnees, Sious [sic], Crows, Blackfeet, and Cheyennes."[17]

Dog Stew

[The pup] was kept on the blaze, with constant turning, until the hair was well singed off, and then cleaned, beheaded, and divided into all imaginable shapes and sizes, and cooked in water for six hours. It was then fished out, and a portion set before us—a slimy glutinous mass, uninviting to the eye, but, nevertheless, most delicate and sweet. Smith laid by one of the hind legs until the next morning; the marbled thin streaks of lean and fat, were most tempting.[18]

The Sego Bulb

The Mormons borrowed more than a little from the local Indians. The sego bulbs mentioned earlier were a staple for the Shoshonean people who shared the Wasatch mountains and valleys. Indeed, the early settlers called their Goshute and Paiute neighbors to the south "digger Indians."[19] The fundamental food-gathering activity of these groups was digging bulbs such as segos, thistles, and wild onions (as mentioned above). For this task, the Indians had developed a rather simple tool—a digging stick.

Just as our previous discussion about the physical elements of Mormon cookery focused on Dutch ovens, a collection of Shoshonean food-related artifacts would not be complete without a digging stick. The curator of the collections of the Utah Museum of Natural History recently displayed several such tools from the earlier Anasazi culture. Varying between three and four feet long, they are as stout as a broom handle and usually slightly curved. One end has a fire-hardened blunt point, the other being squared off.

Within this context, we meet Lorena Washburn Larsen, a Mormon girl growing up in Manti, Utah, circa 1868. She recalled:

> In my childhood our whole group of children used to go east of town, each carrying a sego digger. It was a piece of wood sharpened on one end, and flat on the other. We would just go out of town and look for segos, which were plentiful. When we found them we each went to digging by putting the sharp

The sego lily, Utah's state flower. Goshute Indians taught Mormon settlers to use the bulbs for food.

end of the stick into the ground close beside the sego, and pressing down on the flat end of the digger until it was a few inches in the ground. Sometimes we pounded on the top of the digger with a rock. . . . When the stick was far enough into the ground to suit us, we just pushed it to one side and up came the segos. Then we ate them, and oh how we enjoyed hunting them.[20]

Lorena's mother was an industrious woman. Though she raised her family in Manti, she often traveled to Utah Valley for the good fruit that was raised there. Lorena recalled that her mother's table was always filled with good things to eat. In fact, Lorena remembered the foods of her childhood fondly, with molasses candy and peach preserves at the center of these memories. It would appear that Lorena's sego-hunting expeditions were recreational food ventures, not driven by hunger but by finding joy in the providence of wild places. Though the digging stick was likely a remnant from leaner, hungrier times, Lorena used it for fun. The Indian influences on Mormon settlers continued even when they were not needed for survival.

Sego bulbs showed up in the diet of many early pioneers. We have already noted Emily Barnes and Lorena Larsen. Sarah Flint grew up taking a lunch of sego bulbs boiled in milk for her school lunch.[21] In his later years Aroet Hale cooked up a mess of sego bulbs for his children. Although he had become a prosperous businessman, he wanted his children to eat segos so that they might appreciate what he had endured in his youth.[22] For Hale, the segos were a sacrament of heritage. In fact, the sego lily and its tubers figure so prominently in Utah history that it has been designated as the state flower. As such it is now protected by law and should not be picked. Sego lilies once grew prolifically across Utah's valleys. Today Kentucky bluegrass grows in its place; the sego can only be found in sparse mountain populations. Its striking beauty is amplified by its rarity.

Berrying

In contrast to these early subsistence patterns, some settlers assimilated wild foods for sweetening and garnishes or for the plain joy that only wild berries can offer. Emily Barnes remembered happy excursions into Weber Canyon to gather berries in her youth. Together with her neighbors the Foxleys and also Charles Layton, they went to picnic as they collected service berries, eating as many as they gathered to take home. Emily later wrote: "I took for lunch some boiled potatoes and bread, and I ate so many service berries that I got sick. We remained until the next day, and I picked two bushel sacks full of berries by a spring."[23] Whether they were picking for their own use at home or for sale in the markets is not clear. In reading Emily's autobiography, however, we get the distinct impression that gorging on sweets was not possible except in a wild berry patch.

Other Mormons adapted wild foods to maintain their European ethnic identity. English immigrant Annie Underwood (born November 18, 1823) scoured watercress from streams and ditch banks to make a proper Englishwoman's sandwich for tea. Similarly, by collecting wild plums and currants, Annie could make something resembling an English plum pudding.[24] Other industrious settlers transplanted starts from currant bushes into their farmyards for convenience.

Wild foods still grow in abundance. The pigweed and thistle that sustained Mary Ann Hafen are widely distributed. I often pull them from my garden to make room for tomatoes. It might be easier to grow pigweeds instead of tomatoes. I find the wide variety of wild berries and chokecherries that abound in the foothills and mountains of Utah more appetizing. Some Mormon families and Shoshone Indians make annual expeditions to gather these wild crops. On Highway 36 near Mink Creek, Idaho, cars park bumper to bumper in huckleberry season. In the brutally rugged Mendon hills of Cache Valley, hikers find prolific crops of thimbleberries, if they're lucky enough to show up on the right day. Some Mormon housewives likewise track the maturing chokecherry crop in the canyons and steam the tart juice to make syrup and preserves.

Wild Game in Abundance

Early settlers demonstrated similar patterns in their use of wild animals to sustain their diet in the early years and as luxury items to enrich their meals in later years. Livy Olsen immigrated from Denmark to Utah's Sanpete Valley. While growing up near the Sanpete River he recalled that wild meat was his primary source of protein. With a diverse menu to choose from, Livy ate deer, rabbits, sage hen, trout, suckers, and chubs.[25] It might seem that a domesticated diet limited to beef, pork, and chicken would be a reduction in provender by comparison.

While some settlers used wild gathered foods to augment domesticated menu items, for others the reverse was true. Andrew Christian Nielsen's friends primarily ate wild rabbit, with a bit of wheat. He was horrified to observe: "Their grub was mostly rabbit for breakfast, hare for dinner, and sorghum for supper with a little burnt molasses and cornmeal mush or cooked wheat." When Andrew's wife, Maren Kirstine, arrived, she remarked: "I also learned to prepare what was to become my principal diet boiled wheat and fried jack rabbit. Such food was different than anything I had ever eaten, and it tasted rather good." After several hundred such meals, however, her family began to complain. Her sons prayed that they might be blessed with a shotgun to alter their fare. Taking inspiration from this, she bought a second-hand gun and some ammunition on credit. Her sons provided wild ducks and geese for dinner that night, and there was rejoicing in the land.[26]

A rabbit-hunting party travels on the ice over Utah Lake. Wild rabbits served as a critical source of protein for early settlers.

Rabbit

Put it down to a sharp clear fire; dredge it lightly and carefully with flour; take care to
have it frothy and of a fine light brown; boil the liver with parsley while the rabbit is
roasting; when tender, chop them together; put half the mixture into melted butter,
use the other half for garnish, divided into little hillocks. Cut off the head, divide it,
and lay half on each side of the dish. A fine well-grown and well hung warren rabbit,
dressed as a hare, will eat very much like it.   —*The Complete Cook*, 1864[27]

Fish, Fish, and More Fish

Better known than the use of Utah's big game in feeding the early settlers is the role of
fish. Wilford Woodruff famously fished anywhere there was water. He made frequent
notes in his diary of his fishing exploits in Utah, including an early attack on the trout
of Utah Lake in 1851.[28]

Even earlier in 1849 Parley Pratt had explored the possibilities of fishing in Utah
Lake with optimism but no success.[29] Through these early years a few pioneers made
small stabs at using fish from Utah Lake, but it took an emergency to launch fishing as an industry. In 1856 Peter Madsen settled on the lake near the mouth of the
Provo River, preferring the nostalgic setting, which reminded him of his fishing days
in Denmark. The previous winter had been hard, and grasshoppers soon made things
worse. Madsen commenced fishing with a net cobbled together from parts contributed by other fishermen. This first earnest effort returned hundreds of pounds of fish
with every cast of the net. In the face of starvation, Peter gave fish to anyone who
needed it, working with a small crew to keep the nets hauling around the clock for
several days. With fresh fish in hand, some sat down on the banks of the river to roast
their fish on sticks over small fires, eating them with trembling hands. Others packed
fish in brine and hauled them in barrels back to their homes.[30]

In the spring of 1858 more Mormons showed up in Utah Valley. With word of the
federal army's expedition to Utah, settlers from all over northern Utah abandoned
their homes and retreated in exile to Utah Valley. Without adequate preparations for
the masses of people that descended on the valley, starvation stalked the settlements.
Emily Barnes remembered her father fishing in the lake and salting his catch for preservation before they returned to their home in Kaysville, seventy-five miles to the north.[31]

Once the Mormons and the army learned how to get along, they began a reserved
relationship, trading commodities and cash. The Mormon society had few exports,
because Brigham Young followed isolationist policies. As a result, Mormon cash
flowed out to the eastern states as imports poured in. The army camp offered momen-
tary relief from this cycle. The army payroll provided an influx of cash, and Mormons
jumped at the opportunity to supply some of the soldiers' needs. Albert Tracy, stationed at Camp Floyd, remarked: "The Mormons bring out to us trout from Lake
Utah—cured by drying. We find them excellent, and a most acceptable change from
our former habitual diet."[32]

Mormons continued their use of wild fish long after the settlements in Utah Valley were well established. Elizabeth Kane, traveling through Provo in 1872, mentioned
eating wild trout in Provo, drawn from Utah Lake.[33] As the settlement years drew to

Commercial fishing on Utah Lake. Fish were caught with nets, salted and dried, and marketed throughout Utah.

a close, however, Peter Madsen noted a decline in his hauls of fish. In 1856 he could haul thousands of pounds in a day, but by the 1880s it was down to mere hundreds. In addition, the trout and salmon he once knew were a clear minority compared to the suckers and chubs that filled out the bulk of his nets. In his 1886 effort to revive the fishery Madsen introduced two dozen carp to the lake.[34] Today his carp have overrun the lake, destroying habitat for the endangered suckers that sustained earlier generations. Recently commercial fishers have contracted with state wildlife agencies to fish out millions of pounds of carp in hope of restoring the habitat for Utah's native and endangered species.

Cream Trout.—Having prepared the trout very nicely, and cut off the heads and tails, put the fish into boiling water that has been slightly salted, and simmer them for five minutes. Then take them out, and lay them to drain. Put them into a stew-pan, and season them well with powdered mace, nutmeg, and a little cayenne, all mixed together. Put in as much rich cream as will cover the fish, adding some bits of the fresh yellow rind of a small lemon. Keep the pan covered, and let the fish stew for about ten minutes after it has begun to simmer. Then dish the fish, and keep them hot till you have finished the sauce. Mix, very smoothly, a small tea-spoonful of arrow-root with a little milk, and stir it into the cream. Then add the juice of the lemon. Pour the sauce over the fish, and then send them to table.

. . . Carp is very nice stewed in this manner.   *—The Lady's Receipt Book*, 1847[35]

Sometimes Mormon pioneers turned to wild meat as a celebration of their mountain home. In September 1849 Brigham Young and his entourage traveled to the settlement of Brown's Fort near present-day Ogden, Utah. After spending the day exploring sites for future settlement, some members of the party adjourned to fishing the Weber and Ogden rivers. With a bountiful catch, they repaired to Brown's Fort, where they feasted on broiled trout as well as roasted pork and goat meat. This was not subsistence; this was celebration.

We might imagine that Wilford Woodruff was an instigator in this piscatorial adventure. But, to his chagrin, Woodruff was in England at the time, converting future pioneers to the faith. Woodruff was an ardent fisherman, casting his artificial flies in many of Utah's streams. Soon after his return, however, he redeemed his neglect with a note in his diary: "I went fishing and caught 49 trout."[36] Following the tradition of the apostles of Jesus in their miraculous catch (see John 21:10–11), Woodruff often made a careful record of the precise numbers of fish and fowl he harvested from wild places.

Fried Trout

Fry some slices of salt pork, say a slice for each pound, and when brown take them up, and add lard enough to cover the fish. Skim it well, and have it hot, then dip the fish in flour, without salting it, and fry a light brown. Then take the fish up, and add to the gravy a little flour paste, pepper, salt; also wine, catsup, and spices, if you like. Put the fish and pork on a dish, and, after one boil, pour this gravy over the whole.

Fish are good dipped first in egg and then in Indian meal, or cracker crumbs and egg, previous to frying.   —*Miss Beecher's Domestic Receipt Book*, 1850[37]

Woodruff always seems to have traveled ready for adventure. In the fall of 1867 he journeyed with other apostles to Cache Valley on an extended preaching tour. After preaching to congregations up and down the valley, the party camped on Blacksmith Fork near present-day Hyrum. The next morning Wilford noted, "We took a breakfast of trout which I caught last evening."[38] Even on preaching tours, he carried his fly rod, which is on display in the exhibits at the LDS Museum of History and Art in Salt Lake City.

The arid landscape in Rush Valley offered no trout streams. When Woodruff went out to cut corral poles there, his fly rod stayed home. Still, the likelihood of a sporting adventure lingered. Instead of his fly rod, he carried his fowling gun and prowled the marshes in the evening. "I shot 7 ducks, dressed them & roasted them for our dinner," he reported. A week later he returned for the same chore and shot three sage hens.[39] It seems that he viewed the wild fish and fowl as reliable groceries in a wilderness market. When his travels or farming ventures took him to the mountains, he regularly leaned on wild meat for his meals.

Roasted Duck

Wash the ducks, and stuff them with a dressing made with mashed potatoes, wet with milk, and chopped onions, sage, pepper, salt, and a little butter, to suit your taste. Reserve the inwards to make the gravy, as is directed for turkeys, except it should be

> seasoned with sage and chopped onions. They will cook in about an hour. Ducks are
> to be cooked rare. Baste them with salt water, and before taking up, dredge on a little
> flour and let it brown.   —*Miss Beecher's Domestic Receipt Book,* 1850[40]

Other Mormons used wild foods when away from home as well. In 1857, as the
invading federal army approached, Andrew Allen found himself stationed in Echo
Canyon as part of a militia. A few days earlier he had accompanied Porter Rockwell
and Lot Smith as they raided the supply train that followed the army. In that instance
they killed a fat cow from the herd. As they stood picket guard in Echo Canyon, they
saw no fat cows. To supplement their lean rations, Andrew recorded, "The boys went
out hunting killd [*sic*] too chickens."[41] These were likely sage grouse or sharp-tailed
grouse, about the size of a pheasant. One would make a meal for two people.

> **To Broil a Fowl or Rabbit:** Cut it open down the back, wipe the inside clean with
> a cloth, and season it with pepper and salt. Have a clear fire, and set the gridiron at
> a good distance over it, lay the fowl on the inside, toward the fire, and broil it till it is a
> fine brown. Do not burn the fleshy side. Lay it on a hot dish, garnish it with parsley,*
> and pour over it some melted butter.   —*The Great Western Cookbook,* 1857[42]
> * Andrew Allen probably didn't use parsley on that occasion; he may not have had
>   butter either.

Wild Recreation

On other occasions, Wilford Woodruff pursued wild game simply for the pleasure
and sport of it. In December 1867 he wrote this vividly detailed account of a duck
hunting expedition to the marshes of Great Salt Lake:

> I went down the Jordon with Ezra & Browen Pettet to shoot some ducks.
> Brother Ezra Pettet sen. Took two boats crossed the Hot spring lake &
> Browen went with me in the waggon & met him there. We shot 6 ducks
> then drove down the Jordon with the team some 4 miles further. I then left
> my team with my Indian Boy Sarroquetts & we went down 3 miles near the
> mouth of Jordon. Ezra Pettet rowed down with his boat. While going down
> he shot 3 geese. We rowed our boats into the rushes whare [*sic*] we could hide
> ourselves & as the ducks would fly over or among us we would shoot them on
> the wing. We staid till dark then rowed back to our waggon, drew our Boats
> up on the dry land made up a fire Cooked a duck pot pie Eat our supper made
> our Beds in the Boat & slept all night. . . . We counted our game & found we
> had 40 ducks & 3 geese.[43]

This was after eating a half-dozen ducks the night before.

As Mormon settlements moved from subsistence to opulence, from wilderness
sojourners to domesticated gentlemen and women, people continued to incorporate
and rely on wild foods. At the Territorial Ball of 1860, a high society event, a variety
of wild meats showed up on the menu. Mountain sheep, bear, elk, deer, duck, trout,
and salmon formed the basis of the meat course, with a few domestics thrown in as

A father and son shooting ducks on the Great Salt Lake mudflats for the markets in Salt Lake City.

well.[45] When Brigham Young traveled through the settlements, the locals frequently prepared feasts including wild elements. Whether out of need or for pleasure, Mormon pioneer diets actively incorporated wild foods. Near the turn of the twentieth century retailers in Salt Lake City provided a market for wild ducks and game. Utah hunters shot for the market and killed thousands of ducks annually.

Pot Pie

Take raised pie-crust, line a pot, or small Dutch oven, or a very deep stewpan, bottom and sides, with one-half an inch thickness; lay your fowls and pork, or veal, in very small pieces (the pork is always best boiled first) in, with salt, and pepper, and small pieces of butter, then potatoes, cut in very delicate slices, then a layer of crust, one, again, of meat, then potatoes, then crust. Then pour in the water in which the pork has been boiled, through a hole in the top crust. The pie must be baked very judiciously, or it will be a failure. It is, therefore, always best to cook the meat and fowl, unless they are very young and tender. Lay a sheet of foolscap over the top, to keep it from baking too rapidly.

This is a most excellent dish for a harvest-party, or log-rolling; it can be made at any season of the year; in winter they are very fine, made of sweet-breads, tenderloins, and spare-ribs, finely sliced, or cut up.   —*The Great Western Cookbook*, 1857[44]

As Mormon settlements moved from subsistence to opulence, from wilderness sojourners to domesticated gentlemen and women, people continued to incorporate and rely on wild foods. At the Territorial Ball of 1860, a high society event, a variety of wild meats showed up on the menu. Mountain sheep, bear, elk, deer, duck, trout, and salmon formed the basis of the meat course, with a few domestics thrown in as well.[45] When Brigham Young traveled through the settlements, the locals frequently prepared feasts including wild elements. Whether out of need or for pleasure, Mormon pioneer diets actively incorporated wild foods. Near the turn of the twentieth century retailers in Salt Lake City provided a market for wild ducks and game. Utah hunters shot for the market and killed thousands of ducks annually.

The practice of harvesting food from wild sources continues in Mormon families and communities. Whether from poverty, frugality, family tradition, or a sense of adventure, modern generations of Mormons continue to make a place in their diet for wild meat and vegetables. While it has declined from the pervasive levels of the 1960s, the annual deer hunt still impacts many facets of the Utah economy and society. Utah's earliest pioneers leaned on wild foods out of necessity as they fended off starvation. Later generations embraced wild foods out of nostalgia or adventure. Many modern families continue to gather berries, chokecherries, pine nuts, mushrooms, wild asparagus, and watercress. The reasons for the persistent incorporation of wild gathered foods are probably as diverse as the foods gathered. Wild foods are a defining element of Mormon cuisine, historical and modern.

CHAPTER 7

Put By for Winter

PRESERVED FOODS

Slaughter no more than you can salt, or you will have tainted meat.
—Danish proverb

Flora Clarinda Washburn knew how to set a table. Her daughter Lorena remembered, "Her table was always loaded with good things to eat."[1] In part this was because Manti had been settled for several years by the time Lorena scooted her chair up to eat at the table. Lorena's father, Abraham, had been one of the first settlers in the Sanpete Valley in 1849. Those years provided compound interest on his investment, as he had paid his dues early on. Abraham and other early settlers plowed, planted, and expanded their herds. By the time Danish immigrants arrived years later, Abraham's farm was well established. When Danish farmers were starting from scratch to eke out their existence, the older American and English farmers in the valley had surpluses.

This might account for "good things to eat" in the summertime when gardens yielded their bounty. The Washburns' table was also well appointed in winter, largely due to their cellars. "There were steps going down to the cellar, which was the storehouse for the barrels of pork, molasses, ground cherry and fruit preserves (all made with molasses), dried fruit and dried squash. The bread barrel was there and there were cupboards for milk, butter and cheese. The vegetables were kept in an outside cellar."[2] The humid cellar with its dark, musty smell provided a cool space that facilitated longer-term storage of food. The cellar was not a refrigerator, but it kept things from freezing in winter and cooled milk in the summer. If not for the cellar and its preserved foods, winter would be lean. Such preserved food allowed pioneers to spread the surpluses of summer throughout the winter.

Prohibition of Rot

At the same time Lorena's mother was putting food away for winter in the Sanpete Valley, a group of men in Europe argued about how such food evaded decay and spoilage. The crux of their disagreement regarded the process of decay. Some thought that decay simply happened by exposure to air: oxidation caused decay. This school of thought was influenced by an old theory about "spontaneous generation." Perhaps weevils just suddenly showed up in wheat or flour as a result of exposure to air. Oxygen caused the flour to give birth to weevils. Yeast might spontaneously appear in a sugar-water solution when it stood uncovered overnight.

Others argued that small "animalcules," "airborne infusoria," or "floating matter" existed in the air, smaller than the human eye could see. In 1837 microscopes had examined yeast cells and found them to be living things, but their cycle of life was not yet understood. While the first school of thought concluded that yeast caused fermentation as the yeast colony died and decayed, the new school believed that invisible airborne yeasts were attracted to sugar and consumed sugar as part of the life cycle in regeneration. Louis Pasteur and John Tyndall belonged to this new school of thought. But they had only primitive scientific instruments to work with. The argument was stalemated: neither side could definitively prove its case.[3]

Back in Utah, Mormon pioneers knew nothing of this heated argument that had everything to do with food preservation. Pioneer housekeepers were completely ignorant of bacteria and their relationship to decay. Mormon settlers didn't understand anything about microbiology, but they were experts at working around the problem. In spite of their ignorance, they prevented rot and spoilage all winter long.

The long-term security and stability of any society depends on being able to store food beyond the moment. Today we accomplish this superficially with refrigerators but more fundamentally with a debit card, a grocery store, and a worldwide industrial food network. Our food supply chain and credit provide for our food storage beyond the next meal. During the historic period discussed here, this same security came through different means: a complex system of storage that utilized salting, drying, and smoking; bacteria cultures; alcohol- and vinegar-based antiseptics; anaerobic environments; and trade networks.

Perhaps the pioneer parallel to our modern extended food supply chain might be found in the barns and farmyards of Mormon settlers. A haystack in the field served to give fodder for animals through the winter, ensuring a continuing supply of beef and milk. Root crops stored under straw or manure or in cellars provided ongoing food for pigs in cold months and the possibility of fresh pork in winter. A corncrib fed fowls through lean months. These storage systems for crops not immediately useful as human food guaranteed a diet for the livestock that would become food themselves.

Preservation and Security

Domesticated agriculture can be phenomenally productive, far exceeding the ability of one family to consume. Anyone who has ever made the mistake of planting six tomato plants can tell you that tomatoes will rot on the ground faster than a family can eat them. A Jersey dairy cow can average five or more gallons of milk each day—more than any family could drink. A small flock of a dozen chickens might give eight eggs a day. A larger flock can readily supply eggs for market, creating a bit of extra spending money. All of these food products are perishable and will not last a week without refrigeration. Even with a refrigerator, those daily five gallons of milk soon

A Daniel Weggeland illustration of the Brigham Young Eagle Gate estate. Haystacks, cellars, and barns all served to safeguard food for winter.

become thirty-five gallons over a week. By the time the first five have been drunk, thirty gallons have gone to waste. Do you begin to see the problem?

If all of this produce could be preserved for consumption at a later date, life in Manti circa 1865 might begin to be pleasant. Peach preserves in January might not be quite so divine as a fresh juicy peach in August, but they would ward off scurvy as well as provide a sweet diversion from the heavy, starchy foods of winter. A winter void of vegetables would be not only dreary but possibly deadly. To this end, Patty Sessions made note of eating her first fresh domesticated vegetables each season, in contrast to preserved foods.[4]

Dried Foods

Drying is the simplest food preservation technique. The primary aim is to eliminate moisture as a breeding ground for bacteria. Just as bacteria can fester more easily in a damp rag than on a dry plastic surface, food drying techniques seek to eliminate moisture as a haven for bacteria. Alice Langston Dalton helped her mother prepare the fruit harvest for drying. She wrote:

> The fruits were sun dried on big scaffolds. Fruit became very plentiful and we had more than we could do ourselves.
>
> We would gather a good many bushels and pile them up on the ground then invite all the young folks in some evening, to a "cutting bee" we called it, some would cut and carry them to the scaffolds in baskets made of water willows, and then those on the scaffolds would spread the fruit on the boards. I have seen whole wagon loads of fruit cut and put out in just a few hours that way.[5]

Fruit on racks, drying in the sun. "Fruit drying was a great business in Utah," said pioneer Patience Loader.

Just as we buy dried apple or banana chips at the grocery store today, Utah's early settlers dried and stored their sweet fruits for winter, though apparently in much larger volume.

Dried Apple Pie

3 c. dried apples, ½ c. honey, ¼ tsp cinnamon, butter the size of walnut. Soak apples in water overnight and cook in same water. Add honey when apples are cooked. This makes one large pie.   —Jane Holmes Orton (1839–1909)[6]

A sizable portion of the fruit crop was not for home consumption but rather to be sold, fresh or dried, as a cash crop. As a new bride, Patience Loader planted apple, apricot, and peach trees in 1858, as "fruit drying was a great business in Utah."[7] Living with her husband, a soldier at Camp Floyd, she had a ready market for fresh fruit among the soldiery. Clarinda Washburn also purchased much of her fruit. After driving a wagon from Manti to Provo, she helped to harvest and process the fruit, bringing some of it home with her.[8] John Langston (Alice Dalton's father) used dried fruit more directly as a commodity: "My father, in order to get flour would take his molasses and dried fruits and vegetables north and trade for flour, machinery and other things to use."[9] Dried fruit functioned as a medium of exchange in territorial Utah, in addition to its dietary contributions.

By the 1860s Utah fruit farmers had consolidated into a cooperative of sorts, with the LDS Church acting as its agent. The church set commodity prices by assigning a cash value for tithing donations of produce and negotiated for farmers on large sales in bulk. Small farmers like John Langston and Patience Loader processed and sold their fruit to the church agent, who in turn sold these cash crops to hungry mining communities in neighboring western states. In 1864 alone, Utah farmers sold 200,000 pounds of dried peaches to mining communities in Montana for $150,000.[10] Can you imagine what the crop was before drying? Agricultural produce was one of the very few viable exports in Utah's cash-starved economy.

Sugary Preserves

In another common treatment for fruit preservation, settlers made preserves by simmering fruit in molasses for several hours. Like salt, sugar in sufficient quantities can create a medium hostile to bacterial growth. Lorena Washburn Larsen recalled her mother's annual trips to Utah Valley after fruit: "Mother went home at the end of the fruit season [1868], with the wagon loaded with sacks of dried fruit, barrels of preserves, peaches, plums, pears and apples, cooked in molasses."[11] Likewise, Mary Josephine Knight Bunker remembered, "Peaches was the main fruit taken care of for winter. Some were dried and some preserved, the preserves being put up with molasses in a twenty or thirty gallon barrel, as there were not bottles or sugar to be had."[12] All bacteria and lingering yeasts could be killed off by simmering the fruit for hours. Intense levels of sugar from the molasses kept bacteria at bay.

These thick preserves akin to jam were then stored in barrels and crocks. When the bung plug was hammered tight and the barrelhead closed within its staves, these air-tight barrels were certain to be fairly safe against yeast or bacterial infection. Crocks were a little more tricky. Annie Underwood used a piece of cotton cloth dipped in hot candle wax to close her crocks. With a strip of waxed cloth likewise tied around the crock to hold the cover on, the wax formed a reasonably tight air seal after it dried.[13]

Hattie Snow's Peach Preserves

1 qt molasses or more if not sweet enough—3 lbs. peaches either with or without pits. Simmer for 6 hours. Good filling for Roly Poly.[14]

*Having tried this recipe, I would recommend six pounds of peaches with one quart of molasses. Be careful to simmer, not boil. Simmering the pits and skins with the peaches (straining them out afterward) contributes pectin to help thicken the preserves.

Clarissa Young described a similar approach to fruit and molasses:

> Sometimes we would add a little variety to the monotony of peach drying by making "peach leather." This strictly original product was made by mashing the peaches to a smooth pulp, adding some sugar, and spreading the mixture out in thin layers on a clean cloth. When dried it would be cut into pieces and made a very delicious "chewy" concoction.[15]

This peach leather wouldn't be as versatile as preserves; Clarissa couldn't really use it to make filling for a pudding or to eat with bread and butter. Still, she demonstrated

Sugar beets stored for winter under layers of dirt, straw, and manure. These beets could feed livestock or could be boiled down for molasses. Many different root crops were stored for winter in this manner.

a familiar pioneer theme of using the same ingredients to make a wide variety of food items.

Settlers also dried squashes, pumpkins, and melons for winter use, though they were not as tasty or as versatile as dried peaches. First they cut the squash into long thin rings. These were threaded onto a long stick. Ranks and files of these squash-loaded sticks would hang from rafters until the squash dried thoroughly.[16] The squash was then stored away in muslin bags until it was ready to be reconstituted for a pie or to thicken a soup. In this manner settlers could store surplus summer vegetable vitamins for the winter.

A Squash Pudding

Pare, cut in pieces, and stew in a very little water, a yellow winter squash. When it is quite soft, drain it dry, and mash it in a cullender [*sic*]. Then put it into a pan, and mix with it a quarter of a pound of butter. Prepare two pounded crackers, or an equal quantity of grated stale bread. Stir gradually a quarter of a pound of powdered sugar into a quart of rich milk, and add by degrees, the squash, and the powdered biscuit. Beat nine eggs very light, and stir them gradually into the mixture. Add a glass of white wine, a glass of brandy, a glass of rose water, and a table-spoonful of mixed spice, nutmeg, mace, and cinnamon powdered. Stir the whole very hard, till all the ingredients are thoroughly mixed. Bake it three quarters of an hour in a buttered dish; and when cold, grate white sugar over it.　　*—Directions for Cookery,* 1840[17]

One last treatment of squash deserves mention. Several pioneers noted that squash butter played a role in their seasonal diet. Lorena Larsen was one of these.[18] James Jensen, a Danish handcart emigrant of 1857, also recalled: "Our diet consisted chiefly of bread, and of molasses which my mother made from beets. Butter, in the beginning, we made out of squash."[19] In the spectrum of preserves, jams, and jellies, "butter" refers to a thick spreadable reduction of whatever fruit or vegetable may be handy. Apple butter may be more familiar to modern readers and is still commercially available. Until apple orchards took root in Utah, settlers found squash to be a suitable alternative.

> **Preserved Pumpkin**
>
> Cut a thick yellow pumpkin, peeled, into strips two inches wide, and five or six long.
>
> Take a pound of white sugar for each pound of fruit, and scatter it over the fruit, and pour on two wine-glasses of lemon juice for each pound of pumpkin.
>
> Next day, put the parings of one or two lemons with the fruit and sugar, and boil the whole three quarters of an hour, or long enough to make it tender and clear without breaking. Lay the pumpkin to cool, strain the syrup, and then pour it on to the pumpkin. If there is too much lemon peel, it will be bitter.
>
> —*Miss Beecher's Domestic Receipt Book,* 1850[20]

Salted Foods

In these treatments, pioneers tried to achieve dryness, knowing that damp and decay went hand in hand. From a modern perspective, the aim is to create an environment that is hostile to bacteria. A dried fruit accomplished this in some measure. Pioneers knew that drying was effective with meat, and salt often played a role there as well. Salt served to drive off moisture in meat. But the pioneers didn't know that salt, in concentration, was also an antibacterial agent.

Dried foods often converge with salted foods, as in salted beef, pork, fish, and venison. We have seen Mormon pioneers salting wild meat as part of the process of making jerky. Utah dry goods retailer Holliday and Warner advertised codfish for sale in 1851.[21] These were likely salted and dried on Cape Cod, hard as shingles, to be reconstituted after shipping. Likewise, the fishing industry at Utah Lake employed salting as part of processing the fish for transportation and storage. Some families came to Utah Lake prepared with salt and barrels to process their fish on-site.[22] Others approached the task industrially, processing tons of fish for commercial sale. George Brimhall reported:

> [The fish] are first dressed, then salted about as when going into the frying pan, packed into heaps for about six hours, then laid flesh side upon the grass, in about two hours turned over, and so repeated for three or four days, when they are dried.[23]

Such salting makes a good preservative on two different levels: the hydroscopic characteristic of salt drives off moisture more quickly and thoroughly than drying alone. In addition, salt itself is an enemy to the microbial life forms that rot meat. Just as only brine shrimp can survive in the highly saline environment of the Great Salt Lake, not much can live on a well salted piece of pork. In this context, Elizabeth

Baxter watched as her father took chunks of beef "down to the Great Salt Lake to get salt to preserve it."[24] Once salted, such food is inedible even for humans. It must be freshened again by repeated soaking in fresh water before it is made edible again.

To Dress Salt Fish

Soak it in cold water, according to its saltiness; the only method of ascertaining which, is to taste one of the flakes of the fish. That fish which is hard and dry will require 24 hours' soaking, in 2 or 3 waters, to the last of which add a wine-glassful of vinegar. But less time will suffice for a barreled cod, and still less for the split fish. Put the fish on in cold water, and let it simmer, but not actually boil, else it will be tough and thready. Garnish with hard-boiled eggs, the yolks cut in quarters, and serve with egg-sauce, parsnips, or beet-root.   —*The Ladies' New Book of Cookery*, 1852[25]

Cured Meats and Sausage

Frequently we see references to salting meat simultaneously called "curing." Smoked meat also takes on this misnomer from time to time as well. In truth, curing is a much more specific process in which saltpeter (potassium nitrate) is mixed with salt (and sometimes sugar as well) to be infused into meat. Saltpeter is the chemical responsible for the red color in cured meats like ham and corned beef. These nitrates are used in many modern meat products to aid preservation and deter spoilage. A very small portion of saltpeter is sufficient to treat large volumes of meat. If you imagine trying to spread a tablespoon of butter over 100 pounds of meat, you begin to see the difficulty of the task. To solve the problem, the saltpeter is thoroughly mixed into a larger volume of salt and sugar, which is then applied to the meat. In modern applications this is done by making a saline solution that can be pumped into the artery of a ham, thus infusing the curing mix through the capillaries. Hams can also be submerged in a saline/nitrate mixture in larger containers.

On Lemuel Redd's farm, hog killing and butchering time was a critical season for putting food by for the winter.[26] Hogs were killed after the weather had turned cold. Neighbors came to help; it was a big job. After killing the hog, Redd lifted the hog into the air by means of a derrick and immediately bled the carcass, draining more than a gallon of hot steaming blood. Not only did blood in the meat make it less palatable, but evacuating the blood immediately helped to cool the meat. Next the hog was scalded in hot water and scraped to remove all hair from the skin.

After the sides of pork had cooled completely, Redd butchered out the hams, shoulders, and bacon. Wives stood by waiting to take the first cuts to make into a celebratory meal for the butchering crew. Redd used a dry-rub process for curing his hams, more typical of meat curing for his day. "Then warm salt was rubbed into the meat until no moisture came out," his daughter Ellen recalled. "Sometimes a little sugar was added, but that was harder to get. This meat stood a few days and if any moisture or blood came out, it was evidence that more salt was needed and more was rubbed in."[27]

To Cure Pork

For each 100 lbs. of pork make a pickle of 10 lbs. salt—2 lbs. brown sugar—2 oz. salt petre—1 oz. red pepper and from 4–5 gals. water or just enough to cover meat. First rub the hams with common salt and lay the meat in a tub overnight. Heat the above ingredients, stirring frequently, remove all the scum, allow to boil 10 minutes. Cool and pour over the meat. Take out small pieces [such as bacon or ham hocks] in 2 weeks. Allow hams and shoulders to remain in brine 6 weeks.

—Attributed to Henry Atkin, 1865–1938[28]

Elizabeth Brockbank Hales remembered such cured meats as being common in her family's cellar. "Our home-cured hams were tops," she said. "We also had a barrel of corned beef."[29] Corned beef required a curing process similar to that for hams, particularly for briskets. Roasts and steaks were best eaten fresh, but the brisket, a tough cut of beef filled with fat and gristle, did better with a cure. Slabs of bacon were cured likewise, by packing them in the mix of salt and saltpeter. Salt and saltpeter made up a critical element in the meat curing of Mormon pioneers. We continue to use them in large quantities today.

Brine for Corn Beef: 4 qts. Water—10 lbs. salt—1 level tsp. saltpeter—1 qt. Molasses—¼ lb. soda. Sufficient water to cover meat for 100 lbs. beef. Make brine, let cool then add the molasses and soda, dissolving saltpeter in hot water to be added last. [Cured beef] had to be soaked in cold water overnight before cooking.

—Harriet Robinson Jones, 1871–1945[30]

Hams and bacon continue to hold a strong place in Mormon foodways today. But cured sausages seem to be losing ground. Perhaps this is because much of the meat that was once ground to sausage is now used in pork chops and other single-serving cuts of lean meat. The sausages once fermented from ancestral recipes are now processed as bologna. When we read about butchering pork on the pioneer farmstead, the only cuts we find are hams, shoulders, bacon, and sausage. "It was the custom when a hog was butchered to give to friends and neighbors enough fresh meat for a meal including some of the famous Danish sausage," writes Anna Madsen Bench. She left the following description of her family's tradition of making sausage from her mother, Mette:[31]

This was made by grinding together part of the tenderloin, some fat, and trimming from the hams and shoulders. It was well seasoned with salt, pepper, allspice and sage. Then stuffed in the small casing [the small intestine] which had been cleaned and scraped until it was as transparent as cellophane. The stuffing was done by stretching the casing over a tube which had been made from the horn of an ox or cow, cut the right size, hollowed out and thoroughly polished. The hams, shoulders and side meat were put in the brine until cured, then smoked and hung in a cool place ready for use.[32]

Anna is not completely clear as to whether these sausages were eaten fresh immediately or might have been cured and smoked along with the hams and bacon.

Smoked Meats

Once cured, hams, bacon, and sausage could be smoked. Smoked meats are often referenced as "cured," but smoking alone will not preserve meat. Smoking, like salting, accomplishes two ends. First, the smoke comes with a mild amount of heat (preferably not above 115° F) and helps to dry the meat. Dried meats are less susceptible to rot (see the discussion above). Smoke also contains carcinogens that retard bacterial growth. A well-smoked ham appears quite black with its sooty covering. In this regard, smoked meat is more impervious to spoilage than unsmoked meat. Still, without a saltpeter cure, the meat will soon rot. Smoking alone does not cure beef and pork.

Lemuel Redd's daughter recorded the smoking process that her father used in southern Utah in the 1870s:

> Each piece was hung by cords from the [smokehouse] ceiling, so smoke could get all around it. My father used only corn cobs for fuel. They did not make a big fire or blaze—but smothered it, so only smoke came up, and it lasted a long time. When these hams etc. had been smoked three days, my mother Kezia Butler Redd knew they were ready for the winter.
> —Ellen R. Bryner, 1872–1957[33]

Before homesteads were well established, some pioneers used the chimneys of their fireplace as an improvised smokehouse. Ellen Maria Bailey Humphrey (1856–1951) wrote: "One year Father strung a lot of fish on sticks and then got on the house and put them down the chimney. The sticks held them up. They smoked and dried and were very good to eat."[34] Although fish might be adequately dried for preservation with the smoking process, these fish were likely salted before smoking as well.

Some pioneers also used salt as the primary preservative for vegetables such as cucumbers. Leah Larson wrote:

> I remember when mother used to sort the cucumbers and put them into crocks in the cellar. Then she made a brine of salted water, strong enough to hold up an egg and poured it over the cucumbers; put a board on top, with a rock to hold the board down, and there they stayed until winter. She would bring up a pan full at a time and freshen them. This was done by covering them with cold water, adding a pinch of alum and letting it stand on the reservoir at the back of the stove all day. At night she poured off the salty water and added more fresh water and in the morning the cucumbers were ready to be made into pickles. The cucumbers were covered with vinegar and water until they were just sour enough to be good and they didn't last long on the table.[35]

Here the salting process was used to dehydrate the cucumbers so that they could readily absorb vinegar, which prevented decay. Even so, these pickles would have been rather salty.

Alcohol and Vinegar

In these instances salt is the tool to kill bacteria. In a similar approach, pioneers sometimes used alcohol to inhibit bacteria growth in the interest of food preservation. In fact, alcohol itself is a means of preserving a crop. Barley, corn, apples, grapes, and peaches might all be fermented to a state of alcoholic preservation in the form of beer, whiskey, cider, wine, or brandy, respectively. Wine will keep much longer than grapes, and cider longer than apples. Chapter 11 details some of these approaches. In other instances, alcohol was used as an antibacterial agent to aid in the preservation of other foods. Brandied peaches and mincemeat pie (the mincemeat being soaked in brandy) are the most common examples in this category.

Brandied Peaches

Prick the peaches with a needle, put them into a kettle with cold water, scald them until sufficiently soft to be penetrated with a straw. Take half a pound of sugar to every pound of peach; make the syrup with the sugar, and while it is a little warm, mix two-thirds as much of white brandy with it, put the fruit into jars, and pour the syrup over it. The late white clingstones are the best to use.

—*Miss Beecher's Domestic Receipt Book*, 1850[36]

Alcohol is also just a step away from vinegar, the pioneer's more common preservation medium. Levi Savage, an early settler in Utah's southern wine-making settlements, noted that along with wine production came vinegar production. After the grapes had yielded their first pressing, he flooded the mashed grapes again with water and allowed a second, less controlled fermenting. After a short ferment, he allowed the diluted wine to stand on the grapes, triggering a vinegar bacterial growth.[37] Emily Stewart Barnes reported making vinegar from a fermentation originating on the shells of sweet peas.[38] By using this by-product of the garden for fermentation and vinegar, she saved her hard-won beet molasses for more opulent uses. Just as alcohol can be manufactured from barley, grapes, or apples, vinegar is most often made from beer, wine, or cider.

Cornelia Lund related her grandmother Gustava Capson's recipe for cucumber dill pickles. Although Cornelia identifies this recipe as "Danish,"[39] it seems to contain nothing inherently Danish (such as an excessive amount of cardamom or other spices). The recipe is interesting in that it identifies different strengths of vinegar. In Gustava Capson's food technology, she could moderate vinegar strength by altering the fermentation process. Home production offered a spectrum of variability foreign to the homogeneous consistency of our industrial food systems today. Most vinegar in the supermarkets today carries a standardized acidity of 5 percent. We might dilute this with water to reach a weaker product, but it would be much more difficult to come up with "strong" vinegar today.

Danish Dill Pickles

Peel and cut in two, lengthwise, large cucumbers, scrape out the core with a tablespoon, put in salt water over night; drain well and wipe dry. Scald the cucumbers for 15 minutes in medium-strong vinegar, which [you should] throw away. (A few at a time—do not boil.) Take good strong vinegar, add sugar and a pinch of cayenne. Bring to a boil and then scald a few cucumbers at a time for 10 min. (not boil), place in layers in crocks or jars with a few dill tops and onions if desired, between the layers. When all the cucumbers have been scalded and placed in layers in the jars, pour the hot vinegar over the pickles and seal. When cold they are ready to serve.

—Gustava Lundstrom Capson, 1836–1914[40]

Sauerkraut: Born of Bacteria

More complex preservation methods relied upon bacteria cultures and fermentation. After the earlier discussion of yeast fermentation for the preservation of apples and grapes, we turn our attention again to bacteria. Housewives preserved some food products by adding vinegar; in other cases they cultured bacteria anew. Such is the case with sauerkraut.

Sauerkraut is a naturally wild-fermented cabbage. Like Belgian brewers who rely on wild airborne yeasts to ferment their barley to beer, sauerkraut makers depend on a fermentation process in which the only added ingredient is salt. With a saline environment of approximately 2 percent, the shredded cabbage begins to yield its 90 percent water content. As these juices leave the cabbage, they carry with them sugars inherent in the cabbage as well. Working from this salt-and-sugar environment, airborne coliform bacteria begin to colonize and cause fermentation.

With yeast-based fermentation, the by-products are alcohol and carbon dioxide. But with sauerkraut the fermentation works from lactose instead of sucrose. The bacteria begin to produce lactic acid, and the acidity of the brine starts to rise. Eventually this creates an environment more conducive to successive colonies of *Leuconostoc* and *Lactobacillus* bacteria. *Lactobacillus* (the same bacteria at work in San Francisco sourdough) contributes the sour flavor. These bacteria continue to nibble away at the sugars from the cabbage and produce acids in turn. The final preservation of cabbage in sauerkraut form is a result of the tangy acids, which remind us of tart vinegar flavors.[41]

Sauerkraut

Shred as much cabbage as you want to use. Put shredded cabbage into a stone crock in layers with salt sprinkled between each layer of cabbage, tamping the layers as you fill the crock. When all the cabbage has been added, place a nice white cloth over it and a heavy stone on top of it to keep it down tight. Place in a not too cold place and after fermentation has taken place the sour kraut can be put in the cold cellar and is good to eat all winter. Home made noodles fried and added make a fine meal.

—Mary Richert Helm, 1812–1903[42]

Naturally, none of this microbiology was understood by Utah pioneers. Mary Helm, a pioneer sauerkraut maker from Germany, knew that it was essential to keep oxygen out while fermentation worked its course. And she knew from brewing experience that fermentation was happening. Yeasty residue and escaping gas bubbles told her as much. She specifically mentions a "nice white cloth" as part of her process.

The cloth seems to hint at the necessity of detecting any derailing of the fermentation along the way. Dark patchy residues could be easily cleaned off once the cloth betrayed them. Most sauerkraut recipes also use a plate or board to cover the cloth. The plate (also white) gives a solid surface for Mary's "heavy stone" to bear down upon uniformly as it keeps the cabbage from rising to meet the air and bacterial contamination. Protection from airborne contamination comes by constant submersion under an inch of salty brine. Did Mary simply forget to include directions for using the plate or was that detail overlooked by the second-generation transcriber?

What Mary did understand was that sauerkraut preserved the cabbage crop through the long winter months until fresh vegetables were again available in the spring. Further, in the previous century Captain James Cook had demonstrated to the world that kraut was effective in preventing scurvy. Mary knew that sauerkraut was nutritious and tasty. A complex understanding of microbiology is not necessary for a healthy diet and delicious meals.

Cheese

Having crossed into lactic fermentation, we come next to the wide world of cheese. Like sauerkraut, pickles, bread, beer, and other magical foods, cheese is the result of a fermentation process. This discussion began with the problem of a dairy cow giving five gallons of milk each day. Of course, she's a Jersey cow—Holsteins give closer to ten. (The thought of milking a Holstein makes my hands cramp up with

The Charles Miller Shorthorn dairy in Farmington, Utah, circa 1900.

tendonitis and carpel tunnel inflammation.) Cheese is the answer to the problem of having more milk than you can drink.

Emily Stewart Barnes kept a cow, as did her neighbors. It appears that they alternated keeping their cows fresh,[43] so that only one cow was milking at a time. In this way both families consumed the milk without any wasting or spoilage. "We borrowed milk from our neighbors so that we would have enough to make cheese," she said. "When our neighbors wanted to make cheese, we would in turn take milk to them, so every few weeks we had a cheese."[44] Such interdependent social relationships seem to have been common in agrarian communities, as families and neighbors helped each other with chores such as hog butchering, sheep shearing, or threshing. Beyond all the foodways that have disappeared with the advent of electricity and refrigeration, we have also lost social relationships based on food.

As in the case of Mary Helm and her sauerkraut, Emily Barnes understood the process for cheese making if not the microbiology behind it. She left a detailed description of her cheese-making process:

> We had a tub that we kept for that purpose [cheese making]. We would get all the milk warm and put it in the tub; then we would cut a piece of "rennet" as we called the inner skin of a calf's stomach, and let it soak in a little warm water overnight. In the morning we would pour this into the milk, which in a little while would set up like clabber. Then we would dip off the whey for which we had a pan with holes in it; and after putting a white cloth on it we would put some large rocks on it to hold it down.[45]

As we have seen with other historical foodway descriptions, this one gives us some vital clues and leaves other essential information out. Emily is describing in vernacular detail the process of converting lactose (sugars found in milk) to lactic acid. This is much the same fermentation process that we saw with Mary Helm's sauerkraut. In both cases, the process begins by creating an environment that will nurture the culture. In the case of sauerkraut, bacteria inherent on the leaves of the cabbage began the inoculation. With Emily's cheese project, the inoculation happened without her knowledge. Agricultural publications of the day warned against using wooden buckets for milking because they could not be cleaned thoroughly. Their wooden nature defied cleaning. In Emily's case, however, the porous wooden tub harbored desirable bacteria—an essential part of the cheese-making process. The tub she used to make cheese played host to bacteria cultures from dozens of previous cheese-making episodes. By letting the milk stand in this tub, Emily unwittingly inoculated the milk with her own unique bacteria culture. These bacteria began chewing away at the lactose just as yeast eats sugars in grape juice.

Next Emily added rennet: the inner lining of a calf's stomach. Traditionally, rennet came from the stomach of a calf, kid, or lamb that had not eaten solid food but had only received its mother's milk. This established milk-digesting enzymes in the stomach lining. Today many cheese makers use an artificially created vegetable-based rennet in order to market their product to vegetarians. Vegetable-based rennet tablets and liquids are readily available now. Rennet serves to curdle the milk, separating the milk solids from the remaining liquid, called whey.

After rennet is added to the milk, the same sorts of bacteria at work in sauerkraut fermentation go to work on the lactose in milk. As with sauerkraut, lactic acid is produced. This acid creates the tangy flavors of sharp cheddar cheese. The associated curdling helps to eliminate liquid from the cheese. As we have seen, liquids harbor opportunity for spoilage. Hence drier cheese lasts longer. Emily also used rocks as weights to help squeeze moisture out of the cheese. Modern cheese makers use mechanical and pneumatic presses for more exacting outcomes.

Easy Cheesy at Home

So you want to try your hand at cheese making? Follow these easy steps and you might get something close to Emily's cheese. You'll need:

- 1 gallon whole milk
- 1 pint cultured buttermilk
- salt
- cheese cloth
- rennet (purchase online or buy "Junket" tablets at the grocery store)
- a pressing mechanism (try using a #10 can, both ends removed, with a weight, or a cutting board with a weight).

1. Inoculate the milk by adding the pint of buttermilk to a gallon of milk. Heat both to room temperature and let stand for 2 hours.
2. Add rennet to the cultured milk. Dissolve the rennet in water according to manufacturer's directions. If using liquid rennet, add 2–3 drops to ⅓ cup water. Stir well.
3. Let sit undisturbed until the milk sets up. It should set about as thick as sour cream. This might take up to an hour.
4. Cut the curd. Using a long sharp knife, cut lines ½ inch apart through the curd. Turn 90° and cut again. Then angle your knife and cut again and again to create small cubes.
5. Heat the curd over a low flame until it reaches 98° ("blood warm" as the pioneers would say). Using your clean hands, stir and lift the curd up from the bottom of the pan. "Cook" it this way until the curds reach the texture of firm scrambled eggs. You should notice the whey as distinct from the curds.
6. When it is cooked, turn the curds into a cheesecloth over a colander to drain the whey. Add 2 tsp. salt and mix well without kneading.
7. While they are still quite warm, gather the curds up in the cheesecloth and secure it like a bag. Press the curds in your coffee-can press or under a cutting board and weight. Press overnight, and in the morning you have cheese. You can age it in the fridge or eat it right away with nice bread and your best bottle of homemade cider.

The debate about the spontaneous appearance of yeast and other bacteria cultures raged into the 1870s. Even after Pasteur had moved on to rabies vaccines, his

The spring house at the Fielding Garr ranch was built directly over a spring. The flowing water served to draw heat from milk pans and milk cans to cool the milk before it was made into cheese and butter. Author's collection.

detractors continued to insist that yeasts performed their fermentations as they died rather than to live. Pioneers in Utah carried on with little regard for this debate, which had no effect on their meals from day to day. Emily Barnes made her cheese, Lemuel Redd cured his hams, and Gustava Capson put up pickles, completely ignorant of the microbiology they manipulated.

Barnes, Redd, Capson, Helm, and thousands of other Mormon settlers worked with complex microbiology and chemistry in their daily food processes, with little technical understanding of what they were doing. Still, they turned out food products that they served up for state occasions, wedding dinners, and holidays. More than one or two got fat. We like to think of pioneer food as simple and wholesome with no added preservatives. The foregoing discussion shows the opposite. Utah's Mormon settlers used sophisticated bacteria cultures and chemical processes to preserve food year-round.

Preserved foods define one major difference between modern and historical Mormon foodways. Though many Mormons continue to put up produce and meat products in glass bottles using a pressure cooker, most have abandoned the complex chemistry and microbial cultures once common in Utah's settlements. Bacteria frighten us. We lean on vacuum-packed and temperature-cleansed products or buy food from the store. No doubt many readers will feel uncomfortable with some of the processes described here. Though I don't want to advocate for the Luddites, I would suggest that our world might be more interesting if we would use food processes without being hampered by fear and ignorance.

CHAPTER 8

Brit, Dane, and Swiss

IMMIGRANT FOOD

They also bake good bread in foreign lands.
—Danish proverb

"All we had in the world was our clothes, with the exception of a small frying pan which my wife's mother had given her, to start housekeeping with."[1] This was Hans Christensen's introduction to Utah. As our typical Danish Mormon convert, he left Copenhagen, arriving in New Orleans after a long sea journey. Steaming up the Mississippi, he kept company with other new converts headed for Winter Quarters, the fitting-out point for Utah-bound pioneers. Along the trail he fell in love with a Danish woman in the wagon company. Illness treated her poorly on the trail, and she had no hair by the time they arrived in Salt Lake City. They married anyway and settled with relatives near Kaysville, where Hans worked with his brother in a rented blacksmith shop. Like most emigrants, they came with almost nothing to call their own. Mrs. Christensen carried a bushel basket of her possessions to start their married life together.

This brief anecdote echoes the themes of privation and sacrifice that run throughout the lore of the Mormon pioneers. Perhaps the actual experience of the westward movement was not so traumatic for native-born American settlers, but a severe reduction in economic status seems to have been common for foreign-born emigrants. Whether hailing from the British Isles, Scandinavia, or the German-speaking states of Austria, Switzerland, or Bavaria, European Mormons came to Utah largely without means.

To provide a full plate of Mormon pioneer foodways, the emigrant experience must be given a place at the table. Throughout the course of the pioneer era in Utah, Mormon converts from Europe flowed to the territory by the thousands. In fact, any native Utahn today with more than three generations of ties to the state will likely find a Brit, a Dane, or a German ancestor in the family tree. And if we look hard enough, we will also find a plum pudding, an ableskiver, or sauerkraut in the family food lore.

Still, let us make no mistake. This entirely too brief chapter cannot do justice to these cultures and cuisines. Each deserves a study of its own, perhaps even a volume of its own. All of these distinct traditions manifested complex systems of supply, preservation, and consumption among complex kinship networks. We cannot leave room for the mistaken assumption that Mormons in Utah, or even European Mormon immigrants, shared a common cohesive culture in Utah. My purpose here is simply to establish a foundation for future works and to highlight the living traditions that continue today. Danish, German, and British foodways came to Utah intact, distinct, and vibrant.

Utah's Foreign-Born

To quantify this foreign-born presence in pioneer-era Utah it would be tempting to say that 38 percent of the population was foreign-born, thus continuing to lump all foreigners in the melting pot. The census of 1870 supports such a statistic.[2] When second-generation Danes, Brits, and Swiss are added in, the foreign presence in Utah becomes overwhelming. Demographics and statistics can be elusive, however, and represent just a snapshot in time. In various periods throughout the settlement era, Brits outnumbered Danes, and then Danes surged ahead of Brits. Second-generation immigrants alternately assimilated to a homogeneous Mormon culture then returned to embrace their European heritage. To lump all foreign-born Mormons under a single header would blur our understanding.

Mormon missionary efforts began in England in the 1840s, and some early emigration certainly resulted. Still, the foreign-born population in Utah in 1850 numbered only in the hundreds. By 1870 more than 37,000 European emigrants had made their way across oceans, plains, and mountains to the Utah Territory.[3] Throughout the 1850s and 1860s each of these demographic groups (British, Danish, and Germanic) was in constant flux. British immigration dominated early on but ebbed as Danish and German immigration surged toward the end of the era. As a result, the "dominant" foreign influences in Utah fluctuated constantly. The foodways of European pioneers came to have a significant impact in Utah's territorial cuisine.

The Mormon message found receptive souls in mid-nineteenth century Europe. Religious and economic turmoil combined to put millions of people on the move. Some found faith in the Mormon gospel of modern prophets and a new priesthood. For others, the economic turmoil that accompanied the Industrial Revolution left millions of middle-class workers dissatisfied with their lot. Danish farmers and skilled artisans suffered particularly as social and religious elites fostered economic policies that increased taxes and took the bottom out of the market for their goods. The Irish inheritance structures combined with economic turmoil and a devastating potato blight to rob millions of their ability to make a meal. Industrial conditions in Germany prompted Karl Marx to pen his *Communist Manifesto* as a proposed solution to the economic woes of the skilled working class displaced by factories and

Elsinore, Utah, settled by Danish immigrants, was named for its resemblance to a town of the same name in Denmark.

machines. Thousands of these displaced workers heard the Mormon gospel advocating redistribution of wealth and migrated to Utah, hoping for a kinder, gentler world in the new Zion.

By the 1860 census Utah's foreign-born population was significant, at 32 percent of the total population. This number would increase through the decade and be concentrated in particular communities. "Family and friendship ties combined with a common language seem to have been the prime pull factors in attracting Scandinavian emigrants to Brigham City," Wayne L. Wahlquist wrote.[4] The same would be true in other areas of concentration. In fact, this pattern seemed to manifest throughout Utah, with enclaves of German-speaking settlers established at Cache Valley's Providence, in Midway, and in the Swiss Colony at Toquerville. Scandinavian settlements sprung up in Hyrum, Mantua, Ephraim, and Manti. British strongholds in Bountiful and Salt Lake City demonstrated that even English-speaking emigrants found comfort in neighbors from their country of origin.

Salt Lake City proved to be a melting pot of emigrants to some degree. The 1860 census recorded the ethnicities of city blocks in the Second Ward: "On one block lived two Danish families, a Canadian, an English, and one from Maine; on another, the order of houses was Scotch, Danish, English, two Danish, Irish, English, two Danish; on a third, Danish, Pennsylvania, Vermont, three Danish, New York, English, English."[5] Danish converts settled close to other Danish kin in the Second Ward, but their life patterns wove tapestries that crossed ethnic lines as well, creating unique problems. Charles Walker's diary often made note of being asked to mediate disputes between Danish and English settlers whose language ability kept them apart.[6]

Immigrant Poverty

Whether because of their original poverty before migration or official church policy, these foreign-born emigrants arrived in Utah without much more than the shirts on their backs. The story of Hans Christensen at the beginning of this chapter echoes themes of privation and sacrifice common to the lore of Mormon pioneers. Some American-born Mormons may have brought wealth to Utah, but the European emigrants largely did not. Church publications promoted a spare bundle for emigrants who used the Perpetual Emigration Fund (PEF) to pay their passage. "Harsh words were used in criticism for those who planned to take luxuries. The Editors firmly stated that those who took the most baggage with them were generally the ones who were the most dissatisfied, and those who humbled themselves to a bundle were the very ones who had the spirit of the Gathering in their hearts."[7]

For those pioneers utilizing the PEF, this policy created a poverty that accompanied them to the Utah settlements. Though some ethnic clothing might be packed in a trunk, the traditional foodways of the foreign-born homeland had to be earned once they were settled in Utah. William Ajax, a Welsh emigrant of 1862, lamented the loss of his traditional diet upon arriving in the Salt Lake Valley. "We had the taste of potatoes, and very little else than the taste of them, on 5 occasions," he wrote of his trip across the plains. "We longed more for potatoes, onions, butter, and cheese than anything else, because of having such a long time without them [on the trail]. . . . Potatoes, butter and cheese are not very abundant in the city."[8]

The Ajax General Store, operated by the sons of Welsh immigrant William Ajax in Tooele County.

Potatoes, onions, butter, and cheese form the building blocks of traditional Welsh diet. *Teissenau tatws*, a Welsh potato cake, illustrates the culmination of these ingredients in one dish. By 1862, with more than a decade of farming success, potatoes, butter, and cheese certainly were common in Salt Lake City. Scores of other diaries and newspaper sources indicate as much. By that time Utah had even begun exporting agricultural produce, specifically wheat, potatoes, and butter, to mining communities around the intermountain West. The butter and cheese were there, but the recent immigrant status of Ajax combined with his accompanying poverty to prohibit him from accessing the agricultural wealth of the Mormon communities. This common thread weaves through the foodways of foreign-born Mormon emigrants.

Other immigrants from Britain adapted their traditional seafood-based dishes to Utah's inland waterways. Margaret Cruikshank Morrison immigrated with her husband, William, from Scotland to Utah's Sanpete Valley in the 1850s. She passed her recipe for finnan haddie to her daughter Wilhelmina (born 1859), who continued to make the dish into the 1900s. Traditionally the dish is made with smoked haddock, but Wilhelmina's adaptation directs that the dish be made with dried salted fish, as from the fisheries at Utah Lake. Utahns with Scottish ancestry continue to make the dish in isolated corners of the state.

Finnan Haddie with Tomatoes (Fish)

Freshen fish by pouring boiling water over it & letting it stand till cool. (Remove skin & bones and separate into larger flakes.)

About one & one-half pounds of fish should be used. Melt three tablespoonfuls butter in a saucepan. Add one teaspoon minced onion & cook to a pale straw color.

Add three tomatoes peeled & cut in slices.

Cook over a slow fire till soft.

Add one teaspoonful of minced parsley, one-eighth teaspoonful pepper & a few gratings nutmeg. Add fish & cook over hot water till the fish is very hot.

Arrange boiled rice in a circle on a chefs plate and fill center with fish mixture.

—Wilhelmina Henrietta Morrison Eriksen, 1859–1935[9]

Simple Foods for Cultural Identity

Stripped of many elements of cultural identity, these Germans, Britons, and Scandinavians latched onto simple manifestations of their homeland foodways. For Danes, coffee was part of their Scandinavian culture, much like tea for Britons. Ole Poulson, an early settler in Brigham City, continued to drink coffee as part of his Danish heritage, in spite of its prohibition in Mormon doctrine. His granddaughter remarked that he and his wives were "raised in the old country"; as for coffee, that's just how it was. Still, she felt compelled to defend their moral virtue: Ole's wife was "as good a person as you may ever hope to meet," despite her coffee habit.[10]

Many typically Danish beverages were prohibited by the Word of Wisdom, the health and diet code of Mormonism. William Mulder wrote: "Scandinavians believed they had a special dispensation to drink coffee and their homemade beer. With at least one Dane it was a particular mark of devotion to go without coffee on Sunday."[11] Modern descendants of Danish heritage relate a similar practice of abstaining from caffeinated cola drinks on Sunday as a religious observance. Indeed, it seems that Danes and coffee were inseparable. In other instances, Danes viewed their homemade beer more as a food item than as an indulgent recreational beverage. Anna Bench recalled a dish served by her mother, Mette: "øllebrød" (bread soaked in beer). Often prescribed as a meal for invalids, it went down easily and was kind to the stomach.

> ### Øllebrød
>
> Beer was also used in cooking; bread was soaked in hot beer, thin cream and beaten eggs added while hot to make it the consistency of thick soup. This was a dish given the sick and also used as a main dish for a meal. It was called Øllebrød (beer bread).
>
> —Anna Madsen Bench, from Mette Andersen Madsen, 1834–1896[12]

The English emigrant likewise found no lack of tea from the grocers and dry goods merchants on Salt Lake City's Main Street. The firm of Holliday and Warner frequently advertised its tea offerings in the *Deseret News*, including "30 chests of Imperial, Gunpowder, Young Hyson and Black Teas."[13] Such an abundance of teas in variety makes it plain that the English who could afford it could have what they needed to continue their cultural traditions.

Annie Underwood, an English convert, often had her granddaughter Pearl visit for a teatime tradition of sandwiches with tea. Together they would go out to pick wild-grown watercress from irrigation ditches. Taking the loaf of bread in hand, Grandmother Underwood would spread butter on the cut end and then shave off a slice so thin that it wouldn't stand buttering after it had been cut. With the watercress and a cuppa it made a proper Englishwoman's tea service.[14] This same buttering of the loaf before slicing is also mentioned in the history of Elizabeth Bott Brough, an Englishwoman who settled in Randolph, Utah. It seems to be a marker for English foodways.[15]

With coffee for Danes and tea for Brits, we might think the Germans would have their beer. Instead, the brewing tradition in Utah seems to have belonged to the Danes. German-speaking emigrants settled in Utah's Dixie with the purpose of making wine.[16] For a thorough discussion of the German-Swiss wine tradition, see chapter 11. As for other emigrants, foodways in the new settlements first reflected necessity and ethnic traditions manifested only in simple forms. John Henry Mueller was one of these Swiss emigrants sent to the southern redrock country in 1860. Most of the Swiss emigration that year came in response to Brigham Young's effort to recruit skilled wine makers for the new Dixie settlement. With local stones Mueller built himself a domed oven in the *horno* style of the Southwest. Using simple and locally available ingredients he would often bake a quiche of sorts directly on the floor of the oven. His daughter Rosina Beacham described his process: "We would mix a batter out of flour and cream, and put some salt and chopped onions in it and an egg. We would put this on the paddle, and slip it off into the oven. It made a very good cake."[17] The notion of European immigrants baking quiche-like treats in the deserts of southern Utah gives us cause to rethink many ideas about pioneer food. It seems that many of the earlier representations of old-country foodways were simply various fashionings of flour, milk, and eggs.

Zweibelkuchen **(Onion Cobbler)**
1 quart milk
3 eggs
1 onion, sliced
salt and pepper to taste
Bake either in soda biscuit or baking powder biscuit dough and bake as you would
custard pie.   —Cecilia Ence Tobler, b. Sept 20, 1889[18]

Some Swiss emigrants like Mary Ann Hafen brought seeds from Switzerland to plant more exotic and traditional crops in the hot Dixie sun. More often these settlers found that new American crops were necessary to compete in the arid climate of the West.

Danish settlers in Utah's arid regions likewise started with very little that might remind them of home. Anders Thomsen's crops seem typical of other British and American farmers. Instead of growing Danish crops such as rye and cabbages, he grew more typically English crops: wheat, oats, peas, carrots, turnips, potatoes, and radishes.[19] James Jensen (Danish, of course) recalled of his early settlement days: "Our diet consisted chiefly of bread, and of molasses which my mother made from beets."[20] This would not be the dark Danish rye bread but plain white or whole wheat bread, because wheat and wheat flour were what they could borrow from friends. These early settlers often worked on public projects such as digging irrigation ditches or building roads to the new settlements to repay their debt to the Perpetual Emigration Fund until their farming efforts took hold. They were paid in wheat. Hans Jensen Hals demonstrated this subsistence pattern as he established his first home. He wrote: "I bought a little house for 16 dollars in work, and began to work for others to earn wheat."[21] Like other stable agricultural produce, wheat functioned as a medium of exchange in territorial Utah, with LDS Church leaders setting the rate of exchange through the central tithing system.

For Danes this meant that wheat flour, rather than the rye of the Old World, shaped their daily meals. Rye grows well in colder climates with inferior soil and short growing seasons. Hence it makes sense for Denmark. Wheat grows readily in Utah's long hot summers. Though some might have yearned for the dark, heavy loaves of Europe, wheat flour made a wonderfully light and chewy loaf that the Danes and Germans could eat without giving up many of their former traditions.

Other simple incarnations of flour, eggs, and milk expressed cultural identity for Britons. The classic British formula is called Yorkshire pudding. As a category, puddings define a staple element of British cuisine. Though they may be more or less solid or liquid, sweet or savory, baked, boiled, or steamed, they may all be called pudding. The Yorkshire pudding stands as a quintessential example of English foodways. Like many such foodway anchors for European Mormon converts, the name itself explicitly connects the food and the mother country. Perhaps such symbolic names have preserved various European foodways as part of the Mormon pioneer food tradition, evoking foreign ancestry as the dish is being prepared. This must certainly be the case for Alice Widdison's Yorkshire pudding. The recipe calls to mind the arduous migration of English emigrants and the sacrifices of early settlers. In truth, Alice was born in Utah, the daughter of an

The Bavaria Brewery in Salt Lake City utilized the specialized knowledge of food and brewing processes held by European immigrants in Utah.

English father. Her Yorkshire pudding should be credited to her mother, Mary Elizabeth Layne, a Hoosier farm girl who learned to make it for her English husband.

Alice Widdison's Yorkshire Pudding

1 qt. milk
5 eggs, well beaten
½ tsp. salt
1 c. flour
Mix flour with milk until smooth, then mix with remaining milk and eggs and salt. Bake in a greased pan or better with the drippings left from the roast. Bake until golden brown.   —Mary Alice Wilding Widdison, 1854–1919[22]

For Scandinavian convert settlers, flour and milk combine with butter and eggs to form a variety of oddly named treats. For Swedish pioneers, the result might be "egga cogga." Gustava Lundstrom Capson, a Swede married to a Dane, brought this dish to Utah. Her granddaughter Cornelia wrote: "I recall how my grandmother could turn the egg cake over by throwing it up and out of the pan, and catching it again. The egga cogga filled the pan and was served as you would cut pie."[23] A Danish interpretation akin to a crepe also follows. Both played a role in pioneer Utah.

Egga Cogga

4 eggs, slightly beaten. Little flour. Fry cubes of home-smoked bacon in frying pan, add eggs & milk, salt & pepper. Cook slowly, then turn upside down on plate.
                          —Gustava Lundstrom Capson, 1836–1914[24]

"Egga cogga" is probably a pidgin-Americanized interpretation of what might traditionally be called *pandekager*. These days it is more likely to be served with jam and
butter. Perhaps the pioneer version with back bacon is heartier.

Danish Thin Pancakes
6 eggs, large
3 ½ cups milk
2 cups flour, sifted
1 ½ teaspoons salt

Beat eggs and add 1½ cups milk. Beat in flour and salt. Add remaining milk and beat
well. Cook on hot greased griddle. Pour two mixing spoonful of batter on griddle, tip-
ping griddle around until batter covers the bottom of the pan. Cook until light brown
on both sides. Roll and serve with syrup or jam. Makes 16 or 17 paper-thin pancakes.
—Caroline Berg Osterman, 1831–1913[25]

The pandekager is second only to ableskiver for nostalgic Danish breakfast carbohydrates. The Danes in my family have kept ableskiver as a part of our celebration of heritage through six generations. *Æble*, meaning apple, refers to the spherical
shape of the pastry. Though modern treatments have incorporated all sorts of variations, the historical article was *not* filled with applesauce and chopped apples were
not mixed into the batter (though I suppose you could serve them with applesauce).
We try different recipes now and then, but all that really matters is that they be round
and piled high on a plate. Ableskiver are cooked in a cast-iron pan, usually with seven
half-spherical depressions. The batter is made of eggs beaten to stiff peaks, folded into
a weak batter of milk and flour. With the greased pan not quite smoking hot, a spoonful of batter is ladled into each cup. When it is halfway cooked, a fork or toothpick
is used to turn the ableskiver over in the pan (this takes practice). The remaining
uncooked batter flows again to complete the spherical shape.

Ableskiver
6 eggs, separated
2 cups flour
1 ½ cups milk
2 Tbsp sugar
½ tsp salt
½ tsp cream of tartar

Beat egg whites with cream of tartar. Set aside. Beat egg yolks until lemon colored.
Add sugar, then milk and dry ingredients. Gently fold whites into this mixture. Drop
by spoonfuls into a hot ableskiver pan, turning halfway through cooking. Serve with
butter, sugar, and jam.
—Metta Hansen Peterson, 1855–1917[26]

Immigrant groups formed social organizations to celebrate their ethnic identity. Here the Manti (Utah) Scandinavian Choir goes on tour.

Sauerkraut through Generations

The Danish ableskiver and the English Yorkshire pudding call out for a Germanic entry to stake a claim on this immigrant foodways heritage. Abraham Braegger, a Swiss emigrant of 1865, brought his family formula for sauerkraut to Willard, Utah. Traditions for making sauerkraut, a pillar of Germanic foodways, have descended through the generations of the Braegger family to continue as a living tradition today. Ken Braegger, a grandson of Abraham, still grows his own cabbages in Providence, where he keeps a barrel in the cellar just for making sauerkraut.

Over the course of his lifetime Ken has watched as the kraut-making traditions that once flowed through the community have ebbed somewhat. In his youth, the kraut barrels were made of oak and required soaking in the canal for a few days to swell the staves and make the barrel water tight. Those were the days of community harvests and cooperative production. Today Ken's son helps make just one barrel of the kraut, and a blue polyethylene barrel at that.

Still, Ken insists that his sauerkraut formula is exactly as he received it from his father and his grandfather before that. He still uses the cabbage shredder that once belonged to his grandfather Abraham. Not much about making sauerkraut has changed in 150 years. In fact, the process is rather simple: Ken shares it with you here.

The process given here depends upon lactic fermentation to develop the necessary brine, which preserves the sauerkraut through winter months in the cellar. Fermented preservation techniques are also used in making cheese, pickles, beer, and wine (see chapter 7).

Most Mormon immigrant settlers subsisted on rather simple fare that could be made from garden produce and wheat flour. Sometimes these foods were augmented with wild game. Danish pioneer Andrew Christian Nielsen remarked with horror on the food of his Danish friends, which he reported as primarily consisting of wild rabbit.[28] Andrew left his wife, Maren Kirstine, in Utah with their children when he went to work on the transcontinental railroad. While he was away, Maren leaned heavily on wild rabbit, ducks, and geese as well as boiled wheat.[29] The immediate demand for survival trumped indulgences of foodways from the old country. Newly arrived Danish settlers ate what was locally available while they established a foothold in this strange new land. Their culinary conformity was forced by circumstances, at least until a more rooted existence became possible.

Ken Braegger's Sauerkraut

- Wash your equipment. You'll need a food-grade plastic barrel or a large ceramic crock. In older days they used wooden barrels, which had to be soaked to swell the staves before using. You'll also need a washtub.
- Set up your work space. You'll need a utility table, cutting board, and butcher knife for quartering the heads. A cabbage shredder comes in handy; you can't do it with just a knife.
- Trim off all the dry, discolored, or damaged leaves. Quarter the cabbage heads and remove the core.
- Put the quartered pieces of cabbage, cut side down, into the cutter box of the shredder and press down firmly. Move the heads over the blade to shred.
- Fill the washtub nearly full of shredded cabbage before putting the cabbage into the barrel. After dumping the washtub into the barrel, spread the shredded cabbage out even and level and add about ¾ cup salt, sprinkling it evenly over the cabbage. Use ½ lb. salt to 100 lbs. cabbage.
- Using a large, heavy beating stick, tamp the cabbage vigorously until the salt is mixed well into the cabbage. After a couple of tubfuls are added there should be liquid brine on the top of the cabbage.
- When the barrel is filled, cover the cabbage tightly with a clean white cloth, tucking the cloth down around the sides of the cabbage. Move the barrel into your shed or cellar at this time.
- Put a board or plate on top of the cloth. This should fit the barrel quite well. Put a heavy weight on top of the board. [Ken uses a bucket of cement to weight down a 55-gallon barrel.] The aim is to create a seal, keeping the cabbage submerged under the brine. There should be at least an inch of brine on top of the board.
- Keep the cabbage warm. Fermentation happens faster with warmer temperatures. About 70°F is ideal. Generally no artificial heat is necessary in the early fall weather of northern Utah.
- Each week dip off the excess juices. Remove the bucket, board, and cloth and wash them in fresh water but no soap. A brush might be needed.
- Wipe the fermentation residue from the inside of the barrel and remove any mushy cabbage. There usually is none or very little.
- Replace the cloth, board, and weight. Add about an inch or more of fresh water. The kraut should always be under water.
- Repeat the three preceding steps each week for about six weeks. By then the cabbage should have transformed into delicious kraut. If you cut the cabbage in early September, it should be ready to can by late October.[27]

European foodways served to reinforce cultural identity for immigrants. Here sauerkraut-making tools stand ready for the job. Author's collection.

Such patience in anticipating the future depended on a living memory of the foods and processes that lay dormant. Through the course of my research again and again I have found examples of Danish cooks who kept recipe formulas by memory and handed them down by rote through three generations before the formula was written down. Such is the case with the Thorup family, whose Danish foodways manuscript offers a treasure trove of tradition for interested chefs.[30] Lorraine Hammond's "Var Sa God" demonstrates a similar dynamic.[31] These traditions are not dead yet.

Once farms and settlements began to take root, however, emigrants and pioneers found ways to incorporate foodway traditions from their homeland. Garden-grown cucumbers took the place of wild-grown watercress for English tea sandwiches. Danish traditions likewise made a place for garden greens. Caroline Berg Osterman brought her recipe for *gronkall* (green soup) to Utah in 1868 but probably had to wait a year or two before all the ingredients were readily available. Her granddaughter Ruth Thorup noted: "In Denmark the green soup is made with nine different kinds of greens. When Grandma couldn't find all nine kinds she would go out to her garden and pick a gooseberry leaf and put it in the soup so as to have nine kinds of greens."[32] Emigrants far from home often improvised to keep their traditions alive.

Gronkall (Green Soup)

2 quarts beef stock
1 lb. Spinach
4 green onions
2 sticks celery & leaves
salt to taste
meatballs

Wash spinach, celery sticks and leaves and green onions, carefully; drain and chop or put through the meat grinder. Add to beef stock and cook until the greens are tender. Add the cooked meatballs [recipe below]. Thicken the soup with one tablespoon (rounded) oatmeal for each cup of stock. Strain the stock the meatballs were cooked in into the rest of the soup.

Frickadeller (Danish Meatballs)

1 lb. Lean ground beef
1 egg
½ cup bread crumbs
1 grated onion (optional)
milk, enough to make mixture stiff enough to shape into patties
salt and pepper to taste

Mix all the ingredients together; shape into patties; fry as you would hamburgers. This mixture may also be used for meatballs. Shape in small balls, about one inch in diameter, cook in boiling water until done. Serve as meat dumplings in vegetable soup or in brown gravy.[33]

This one-pot meal from Denmark served as hearty comfort food, reminding the feasters of their heritage and days gone by. In the German-Swiss tradition of the Mormon pioneers, it would be a slow-cooked pot filled with sauerkraut, sausages, and potatoes. In the English tradition the beefsteak pie serves this function. A one-pot meal in its own crust, this quintessential British dish came to Utah by way of India with Sarah Elizabeth Caroline Scott McCune. As it traveled around the globe this recipe provided an anchor of British identity and food culture for the McCunes.

Beefsteak Pie

1 ½ lbs. steak

½ cup flour

2 or 3 small carrots

2 or 3 small potatoes

1 large or 6 small onions

Pound flour into both sides of steak and cut in small pieces. Brown in drippings in skillet, cover with water and simmer until steak is tender. Add carrots cut in rounds, dice potatoes and slice onions. Add more water and cook until vegetables are tender. Put a handleless cup upside down in a 2 qt. casserole and pour stew around it. Top with rather thick biscuit dough. Bake for 20 minutes.

—Sarah Elizabeth Caroline Scott McCune, 1811–1877[34]

Once settled comfortably, Mormon immigrants resurrected the foodways of their homeland with more indulgence. For some, this may have happened quickly. Christina Crego Hammer came to Utah from Denmark in 1869 and settled in the growing Salt Lake City metropolis. There she found many of the ingredients for recipes that she had learned while working in upscale hotels in Denmark. With the arrival of the transcontinental railroad, it didn't take much for Christina Hammer to re-create her delicacies. The recipes of Caroline Berg Osterman and Sena Mikkelsen Sorensen (from Danish and Swedish families, respectively) found a place in Utah's Johnny-come-lately homesteads before the transcontinental railroad. Before the turn of the twentieth century Sena's family had resurrected the Santa Lucia celebration of Sweden in their new Utah home. Melding the religious traditions of Lutherans and Mormons, Sena Sorensen crowned her daughters with the flaming candles of her childhood tradition and prepared *lutefisk*, that infamous Scandinavian treatment for salted herring. Though these second- and third-generation Swedes found meaning and tradition in the dish, the fifth and sixth generation found none and happily omitted the "stinking lutefisk" from their Christmastime smorgasbord.[35] Families of Scandinavian descent in Manila, Utah, still serve lutefisk at Christmastime.

Other European pioneers found themselves in isolation in the far-flung settlements of the Utah territory. A return to the foods of their youth took time, as their farmsteads acquired enough capital to support dietary indulgences. Lena Knecht Ence stands as an example. Born in Switzerland in 1869, she came to the Swiss Colony in southern Utah at the age of four. She married John Ence, who also came from Switzerland to the southern settlement with his father, Lenare, in 1869. At this time the Swiss Colony had been settled for almost a decade, and agricultural efforts were beginning to create tangible successes. The wine culture for which the region was to become famous had begun to produce fruit on vines planted several years previously.

Swiss culture along the Virgin River flourished in this era. As Lena Knecht grew up in Utah's Dixie, Swiss culture grew up around her.[36]

Lena's daughter Cecilia was born in Santa Clara, Utah, in 1889 and was living with her widowed grandfather Lenare at the time of the 1900 census. Cecilia married Ernest Tobler (another second-generation Swiss) and eventually had a daughter of her own, teaching them the Swiss recipes that had been circulating in Santa Clara when Lena Knecht was a girl. These recipes formed a cohesive body of nouveau Swiss food culture, which Cecilia was kind enough to share with us.

Egg Bread

2 sieves flour
1 tsp salt
2 Tbsp sugar
1 c. potato water
½ lb. butter
1 c. yeast

Mix into a soft batter, let rise then knead down and let rise. Make into biscuits or braid into braids, let rise until light then bake and brush with egg and sugar as soon as it comes from the oven.

Barawackie **(Pear Rolls).** Use dried pears. Cook until tender and then mash and add sugar, pinch of salt, cinnamon, scant cloves and nutmeg, a piece of butter and nuts, use this mixture to spread on egg dough rolled out to ¼ in. thick. Then roll dough and mixture into a roll, stick with fork and let rise until light, bake ½ hour. Cook pears until juice is cooked in, then use grape juice for liquid.   —Cecilia Ence Tobler, b. 1889[37]

Foreign immigration to Utah continued to rise through the end of the nineteenth century. The British wave that had dominated the early years ebbed while Danish pilgrims surged in the last twenty years. By the end of the century more than half of Utah's foreign-born population was Danish, and Danes held LDS worship services in their native language throughout the state. The Scandinavian caucus became such a dominant and divisive political force within the Mormon Church that eventually LDS leaders were forced to quash it with orders for the Scandinavian populace to assimilate to the English language and a homogeneous Utah Mormon culture.[38] While foreign-born immigrants never outnumbered native-born Americans in Utah, they remained a prominent presence, particularly in concentrated settlements known for their ethnic core.

Here I have explored just a few of the notable foods that stand as examples of each of three cultures. I had to pass up many other interesting foods in the interest of space. In addition, other cultures and nationalities present in Utah during the era of our study hold stories of their own, although they never reached prominence in numbers. Of course, the British, Danish, and Swiss pioneers also integrated other American foodways not discussed here. Some of these are mentioned in other chapters.

In any case, Danish and Scandinavian cultural influences continue as a theme in contemporary Mormon culture. Accents of the Cache, Sanpete, and Star valleys betray a Scandinavian linguistic connection. Midway, Utah, continues to hold its Swiss Days celebration. October ushers in Providence's annual sauerkraut dinner. Ephraim, Utah, calls itself "Little Denmark," hosting its Scandinavian festival each year over Memorial Day weekend. And on Christmas Day some Mormons still eat lutefisk, sauerbraten, English plum pudding, or abelskiver.

CHAPTER 9

Uncommon Fare

NOTABLE AND EXOTIC MEALS

Dispense with your multitudinous dishes, and, depend upon it, you will do
much towards preserving your families from sickness, disease and death.
—Brigham Young, *Journal of Discourses*, vol. 13

On a cool September morning in 1849, Brigham Young's entourage set out for an
excursion. The party headed north to the settlements on the Weber River. Miles
Goodyear, a fur trapper from earlier days, established the fort shortly before the
Mormons arrived in the valley. The community now went by the name of "Brown's
Fort" or "Brownsville" after James Brown, a veteran of the Mormon Battalion. The
company consisted of Brigham Young, several counselors and secretaries, and Pitt's
Brass Band. Upon arriving at Brownsville late in the afternoon, Brown refreshed the
party with a feast of watermelons.

> **Roast Kid**
> *"A Kid* is very good eating when a suckling, and when the dam is in fine condition.
> Roast, and serve it like a fawn or hare.
> "... *A Fawn* should be dressed as soon after it is killed as possible; when very
> young, it is dressed the same as a hare; but they are better eating when the size of
> the house lamb, or when they are large enough to be roasted in quarters. The hind-
> quarter is considered the best. Fawns require a very quick fire. They are so delicate that
> they must be constantly basted, or be covered with sheets of fat bacon; when nearly
> done, remove the bacon, baste it with butter, and froth it. Serve with venison sauce.
> —*The Complete Cook*, 1864[2]

The next day several from the company strolled through the foothills to the east
and bandied about possibilities for the future site of what would become the city

A scene from an early watermelon feast in Green River, Utah. Feasting on watermelon to excess was a common mode of Mormon celebration.

of Ogden. Everyone ended up back at the fort again that afternoon. Brigham Young and other brethren preached for a bit while the rest of the party worked up an appetite. When the speeches finally ended, a watermelon feast ensued, followed by fresh roasted goat and pork. Pitt's Brass Band played for the dancing.

The following day Brigham went on to visit another settlement in the region. "The President and his party visited Brother Burch's house to eat watermelons; two long seats were fixed for the visitors and a great number of melons were brought in and eaten."[1] Brigham Young found his passion for watermelon long before he came to Utah.

Eagle Gate Resources

One of the greatest challenges in the study of Mormon food history is determining the relative place of a dish or recipe within the greater scope of culture. So far I have presented ample testimony from people who ate weeds, but theirs was not standard fare. Eating weeds gets lots of attention because it is such an unusual thing to do. Likewise, Brigham Young's meals were often notable compared to lumpy dick or hasty pudding. As a result, historians and diarists frequently made note of these exceptional occasions. These dinners were naturally more exotic and indulgent than those eaten by nameless Mormon farmers living in dugouts and log cabins on the edges of the kingdom. Brigham Young's diet does not include many mundane or representative dishes but rather the notable, the exceptional, and the exquisite. Still, it seems that foods attributed to him often become the defining elements of what many want to claim as the essential Mormon meal.

A view of Fort Buenaventura, re-created on the site of Brown's Fort, based on archaeological investigation. Author's collection.

Two distinct qualities separate Brigham Young's diet from that of other early Mormon settlers. First, as one of the wealthiest members of Mormon society, Brigham had greater access to a broad array of hard-to-get specialty items. And rightly so: his Beehive House functioned as the seat of government. Brigham served as the head of state for a small empire and often hosted diplomats and dignitaries from abroad. With plenty of negative press already circulating, it would not do to confirm such opinions. Instead these special guests feasted upon the best food of the territory. The finest fresh fruits, salted cod shipped from Massachusetts, fresh live oysters from the Chesapeake Bay, tea from China, and all manner of spices from around the world were eaten at the Beehive House.[3]

A second primary difference between Brigham's table and that of more common pioneers is that his personal wealth allowed a greater volume of food. While some had to ration their flour, Brigham could afford more than he wanted. The sheer size of his estate, providing for multiple wives and dozens of children, necessitated huge amounts of food. A meal for five in another home became a meal for fifty in the Lion House. Food had to arrive by the bushel instead of by the teacup. Food patterns in Brigham's world reveal an aspect of leisure and indulgence not often found elsewhere in pioneer Utah.

The Eagle Gate estate was larger than most other Mormon farms of the day. Brigham Young's compound blurred boundaries with the church tithing yards and barns to cover almost the entire city block. Nuanced distinctions often failed to define what was Brigham's and what was the Lord's. This agricultural and economic engine extended up City Creek Canyon as well. Peach and apple orchards stretched up to the

A view looking east on the Brigham Young Eagle Gate estate. Note the common wall enclosing the Beehive House and Lion House as well as the Bishop's General Storehouse and Tithing Yards.

foothills, and the site owned the first rights for irrigation on Red Butte Creek. With a tight grip on this valuable water supply, the Eagle Gate estate was sure to produce superior crops of fruits and vegetables. Beyond the Eagle Gate estate, Brigham had other holdings in the territory, such as the Forest Farm—an experimental farm and dairy operation on the southern edge of Salt Lake City.

At the Eagle Gate estate Brigham employed several workers to help manage the production of crops and livestock. Other domestic servants helped in the kitchen. Young's daughter Clarissa remembered that their gardener could make anything bloom under glass.[4] When glass windows were a luxury for most farmsteads in the territory, Brigham's hired gardener was using them to grow luxury food items. First crops of strawberries showed up earlier on the Eagle Gate estate as a result. William Staines, the gardener, could set tomato and cabbage plants out in the garden in a more mature state and thus harvest earlier and bigger crops than the neighbors.[5]

Clarissa also remembered the domestic side of production once farm produce arrived at the Beehive House. Vast stone-lined cellars extended below the house. Separate stone rooms contained overflowing stores of dairy products, hams, and preserved foods. A large stone-topped table in the cellar provided a work space for making huge batches of pie crusts and turning other rough commodities into more refined ingredients.[6] Butchering of small game occurred in the laundry shed nearer the garden.

Yankee Food in Utah

A separate cellar in the garden held potatoes and root vegetables as well as barrels of hard cider in the tradition of New England. Clarissa recalled:

One day Father's manager sent two of his boys up there to sprout potatoes. After a time the attention of one of the boys wandered from the potatoes to a number of kegs that were stored in the rear of the cellar. "I'll bet there's cider in those kegs," he remarked to the other. . . . "I'll show you," said the more ingenious one and, going out, he returned with a number of full-grown onion tops. The next step was to find a keg with a plug in the top that could be withdrawn, and when this had been accomplished both boys lay on top of the barrels and drank cider through the onion reeds until they actually rolled off.[7]

Cider Wine.—Take sweet cider immediately from the press. Strain it through a flannel bag into a tub, and stir into it as much honey as will make it strong enough to bear up an egg. Then boil and skim it, and when the scum ceases to rise, strain it again. When cool, put it into a cask, and set it in a cool cellar till spring. Then bottle it off; when ripe, it will be found a pleasant beverage. The cider must be of the very best quality, made entirely from good sound apples. —*Directions for Cookery*, 1853[8]

Though many of the commodities stored in the cellar may have been commonly available in other homes in the territory, the quantity of food required for Brigham's household knew no bounds. The quality of the stores was also a notch above. Clarissa remembered that she preferred to eat with her father because the food on his table excelled that of any other. "To be sure, there was corn-meal mush and milk, which was no great treat, but there were also hot doughnuts and syrup, codfish gravy which Mother was very adept at making and which Father loved, squabs from the pigeon house, and some little delicacy from our own garden."[9]

Brigham's Doughnuts

1 quart buttermilk
2½ cups sugar
4 eggs
6 tablespoons butter
3 teaspoons nutmeg
1 teaspoon baking soda
1 teaspoon salt
Flour
Lard

Combine ingredients, kneading in enough flour to make a soft dough, not too sticky. Roll out and cut into doughnuts. Fry in deep, hot lard.
—Emily Partridge Young, 1824–99[10]

Clarissa recalled another product of the Eagle Gate estate that frequently contributed to Brigham's breakfasts: squab. Early in the morning she would run out to the barn to find the overseer, who would send her back with a pair of these fat young pigeons.[11] Squab is traditionally defined as a young pigeon that has not taken flight.

As the birds work through their maturation process, their bodies take on tremendous bulk, which is then transformed into energy to grow the feathers necessary for flight. Brigham enjoyed eating them at this preflight stage. Two birds made a fine meal when served with codfish gravy.

Squab
Pigeons, when stuffed, require some green parsley to be chopped very fine with the liver and a bit of butter, seasoned with a little pepper and salt; or they may be stuffed with the same as a fillet of veal. Fill the belly of each bird with either of these compositions. They will roast in about twenty or thirty minutes. Serve with parsley and butter, with a dish under them, with some in a boat. Garnish with fresh parsley, fried bread crumbs, bread sauce, or gravy.   —*The Complete Cook*, 1864[12]

Codfish gravy? Brigham Young hailed originally from New England. In these days before the global collapse of Atlantic fisheries, salted codfish was a staple of Yankee life. After fishermen hauled their catch home, they filleted the fish flat and salted them liberally then left them to dry in the sun. The fish finished out as hard shingles that would store indefinitely. To reconstitute the fish they were soaked in fresh water to drive off the salt.

Cod Fish Gravy
1 cup cod fish
4 cups milk
½ cup flour
½ cup water
salt and pepper to taste

Shred or otherwise break up 1 cup salt cod fish and put in a sauce pan, add 1 qt. milk and heat. When warm add ½ cup flour mixed with ½ cup water and stir constantly until it thickens. Add salt and pepper to taste. Serve over hot biscuits.
                    —Harriet Glines Thorn, 1826–1913[13]

Salt cod is still available in the modern grocery store throughout the West. Look for the little wooden box in the refrigerated seafood display.

Despite becoming such a western icon, Brigham Young maintained a distinct Yankee sensibility throughout his life. Fishmongers in territorial Utah offered salted salmon, trout, carp, and chubs, yet some Brits and Yankees insisted on the salted cod of their homeland. Shipments of New England salted cod allowed Brigham to maintain a connection to his heritage just as some Danish pioneers toted their cast-iron ableskiver pans from the Old World. But while one ableskiver pan can turn out thousands of pastries with only a small amount of flour, Brigham could not multiply his fishes similarly. They had to be shipped repeatedly.

Neither of these dishes is remarkable in itself. Ingredients for each were readily affordable but would constitute a special treat for most Mormon settlers rather than

PLANS OF THE LION HOUSE.

BASEMENT STORY.

PRINCIPAL STORY.

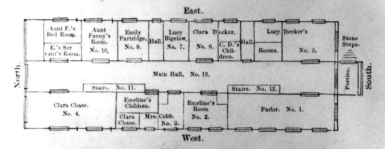

UPPER STORY.

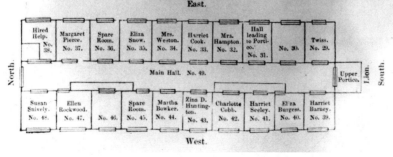

A floor plan of the Lion House, taken from *The Mormon Prophet and His Harem* (Chicago: J. S. Goodman and Company, 1866). It shows nearly all of the lower level devoted to foodways activities, with cellar, pantry, kitchen, and dining room.

a frequent indulgence. Lard production during hog butchering was a labor-intense process, and lard was highly esteemed. The lard required for deep frying of dough-nuts would have been an infrequent indulgence in many homes but a common-place occurrence in the Beehive House. Pigeons are not exceptional in themselves; employing an overseer to manage such breakfast items on a regular basis is. These dishes become exotic in Brigham's home by their frequent appearance, produced by hired hands for a man who appreciated good food as a mark of good living.

Roll Out the Red Carpet

Brigham's appetite was legendary, and his passion for feasting may remind us of an alcoholic binge. This element combines with his special status as prophet and gover-nor. People courted his favor whenever they had the opportunity to share meals with him. When he was hosted in individual homes, the hostess served expansive meals on the best china. On other occasions Brigham broke bread in less formal settings, but luxuries still found a place at the meal.

On one occasion in 1847 Brigham's wagon company headed east from the Salt Lake Valley, returning to Winter Quarters to wrap up business there. Somewhere in Wyoming, his company rendezvoused with another group of Mormons headed west. Naturally a feast broke out. The menu was reported as fresh roast beef, boiled beef, biscuits with butter, pies, and cakes served with a nice peach sauce.[14] Peaches on the Wyoming plains! These were probably brandied peaches put up in stoneware crocks. They might also have been preserves set in molasses stored in crocks or dried peaches, reconstituted. In any case, peaches represented luxury items when contrasted with the bare staples of a provisions list for the trail.

Peach Sauce

Take one pint of water, one cup of sugar, wipe your peaches clean, and boil them in the water and sugar; boil an hour. This is a delicious sauce or preserve, but will not keep good more than two or three days.

—The New England Economical Housekeeper, 1845[15]

Plain Cake

3 lbs. of sugar
1 quart of yeast
3 lbs. of butter
1 quart of milk
9 eggs
2 gills of rose-water
½ oz. of mace
½ oz. of nutmeg
9 lbs. of flour

The flour nicely dried, the eggs well beaten separately . . . beat the rose-water and butter to a cream, add the sugar, then the cream and other ingredients, mix well, bake immediately.   *—The Housekeeper's Assistant, 1845*[16]

Such occasions continued throughout Brigham Young's tenure as head of the church. In December 1872 he traveled south to Saint George, staying with a dozen families along the way. Colonel Thomas and Elizabeth Kane accompanied him on the trip, and Elizabeth recorded many details. Of their meal in Provo, she noted: "What had we for dinner? What had we not! Turkey and beef, fresh salmon-trout from the lake, wild duck, chicken-pie, apple fritters, wild-plum, cranberry- and currant-jellies, a profusion of vegetables; and then mince-pies (drawn from the oven *after* grace was said!) smoking plum puddings for *us*, and wholesome plain ones for the children (who preferred the *un*wholesome!); pears, peaches, apples and grapes, pitchers of cream and scarcely less creamy milk, cakes, preserves and tarts numberless, and tea and coffee."[17] This was the home of Abraham Smoot, stake president, bank president, lumber mill owner, and husband to four wives and households in Provo.

English Plum Pudding

Into a large bowl put the following: 3 cups flour sifted with 3 tsp. baking powder, 1 tsp. cinnamon and 1 tsp. nutmeg, 1 egg, 1 cup ground suet (rub little flour into the suet), 1 cup sugar, 1 pkg. raisins (rub little flour on raisins). Use milk to make a batter a little stiffer than for fruit cake. Put the batter in a damp cloth, gather the cloth together and tie real tight. It needs no room to swell. It will do it. Have a large kettle with boiling water and put pudding in. Water must boil at all times, and when more water is needed this should be boiling water. Boil for 3 hrs. Remove cloth immediately. Serve with any good pudding sauce.   —Harriet Grace Webb, 1841–1911[18]

To achieve the unwholesome qualities that Elizabeth Kane mentioned, we recommend:

Hard Sauce for Puddings

Two tablespoonfuls of butter.
Ten tablespoonfuls of sugar.
Work this till white, then add wine [or brandy, rum, or other spirits] and spice to your taste.   —*Miss Beecher's Domestic Receipt Book*, 1850[19]

The scene was repeated again a few days later at the home of Jacob Gates in the tiny settlement of Pintura. Here the dinner featured "mountains of rolls, the piled-up dishes of steaming potatoes, the steaks and chickens that our party made an end of before the more fanciful edibles, the cakes, and pies, and preserves."[20] Brigham Young lived comfortably, as did those who hosted him.

Feasting on Fruit

Many of these examples illustrate another facet of the Brigham Young diet: feasting on fruit. As the figurehead of the church, Brigham frowned on alcohol as a vehicle for celebration. Instead he yearned for fruits as a symbol of God's grace. Feasting on fruits that had been wrought from desert sands gave a celebratory affirmation of believers as Saints. In this vein, Wilford Woodruff took note of a meal that Brigham provided one September Sunday. With sermon after sermon, the apostles preached the word.

Brigham Young on His Travels, an engraving taken from *Harper's Weekly*. Red carpets were unrolled and parades erupted spontaneously when Brigham came to town.

During a brief break between meetings, Woodruff reported, "President Young feasted the brethren upon peaches and grapes as we had so many meetings we had no time for eating through the day."[21] We can imagine a table spread with the fruits of the season and famished fevered preachers wallowing in the bounties of the desert.

On other occasions Brigham entertained foreign dignitaries in similar fashion. Lord Richard Grovesnor, son of the Marquis of Westminster, visited the Utah territory two years later. Lord Grovesnor, a young man in his twenties, dressed and acted with the unassuming manner of a farmer. Even so, Brigham granted him an interview and feasted him on grapes and fruit.[22]

For Mormon settlers, abundant fruit offered opportunity to indulge in sweets that were otherwise impossible with the rough molasses sweeteners that were commonly available. Fruit not only represented the taming of the wilderness by the grace of God but also showed that Utah had access to the finer points of civilization. Vegetable gardens were nice, but fruits hearkened back to images of Greek gods. Wilford Woodruff had apple scions and grape root stock shipped from the eastern states in tin canisters soldered shut against any injury during shipping. In such manner, he procured the first Isabella grape roots, from which sprung the famed Dixie vineyards.[23] From these apple scions, orchards grew up around the valley. On New Year's Day, 1866, as the apostles visited each other in their homes, Woodruff reported: "We then called upon G. A. Smith's family. Was treated to a fine feast of apples."[24] This was not just a gastronomic indulgence. It was a spiritual witness that Mormon farmers had fulfilled prophecy: the desert had been made to blossom as a rose.

Ice Cream: A Mormon Tradition

On other occasions eating with Brigham Young simply meant eating the best that was available. When Horace Greeley visited from New York, Brigham's Globe Saloon served him ice cream.[25] Such a treat at the Globe might be the norm for a special visitor. Ice cream was also common at the Beehive House. Although cream was quite affordable in this agrarian culture, the ice to make ice cream in the middle of summer came at quite a price. Brigham's daughter Clarissa remembered: "My brother, Feramorz, together with Richard W. Young and Heber J. Grant, frequently used the laundry room for making ice cream. Each boy furnished part of the 'makings' and mother showed them how to cook the custard, in which art they became quite expert."[26]

Home-made Ice Cream

Beat 13 egg yolks very lightly and add thereto four cupfuls sugar and stir well. Add to this, little by little, three pints of rich milk that has been heated to the boiling point, beating all the while, then put in the whites of the 13 eggs beaten to a stiff froth. Cook the mixture in a pail set inside another containing hot water. Boil about 15 minutes, or until it is as thick as boiled custard, stirring steadily. Pour out into a bowl to cool. When quite cold beat into it three pints of rich sweet cream and 5 tsp of flavoring. A pinch of salt is sometimes desirable to bring out the flavor. This makes six quarts of ice cream after freezing. All conditions being perfect the ice cream will be frozen within the hour, in a freezer with a hand crank and revolving dashers, if it is kept moving. The freezer should be packed with cracked ice and salt—rock salt—not the common variety—three-fourths ice and one-fourth salt.　　—Mary M. Vogt Garn, 1820–1915[27]

Pigeons, doughnuts, and ice cream are not particularly exceptional. Any Utah pioneer could have eaten these occasionally. Though they were not staples or daily indulgences for most, in Brigham Young's world they were commonplace. When we take a closer look at particular meals at his Globe Saloon, we start to venture into truly exceptional foods. In January of 1857 Wilford Woodruff recorded: "We dined upon a sumptuous dinner given at the Globe by Capt. Hooper of Oysters, mountain sheep, Beef vegetables pies Cakes nuts &c."[28] Did he say *oysters*?

Exotic Foods

In the early 1850s the *Deseret News* began using its editorial goad to suggest that some enterprising fellow should introduce oysters to the Great Salt Lake. With the early date of this exotic menu at the Globe it is more likely that the oysters were tinned. Holliday and Warner and other grocers had begun offering oysters in tins by 1850. The *News* editors continued to push for a local fresh oyster enterprise but lamented that getting oysters to Utah alive was the sticky wicket. On February 12, 1868, the editors finally announced:

> We are under obligations to Theo. F. Tracy for a box of fresh oysters by rail and stage from the east. These delicious bivalves in a fresh condition, will become less rare here, as the distance between the ocean coast and this city is lessened, and if "oysters on the half shell" should not become so popular as they are in some places, "fresh from their native element" may become so.[29]

Certainly the narrowing gap between the railroad terminus and Salt Lake City played a large role in providing fresh oysters to the market. Only after the Golden Spike was driven did oysters become readily available in the desert.

Samuel Arnold's food history *Eating Up the Santa Fe Trail* gives us a clue about how these oysters might have been brought to Utah in such a fresh state. Arnold reports that in the 1860s oystermen arranged the live oysters in boxes with their shells aligned and facing up. The oysters were then covered in layers of chipped ice and shipped by rail as far as possible. Along the way agents sprinkled cornmeal on the ice, which filtered down to the oysters as the ice melted. At the railroad terminus, agents

Brigham Young in an engraving circa 1870, nearing his final years.

packed the oyster crates onto a stage express, which then rushed the oysters on to Utah. They arrived in fatter condition than when they began their journey.[30]

Oysters to Stew.—Open and separate the liquor from them, then wash them from the grit, strain the liquor, and put with the oysters a bit of mace and lemon peel, and a few white peppers.   —*The Housekeeper's Assistant*, 1845[31]

When we combine these vignettes, we see an epicurean portrait of Brigham: insistent on having whatever pleases him at the moment, from squab, oysters, and codfish to fresh fruit and ice cream. In addition, we see an absence of pigweed and sego bulbs. Brigham had plenty of everything that mattered.

Despite this appearance of fresh oysters on the half shell in pioneer Utah, Mormon pioneers of course did not live predominantly on such delicacies. Oysters are the exception that deserves notice, just as eating pigweed gets plenty of attention. A handful of other exotics likewise deserve mention.

Special Occasions

Many times a special occasion received particular notice from diarists or other observers. Christmas dinners often show up in exquisite detail, while supper on Wednesday evening often goes unnoticed. Wilford Woodruff left this detailed menu of a Christmas dinner in London in 1840: "The dinner consisted of Baked Mutton, Goose, Rabit [*sic*] Pies, Minced Pies, & Plum Pudding & bread & cheese, Porter & Water."[32] The menu is notable in several details: its diversity of dishes, its richness in meats and sweets, and the exotic wild meats reminiscent of Victorian England set this dinner beyond the norm. Just as your Thanksgiving dinner is an anomaly, notable pioneer dinners should not be taken as representative of daily life.

After settling in the Salt Lake Valley following her ordeal with the Willie handcart company, Patience Loader lived for a time with a local bishop. Shortly after she arrived, she helped prepare a wedding dinner for the bishop's second (plural) marriage. The dinner consisted of fresh roast beef served with peas and new potatoes. The desserts were a little more exceptional. Her host provided her with currants, raisins, and "sugar plenty to make a cake."[33] In these early days crude home-manufactured molasses was the ubiquitous sweetener.[34] Patience found it notable that she was given plenty of sugar for her cake as well as dried fruit. Although the meal may have been nice but plain, the cakes and pies were rich. On another occasion Wilford Woodruff made special mention of sharing wedding cake with Brigham Young, leftovers from his daughter Susan's wedding.[35] These wedding cakes deserved particular notice.

Bride's Cake

Two pounds of sifted flour, two pounds of sifted loaf-sugar, two pounds of fresh butter, eighteen eggs, four pounds of currants, one pound of raisins, stoned and cut up; one half-pound of almonds, blanched and chopped; one half-pound of citron, one pound of candied orange and lemon-peel, cut into thin slices; a large nutmeg, grated; half an ounce of ground allspice; of ground cinnamon, mace, ginger, and corianders, a quarter of an ounce each, and a gill of brandy. Put the butter into a suitable vessel, in a warm place, cream it with the hand, and mix it with the sugar and spices for some time; break in the eggs by degrees, and beat it twenty or thirty minutes; stir in the brandy, and then the flour, gradually; beat it well; then add the fruit, sweetmeats, and almonds, and mix all lightly together. Put it in a cake-pan, and bake it four hours or more, in a slow oven. The goodness of a cake depends very much on its being well baked. When it is nearly cold, ice it, according to the following receipt.

Icing

Take a pound of double refined loaf-sugar, pounded and sifted through a fine sieve; beat the whites of six eggs into a froth; put in the sugar gradually, beating it well; then squeeze in the juice of a lemon, or sufficient essence of lemon to flavor it, and beat it till it becomes quite thick. Spread it over the top and sides, as smoothly as possible, before the cake is quite cold.   —*The Great Western Cookbook*, 1857[36]

When traveling through Utah, Sir Richard Burton made note of another special occasion dinner: the Territorial Ball of 1860. Such occasions provided opportunity for Utah politicians and church leaders to flaunt the agricultural wealth of this stronghold in the West. The menu for the Territorial Ball certainly did just that. Featuring a broad array of grains, roots, and fruits, seven kinds of domestic livestock, and several imported delicacies, the menu boasted of Brigham Young's colonizing success. Burton, an outsider to the Mormon religion and settlements, made note of the meal in his travel memoir on Mormon culture, *City of the Saints*.[37]

Any number of unusual elements show up in this menu. Domestic and wild meats appear in equal numbers. The menu features Italian vermicelli and blancmange (a French gelled custard), though the Italians and French formed only a small fraction of Utah's immigrant population, most of whom came from England and Scandinavia. The immense variety of dishes is a departure from everyday meals. And what should we make of hominy served at a state dinner?

TERRITORIAL AND CIVIL BALL,

SOCIAL HALL, February 7, 1860.

BILL OF FARE.

First Course.

SOUPS.

Oyster	Vermicelli
Ox-Tail	Vegetable

Second Course.

MEATS.

Roast.	*Boiled.*
Beef	Sugar-corned beef
Mutton	Mutton
Mountain mutton	Chickens
Bear	Ducks
Elk	Tripe
Deer	Turkey
Chickens	Ham
Ducks	Trout
Turkeys	Salmon

STEWS AND FRICASSEES.

Oysters and Ox Tongues	Chickens
Beaver tails	Ducks
Collard head	Turkeys

VEGETABLES.

Boiled.	*Baked.*
Potatoes	Potatoes
Cabbage (i.e. greens)	Parsnips
Parsnips	Beans
Cauliflower	
Slaw	

Hominy

Third Course.

Pastry.	*Puddings.*
Mince pies	Custards
Green apple pie	Rice
Pineapple pie	English Plum
Quince jelly pie	Apple soufflé
Peach jelly pie	Mountain
Currant jelly pie	Pioneer

Blancmange   Jellies

Fourth Course.

Cakes.	*Fruits.*
Pound	Raisins
Sponge	Grapes
Gipsy	Apples
Varieties	Snowballs

Candies   Nuts

Tea   Coffee

The Bill of Fare from the Territorial and Civil Ball of 1860, as recorded by Sir Richard Burton in *City of the Saints*.

Vanilla Blanc-Mange.—Chip fine an ounce of the best isinglass, and put it into a small sauce-pan, with a jill of cold water, and boil it till entirely dissolved. In another sauce-pan boil half a pint of rich milk and a vanilla bean. Boil it (with the lid on) till the flavour of the vanilla is well extracted. Whip a quart of rich cream to a stiff froth. Separate the whites and yolks of four eggs. Beat the whites till they stand alone. Then, in another pan, beat the yolks, and when they are very light and smooth, add to them, gradually, a quarter of a pound of powdered loaf-sugar, beaten in very hard. Then (having strained out the bean) mix with the cream the milk in which it was boiled. Then beat in, by degrees, the yolk of egg and sugar; then the white of egg; and, lastly, the melted isinglass. When all the ingredients are united, beat and stir the whole very hard. Rinse your moulds in cold water. Then put in the mixture, and set it on ice, for two hours or more, to congeal. When quite firm (and just before it is wanted) dip each mould down into a pan of lukewarm water (taking care that the water does not reach the top) and turn out the blanc-mange on glass or china dishes. Keep it on ice, till the minute before it is served up. It will be found very fine.

—*The Lady's Receipt Book*, 1847[38]

Hominy for State Occasions

We also like it baked to serve with spareribs or roast pork or beef. To bake it I take a cup of hominy, a pint of milk, a tablespoon of butter and salt and pepper to taste. I stir in two well beaten eggs the last thing and bake it in a buttered dish until it is brown. I hope some one will try this old fashioned hominy dish.

—Isabella Rogers, 1858–1951[39]

Sometimes exotic meals and ingredients show up as mementos of a former adventure in life. Such is the case with the McCune family, who maintained their connection to the Indian subcontinent over several generations. Major Matthew McCune (a doctor with the British royal army) was assigned to India before coming to Utah. Sarah Elizabeth Caroline, his new bride, accompanied him and managed a household staff of forty servants near Calcutta. While there, they converted to Mormonism and struggled with the doctrine of polygamy. Political stability fell apart in the 1850s as British colonial states around the globe began to falter. In 1857 the McCunes beat a hasty retreat, narrowly escaping "the mutiny which killed so many white people."[40] This may well have been an insurgency aimed at overthrowing British colonial oppression. Instead of returning to England, the McCune family followed the Mormon migration to Utah.

Once settled in Utah, the McCunes still indulged in recollections of their time in India. Their palates had made a comfortable place for the exotic spices that they discovered there. Spices, unlike tinned oysters or salted cod, weigh very little and are easy to transport. With a small store of curry powder, Elizabeth McCune continued to spice special dishes, served for teas and luncheons with her friends.[41]

East India Curry and Rice

3 medium onions
1 lump butter or fat
2 lbs. round steak
1 tsp. salt
1 medium large potato
1 No. 2 can peas
4 hard-cooked eggs
1 c. rice, cooked
4 tsp. curry powder
lemon wedges

Slice onions and cook in butter until tender. Cut steak in cubes, removing fat. Brown meat, sprinkling with salt and curry powder and continue to brown until spices are cooked with the meat. Pare potatoes and cut into cubes and add to meat and onion. Cover with water and cook until meat is tender. Add entire can of peas and cook until part of liquid is absorbed. Just before ready to serve, peel shell off eggs, cut in half lengthwise and drop into the curry. To serve, make a nest of the rice on hot dinner plate. Place half an egg on top of each nest and cover generously with curried meat. Use lemon wedge for squeezing juice over entire dish. Curry is much better if made the day before serving.[42]

Bengal Chutney

4 oz. raisins
½ lb. sour apples
1 oz. garlic
4 oz. sugar
2 oz. powdered ginger
2 oz. salt
¼ oz. cayenne or fresh hot red peppers

Put raisins, apples and garlic through food grinder, then add other ingredients. Place in heavy kettle on stove and add enough vinegar to make the consistency of thick cream. Heat and boil for 5 minutes stirring constantly. Bottle and seal.

—Sarah Scott McCune, 1811–77[43]

This chapter presents some of the haute cuisine of pioneer Utah. It was not typical daily fare. Many pioneers subsisted on a diet of wheat, weeds, and jackrabbits for years before their settlements offered the pleasures of life. In theory, widows and orphans could appeal to their church leaders for assistance. The more common reality was that "welfare" in Mormon settlements was dependent on the goodwill of neighbors. Often this meant just enough flour to make a loaf of bread or a batch of biscuits. Others living closer to Salt Lake City had greater access to exotic food items. As happens everywhere, an individual's station in life affected access to higher living.

Shoemaker William Stewart in Kaysville lived on meager terms for decades, while Brigham Young ate well almost from the start.

In his office as president of the LDS Church, Brigham Young (and his counselors) often had greater access to prime food items, with plenty of indulgence in excess and the exotic. His girth was a testament to his appetite. Still, he was a Yankee farmer at heart, and nostalgic returns to simple pleasures were not lost on him either. Clarissa recalled evening meals composed of fresh popped corn in a bowl of rich milk.[44] When you're not starving and have plenty of everything, such a dish can be a sentimental treat.

CHAPTER 10

The Complete Confectioner

SWEETS AND TREATS

> Sing, sing, what shall I sing?
> The cat's run away with the pudding string.
> Do, do, what shall I do?
> The cat's run away with the pudding too!
> —English nursery rhyme

Lorena Washburn held her sister's hand tightly, anticipating the excitement of the coming evening. Down the dark lane she could see firelight coming through the windows. The boys were already started.

Bursting into the cabin and giggling, the girls found a crowd gathered in front of the small hearth. One boy stood by watching a pot, with a long-handled spoon in hand but not stirring. The pot hung from a crane close into the fire. The quick flames licked the pot before disappearing up the chimney, causing its contents to roil in a steady boil. Occasionally the pot would nearly boil over, but the watchful boy quickly swung the crane away from the fire and back again as it settled.

When sufficient time had passed, other boys prepared small tin molds on the table. One by one, the kettle kissed the molds, pouring out boiling hot sugar. With a wooden spoon, Lorena scraped every drop of molasses from the pot. Together they waited for the candy to cool.[1]

Pursuit of Sugar

Lorena was not alone in her pursuit of something sweet. In addition to her friends in Manti, thousands of other children and teenagers in Utah begged an egg from their mother to pay for a stick of candy at the store. They pleaded for the by-products of the molasses mill for their candy projects. Adults likewise exerted inordinate efforts to get sweetening. In the fall of 1857 Wilford Woodruff spent the better part of a month working night and day to produce molasses for his family.[2] His 1858 production almost doubled the previous year's, reaching more than 250 gallons of molasses syrup. As a member of the Deseret Agricultural and Manufacturing Society, Woodruff had made a careful study of how to grow the best cane and created designs for state-of-the-art molasses extraction equipment.

We don't *need* sweets, as we do salt or carbohydrates. Yet we pursue sugar addictively. Today we find high fructose corn syrup on nearly every label. Wilford Woodruff and Lorena Washburn could not afford such an addiction, as molasses was dearly paid for. An indulgence in molasses candy showed that Lorena was not poor. She had enough extra for candy. For these young people, a little sugar became a social facilitator, allowing a joyous opportunity to come together in an otherwise hard-working farm community. For Woodruff, his molasses sated the sweet teeth of the multiple households for which he provided.

Sweet things served several important purposes for the community. They gave young people an excuse to mingle and flirt. Sweets also served to punctuate special events, such as a wedding or a holiday. Sugar was a punctuation of the notable moments in the seasons that marked a Mormon community. Though refined sugar and molasses were often reserved for special occasions, children were sometimes given molasses by-products to satisfy their sweet tooth. Eliza Brockbank Hales remembered: "In the summer we went to the molasses mill and got skimmings to make candy."[3] Eliza didn't get molasses but skimmings—the discolored scum that was discarded from the molasses production process. Likewise, Mary Josephine Knight Bunker noted that "molasses served the purpose very well when we were not accustomed to sugar. One of its many uses was for candy pulls. We always had plenty of these and perhaps enjoyed them more than the children of today who have the best of materials for making candy."[4] Do children today even make candy?

Molasses Candy: Boil a quart of molasses half an hour; add a tea-spoonful of saleratus, to make it stiff and brittle; boil it until it is stiff enough to pull; butter a dish, pour it in, and let it get cool; pull it in a cool place. You may add any kind of nuts, or popped corn.   —*The Great Western Cookbook*, 1857[5]

As discussed in chapter 3, the problem of sugar was multifaceted. Transportation, politics, the economy, and technology all played a role in determining the consumption habits of Mormon settlers. In the early days sugar in the white crystalline form was only available when shipped by mule trains from the east or west coasts. Such shipping costs got bundled into retail prices for consumers in Utah, pushing sugar out of reach for daily consumption. Furthermore, Brigham Young's fiscal policies determined that hard-won local currency should not be exported for such items, unduly robbing the territory of its cash. Local farmers eventually found beet and cane seed for crops that yielded sufficient molasses to satisfy an indifferent tongue, but technology to reduce the molasses to sugar remained out of reach for most of the settlement period. As a result, molasses became the standby sweetener for most applications.[6]

Let Them Eat Cake
Expensive sweetening didn't show up every day. For day-to-day meals, bread from whole wheat flour was the staple carbohydrate. Many meals consisted primarily of bread, sometimes sopped in milk and at other times accompanied by a bit of meat.

Molasses evaporation facilities, a long way from the FDA. After juice was crushed from sorghum cane, settlers boiled it down to a thick black syrup in a large evaporating pan over open fires.

Special times called for turning flour into cakes, which required sweetening. Some cakes called for yeast leavens. Others used egg whites beaten to stiff peaks. Less notable cakes used soda for a chemical leaven. All of them demanded sweetening.

Earlier cake recipes lean on beaten eggs as the leavening for the cake. Cooks first whipped air into the eggs then gently folded these air pockets into their batter. This tedious and exhausting job may be partly responsible for the place of honor that cake holds. No cook in her right mind would go to such effort for common meals. Eliza Leslie illuminates the technique required to beat eggs properly to yield a nice light cake:

> Persons who do not know the right way, complain much of the fatigue of beating eggs, and therefore leave off too soon. There will be no fatigue, if they are beaten with the proper stroke, and with *wooden* rods, and in a shallow, flat-bottomed *earthen* pan. The coldness of a tin pan retards the lightness of the eggs. For the same reason do not use a metal egg-beater. In beating them do not move your elbow, but keep it close to your side. Move only your hand at the wrist, and let the stroke be quick, short, and horizontal; putting the egg-beater always down to the bottom of the pan, which should therefore be shallow. Do not leave off as soon as you have got the eggs into a foam; they are then only *beginning* to be light. But persist till after the foaming has ceased, and the bubbles have all disappeared. Continue till the surface is smooth as a mirror, and the beaten egg as thick as a rich boiled custard; for

till then it will not be really light. It is seldom necessary to beat the whites and yolks separately, if they are afterwards to be put together. The article will be quite as light, when cooked, if the whites and yolks are beaten together, and there will then be no danger of their going in streaks when baked. The justly-celebrated Mrs. Goodfellow, of Philadelphia, always taught her pupils to beat the whites and yolks together, even for sponge-cake; and lighter than hers no sponge-cake could possibly be.   —*The Lady's Receipt Book*, 1847[7]

Emily Barnes recalled the plain cakes of her childhood before her father was able to provide adequate groceries, which only came with dues paid in years of settlement. "Once in a while we would have something special for dinner," she recounted. "It was a cake made with light dough into which [Mother] would put one cup of squash, a piece of butter, and a few dried service berries."[8] This appears to be a yeast-leavened cake. The cake's sweetness, such as it was, came from the natural sugars in squash and berries. Without molasses, Emily often turned to sweet things that could be gathered wild.

Ruth Mosher Pack's molasses cake is a step up from this meager existence. Although it also seems to be in the plain tradition, she uses molasses to stretch her sugar as well as soda to leaven. Lacking any spices, it employs coffee as its flavoring agent. Such a cake might be good enough for a social at the church house but was inadequate for Christmas.

Molasses Cake

1 cup molasses
1 cup coffee
1 tsp soda
1 cup sugar
⅔ cup shortening
3½ cups flour

Beat 2 eggs and add liquids together. Add soda to flour and mix well. Bake in a moderate oven 1 hour.   —Ruth Mosher Pack, 1824–1914[9]

Cakes also show up frequently in upper-class meals. The menu and bill of fare for the Territorial Ball of 1860 lists pound, sponge, "Gipsy," and other "varieties" of cakes. Brigham Young's daughter Clarissa remembered her father's fondness for a particular shortcake and its frequent appearance in the Beehive House. "Mother's shortcakes were without an equal," she boasted, "and we all just loved them—Father especially."[10] Like many Beehive House food items, the shortcake was not a rough item made with bran flour and molasses. It required fresh eggs, the best new butter, sifted white baker's flour, and fine white sugar. Lucy Young served it with fresh berries in season. When contrasted with the diet of boiled wheat mush and jackrabbits of pioneer Andrew Christian Nielsen, this makes a distinct statement about the place of cake for early Mormon settlers.

A sorghum crop waits for harvest. The Deseret Agricultural and Manufacturing Society experimented with different varieties of sorghum cane and sugar beets in search of a workable substitute for sugar in Utah.

Strawberry Shortcakes

Sift a small quart of flour into a pan, and cut up among it half a pound of the best fresh butter; or mix in a pint of butter if it is soft enough to measure in that manner. Rub with your hands the butter into the flour, till the whole is crumbled fine. Beat three eggs very light; and then mix with them three table-spoonfuls of powdered loaf-sugar. Wet the flour and butter with the beaten egg and sugar, so as to form a dough. If you find it too stiff, add a very little cold water. Knead the dough till it quits your hands, and leaves them clean. Spread some flour on your paste-board, and roll out the dough into a rather thick sheet. Cut it into round cakes with the edge of a tumbler, or something similar; dipping the cutter frequently into flour to prevent its sticking. Butter some large square iron pans or baking sheets. Lay the cakes in, not too close to each other. Set them in a brisk oven, and bake them light brown. Have ready a sufficient quantity of ripe strawberries, mashed and made very sweet with powdered white sugar. Reserve some of your finest strawberries whole. When the cakes are cool, split them, place them on flat dishes, and cover the bottom piece of each with mashed strawberry, put on *thickly*. Then lay on the top pieces, pressing them down . . . ornament the top of every cake with the whole strawberries, a large one in the centre, and the smaller ones placed round in a close circle.

—*The Lady's Receipt Book,* 1847[11]

Christiana Thompson Galli kindly left another recipe for a rich and indulgent cake. Born in Utah in 1853, she came from a family of Danish immigrants. Christiana married early in life, but her husband soon died. After marrying a Swiss immigrant, she settled in Midway, a Swiss community east of Provo. Her husband eventually entered a polygamous marriage. This cake lends Christiana a distinct identity, separate from the younger second wife.

Mrs. Joseph Galli's Sweet Cream Cake

Beat until thick and lemon-colored 2 eggs; then beat in well 1 c. sugar and 1 tsp. flavoring. Sift together 1¾ c. sifted flour—2 tsp. baking powder—¾ tsp. salt. Add sugar mixture alternately with 1 c. sweet cream. Bake in 2 8" tins—35 minutes.[12]

Pudding

Cake is a familiar concept and still marks special events in modern society. The birthday cake and the wedding cake distinguish important occasions. Less familiar to the modern palate is pudding. Certainly we must concede Bill Cosby's domain of Jell-o brand custardy puddings. But these are far from the puddings of Mormon pioneers. Refusing any singular definition, puddings may be any mixture of flour, milk, eggs, fruit, and even meat. Puddings may be steamed, boiled, or baked in a sack, a tin, a ceramic container, or a jar. They can be savory or sweet, served with gravy from meat drippings or with a "hard sauce" made from butter, sugar, and brandy. Scottish haggis is a pudding; so is rhubarb pie.

Further description will help to avoid confusion. In the eighteenth century puddings were usually boiled in a cloth sack or, in the case of haggis, in a stomach or intestine. Writing in 1843, Charles Dickens described the English boiled Christmas pudding in detail:

> Hallo! A great deal of steam! The pudding was out of the copper. A smell like a washing day! That was the cloth. A smell like an eating house and a pastry cook's next door to each other, with a laundress' next door to that! That was the pudding! . . . the pudding, like a speckled cannonball, so hard and firm, blazing in half of half a quartern of ignited brandy, and bedight with Christmas holly stuck into the top.[13]

Such puddings were quite substantial dishes, often serving as the main course. Bread crumbs and flour-based batters filled out the bulk of the pudding. In winter sweeteners, fats, and dried fruit showed up more frequently, giving the pudding a heavy calorie load and more of a paste texture before cooking. Summer puddings tended to be more savory, such as an English Yorkshire pudding.[14]

Thus puddings come in a wide variety of shapes and textures. The Territorial Ball of 1860 itemized the puddings: "Custards, Rice, English Plum, Apple soufflé, Mountain, Pioneer, Blancmange Jellies." Some of these seem familiar, others completely foreign. We can only guess at what the actual puddings described as "Mountain" and "Pioneer" may have been. A possibility for the Pioneer pudding may be found in a pudding of the same name associated with pioneer Martha Bitter Ricks. Though of a later date, it still retains the cloth pudding sack of the previous century. This pudding is savory, defying our modern divisions of desserts and main courses. Serve it with gravy, as is typical of the genre it represents.

Pioneer Suet Pudding

1 cup bread crumbs—1 cup ground suet—1 cup flour—½ tsp. salt. About ¾ cup milk to mix. Mix milk with other ingredients to make a stiff batter. Put in a [well-floured muslin] sack and tie tightly. Cook covered with boiling water for three hours. Cut and serve with brown gravy.   —Martha Bitter Ricks, 1860–1946[15]

By the mid-nineteenth century (the period of our study) the steamed pudding in a bag described by Dickens was nearly an antiquity. Some older recipes still call for this treatment, marking a contrast with the advent of tins and ceramics and the transition from steaming to baking. Sarah Annie Clark Hale's recipe for English plum pudding illustrates this early school of puddings. This would be the common pudding served at formal dinners as a dessert in fall and winter, as illustrated at the Territorial Ball. Elizabeth Kane noted such a pudding being served in Provo at a dinner for Brigham Young in 1872.[16] This pudding also would certainly have been served at Christmas dinner in the homes of British immigrants.

As with all English plum puddings, the "plum" means raisins. Though the recipe bears all the hallmarks of an early period, it appears to have been written down by the author late in life. She is careful to include information that would have been common knowledge to her mother but would be foreign to her daughter. The baking powder may originally have been soda (though English immigrant Caroline Hopkins Clark expressly mentioned baking powder in 1866).

English Plum Pudding

2 bowls flour, 1 bowl suet, 1 bowl raisins, 1 bowl currants, 1 teacup sugar, ½ teaspoon each cinnamon, ginger, cloves, and nutmeg; a little salt, 2 heaping teaspoons baking powder, 6 eggs. Mix to a stiff batter with milk. Boil 5 or 6 hours in a heavy cloth bag. For the bag use a heavy cloth about 27 inches square wrung out in warm water. Flour the inside well and pour on the batter. Pull up the corners and tie with a strong string leaving just enough room for the pudding to rise. Place upside down in a kettle of boiling water on a rack, so it won't burn on the bottom and keep boiling and fully covered with water in a covered kettle the entire time. Add more boiling water if needed during cooking.

Sauce or "Dip"

2 cups sugar and ¼ pound butter, 1 quart of water and boil until all dissolved. Thicken as for gravy. Flavor with brandy or lemon extract. As a variation, caramelize sugar and butter and just before serving add 1 cup whipped cream. Leave out flavoring.

—Sarah Annie Clark Hale, 1842–1918[17]

The indulgent use of sugar, spices, and dried fruit distinguishes this pudding as one for special occasions. Pioneers Patty Sessions and Emily Barnes noted that they brought starts for wild berries from the canyons and foothills to plant in their gardens, specifically for the purpose of making puddings. More ordinary winter sweet puddings may have called for a few dried fruits but fewer spices and less sugar.

Another odd pudding not mentioned at the 1860 Territorial Ball but common as dirt in pioneer Utah is the roly-poly. This genre marks the beginning of the transition from steamed to baked and from cloth bags to pastry-lined tins and baking dishes. The preparation calls for a puff paste outer shell, filled with fruit and preserves. The fruit is rolled up in the pastry, which is then tied and curled around into a circle and steamed or baked in a Dutch oven. One observer suggested that perhaps the name referred to the little creepy crawly hard-shelled bug by the same name that children play with (also called a potato bug).

Plum Roly-Poly Pudding

3 cups flour, 2 heaping teaspoons baking powder, 1 cup suet, pinch salt. Mix with sweet cream, pat out flat and cover with stoneless Pottawatamie plums,[18] roll up and place in a buttered double boiler and cook 3 hours. Serve with this sauce: 8 tablespoons sugar, 2 tablespoons flour, boiling water, nutmeg, butter and lemon if desired.

—Mary Stoddard Hill, circa 1860[19]

Lucy Jane Barkdull's apple dumplings are a close relation to these steamed puddings. Here we again see the use of a pastry crust as puddings merge into pie. These dumplings still employ the cloth bag for boiling, but it's not a far stretch from there to later recipes. If Lucy Jane made it as one large dumpling, she could almost call it a pie. With the pastry entirely removed and the ingredients put in a baking dish, we would have Sarah Scott McCune's brown betty. Some chefs say that there is no such thing as a new recipe: every dish is simply a slight tweak on something that has gone before. Instead of steaming puddings in a cloth bag, we steam them in their own pastry shell or line a plate with pastry and bake it. A biscuit is just a very stiff cake. A stew is just a very thick soup.

Apple Dumplings

Make a rich biscuit dough or short cake dough. Roll out to about ½ in. thickness. Heap sliced and spiced apples in the middle, gather the edges of the dough up to the top and pinch together. Put in a cloth bag large enough to allow expanding and drop into boiling water; cook until the apples are tender, about 45 minutes. These can be made into one large dumpling or small for individual servings. Serve with favorite sauce or cream.

—Lucy Jane Barkdull, 1830–1914[20]

Brown Betty Pudding: 2 c. finely chopped apples—½ c. chopped walnuts—cinnamon and nutmeg to taste—½ c. brown sugar—½ c. bread crumbs—piece of butter. Butter baking dish. Put in layer of apples. Sprinkle with sugar, bread crumbs, walnut meats and spices. Dot with butter. Put in another layer of apples, etc., and repeat until all the ingredients are used, finishing with the bread crumbs on the top. Serve with warm sauce.

—Sarah Scott McCune, 1811–1877[21]

Cookies

Through the course of this study I have received several recipes that tell the story of the life of Sarah Scott McCune. A world traveler, she was born in England and arrived in Utah after spending time in Calcutta. The brown betty above is just one recipe along this journey, apparently from later years in Utah. Her cookie recipe, however, seems to come from her time in India. As a woman of refinement in English society, married to an officer, she hosted social teas for her friends and colleagues. Her recipe for "Conversation Biscuit" is made in large volumes for a party. She continued to use this recipe as she hosted quilting bees and social luncheons in Utah.

Conversation Biscuit
2 pounds of flour
8 ounces of salt butter
16 ounces of loaf sugar
1 hare vol. Salts
4 hen eggs
16 drops Ess. Lemon
1 Gill Milk
n.b. Dough without water.
stamp—oven solid   —Sarah Scott McCune[22]

The fine Spencerian hand that transcribed the recipe nearly defies reading in the twenty-first century. Some of the ingredients and terminology seem quite foreign to the modern cook as well. "Volatile salts" likely refers to a chemical leaven like baking soda. McCune's cryptic notes on the preparation and cooking also evade our efforts to make these biscuits. "Stamp—oven solid" probably tells us to roll them out firmly and use a cookie cutter or stamp to shape them. This recipe calls us to a challenge.

Many of these recipes required expensive ingredients and extensive preparations. At the end of the day we often wish only for a simple cookie and a cup of cambric tea before bed. Cookies don't get much press in pioneer-land, but they most certainly had their place. In one of her lowest moments on the trail to Winter Quarters, Patty Sessions took heart with a batch of cookies.[23] Some of our most profound moments might come as we share such a simple treat across a century and a half. Humanity just needs a cookie in any era.

Mary's Cookies
2 level c. lard—1 c. sour cream—2 eggs—1 c. seeded raisins—½ c. currants—pinch of salt—1 tsp. soda—1 tsp. cloves—1 tsp. nutmeg—1 tsp. cinnamon—1 tsp. allspice. Add enough flour to make a dough as soft as can be rolled out and bake in a hot oven.
—Mary Dunn Ensign, 1833–1920[24]

Many of the choicest sweets and treats came from rich cream and milk. Emily Barnes and several others mentioned "clabber" in their descriptions of thickened cream. Gustava Capson, a Danish pioneer of 1855, ate clabbered cream with sugar as a dessert dish. "Crocks or pans of milk were placed in a cupboard in the cellar and

A nostalgic farm scene posed by Utah photographer George Anderson. Treats like clabbered cream originate in the farmyard.

it soon clabbered in the warm summer," remembered her granddaughter Cornelia Lund. "The thick cream was left on top to which was added a layer of sugar. This was served in large mush dishes by taking a spoon and cutting down into the pan, so as to get some of the cream with it. This was cool and delicious and was served with sweet cream if desired."[25] Who doesn't desire a little sweet cream?

Clabbered cream is made by first separating cream from raw (nonpasteurized) whole milk. The cream is left to stand at room temperature overnight, as Emily Barnes described in the first step of her cheese-making process. Naturally existing bacteria and enzymes in the milk begin converting the lactose to acids, thickening the milk and cream. The next morning the cream is thick and sweet, almost like a custard or crème fraiche. Served with sugar, it is divine. You can't make this from store-bought cream, because the pasteurization process kills the necessary bacteria. Modern food safety eliminates many of the bacterial cultures that were standard practice for Mormon pioneers. Try buying some raw milk straight from the dairy farmer to make this exquisite treat.

In the wide field of early Mormon cookery, many food items require no formula whatsoever. A soup, a beverage, and a biscuit all appear so intuitive that writing an actual recipe seems redundant. Other food processes defy distillation, approaching an artisan level of craft. With the sweets, puddings, cakes, and cookies presented here, the formula is essential and easily conveyed. In what has traditionally been a woman's

A watermelon feast at the Pace Ranch in Castle Valley, circa 1900. Although the bib overalls indicate a later period, the feasting activity is timeless in Mormon culture.

realm, many of these recipes have been carefully passed from mother to daughter over generations.

Bread is a necessary part of many modern diets. Some would argue that cookies, cakes, and candy are likewise necessary. Clabbered cream, while not strictly needed, provides a simple pleasure that makes life seem just a little more worthwhile. Pioneer mothers understood these things. Many of these recipes were first compiled by the Daughters of Utah Pioneers under the direction of Kate B. Carter in the 1940s. I am indebted to the early efforts of these women, who captured many foodways from still-living pioneers.

CHAPTER 11

Wetting the Whistle

B E V E R A G E S H O T A N D C O L D

Take away the strong whiskey,
Coffee black and cup of tea.
Cool water is the drink for me
Since I became a Mormon.
—Mormon folksong

For many Mormons and non-Mormons alike, the beverage prohibitions defined in Doctrine and Covenants (Section 89) are among the defining elements of what it means to be a Mormon. Since Joseph Smith revealed his Word of Wisdom in 1833, these proscriptions have been the subject of sermonizing, contention, debate, prevarication, and jest as well as the source of guilt for both observant and irreverent believers. What we drink is as much a part of Mormon food tradition and belief as any pudding, roast, or biscuit.

Mormon opinion as to this word of wisdom ("given not by way of commandment") has been torn for more than 170 years. Some say it originated from Emma Smith's complaint. Others say that God has given it as His people were ready to receive it. Perhaps the commandment served as a religious reflection of the same health fad of the early and mid-nineteenth century that inspired Graham crackers and cold showers. Some early settlers flaunted the rule entirely; others obeyed it— religiously. Even today, while the Word of Wisdom remains a litmus test for piety in the church, grocers do a booming business with churchgoing backsliders.

Many Beverage Choices

The advertisement of a popular buffet restaurant in Salt Lake City recently boasted of forty-four beverage choices included with the buffet. This gastronomic excess is not an invention of the twenty-first century. When we consider the dozen kinds of tea, an equal number of beers and wines, and further varieties of coffee and soft drinks all advertised for sale by Mormon merchants in the pioneer era *Deseret News*, it becomes

Godbe's Famous Soda Fountain, now on display at Lagoon Amusement Park's Pioneer Village. Marble with brass fixtures, this fountain dispensed wholesome, refreshing pleasures in the 1850s. Courtesy Lagoon Corp.

apparent that consumers in territorial Utah had as many choices as they had dollars or credit to spend. The advertisements of W. S. Godbe reflect the stylish and casual consumption of sodas: "The celebrated SODA FOUNTAIN (the only one in the Territory) in full operation! Also delicious ice drinks for the warm weather. An abundance of ice for sale."[1] In addition, individual diaries note dozens of home concoctions that may have never found retail viability but certainly figured prominently in local subsistence.

Soda Syrup, with or without Fountains.—The common or more watery syrups are made by using loaf or crushed sugar 8 lbs.; pure water 1 gal.; gum arabic 2 oz.; mix in a brass or copper kettle; boil until the gum is dissolved, then skim and strain through white flannel, after which add tartaric acid 5 ½ oz.; dissolved in hot water; to flavor, use extract of lemon, orange, rose, pine-apple, peach, sarsaparilla, strawberry, &c., ½ oz. to each bottle, or to your taste. Now use two or three table-spoons of the syrup to three-fourths of a tumbler of water and one-half tea-spoon of super-carbonate of soda, made fine; stir well and be ready to drink, or use the soda in water as mentioned in the "Imperial Cream Nectar"; the gum arabic, however, holds the carbonic acid so it will not fly off as rapidly as common soda. The above is to be used *without* fountains, that is to make it up as used, in glasses, or for the cheaper fountains which have an ounce of super-carbonate of soda to the gallon of water; but for the fountains which are charged, in the cities, with carbonic acid gas, no acids are used in the syrups.

Cream Soda, without a Fountain.—Coffee sugar 4 lbs; water 3 pts.; nutmegs grated 3 in number; whites of 10 eggs well beaten; gum arabic 1 oz.; oil of lemon 20 drops; or extract equal to that amount. By using oils of other fruits you can make as many flavors from this as you desire, or prefer. Mix all and place over a gentle fire, and stir well about thirty minutes; remove from the fire, strain, and divide into two parts; into one-half put supercarbonate of soda eight ounces; and into the other half put six ounces tartaric acid; shake well, and when cold they are ready to use, by pouring three or four spoons, from both parts, into separate glasses which are one-third full of cool water; stir each and pour together, and you have as nice a glass of cream soda as was ever drank, which can also be drank at your leisure, as the gum and eggs hold the gas.   —*Dr. Chase's Recipes,* 1864[2]

On the Trail

We might begin the discussion with a look at beverages from the trail. Trail beverages had three simple requirements: they must be easily portable; they must be quickly prepared; and they must have real nutritive or sustaining value rather than offering the simple sheer indulgence that typifies many casual beverages. John Bond, a Martin company handcarter, recalled that his father brewed ginger tea to revive the entire company of frozen handcarters.[3] Ground ginger root would have been kept as a medicinal herb more than as a culinary flavor agent. And the warming effect of tea certainly offered value to handcarters stuck in the snow.

Ginger Tea
Pour half a pint of boiling water on to a teaspoonful of ginger;* add sugar and milk to the taste.   —*Miss Beecher's Domestic Receipt Book,* 1850[4]
    * On the trail, this was probably ground dry ginger. You might also try using minced fresh ginger. Commercially prepared options also available.

Alcohol also found a place on the trail. Beer, cider, and wine consumed too much weight and space to be practical for trail use; distilled alcohol was more sensible. When Caroline Barnes Crosby hosted guests in her camp, she "treated them to a drink of whisky alcohol. We had a very sociable time with br. F. who staid with us until bedtime."[5] Patty Sessions also made note of alcohol as part of her social entertainments on the trail, celebrating her birthday in Winter Quarters over brandy with friends. For many others, however, coffee was more affordable.

Coffee

Contrary to the proscriptions of the Word of Wisdom, tea and coffee played an important part of the story of food on the trail. Overland emigrants reflected this attitude in their provisions of coffee. Daniel Jones, a rescuer for the Martin handcart company, recalled that his surviving winter at Devil's Gate in 1856–57 was due to a diet of boiled rawhide, weak soup, and plenty of strong coffee.[6] Local dry goods merchants offered thousands of pounds of coffee for sale in their advertisements in the *Deseret News*.

Once in the Salt Lake Valley, settlers had access to a wider variety of beverages. Coffee and tea continued to be staples, as evidenced by vigorous advertising in the *Deseret News*. But in addition settlers made use of gardens to supply herbal teas of all varieties. Pioneer seedsman Joseph Johnson published his first seed catalog in 1864 and offered seeds for chicory ("a new substitute for Coffee"), French mint, hyssop, jasmine, "lemon plant," lemon balm, peppermint, savory, strawberries, and hops.[7] Many of these herbal teas served as medicinals as well. Mint cleared the sinus, jasmine and chamomile calmed the nerves, and hops aided digestive complaints. Though pioneers probably didn't understand the precise nutritive value, rose hips provided an important source of vitamin C when citrus fruits were harder to come by.[8]

During this early era settlers purchased coffee as raw green beans. Individual grocers might roast and grind beans for customers, who would use the grounds immediately. Not until 1865 did the Arbuckle Coffee Co. invent the process for coating roasted beans in egg white as a flavor seal during transportation. The Globe Coffee and Dining Room proprietors (with Brigham Young as principal investor) operated in Salt Lake City and frequently bought advertising in the *Deseret News*. Using green coffee beans, the chef roasted his own beans and then ground them fresh each day.

Coffee and tea were also enjoyed at church functions in the Salt Lake Valley. A missionary homecoming in 1855 was held in the spacious kitchen and dining room of the Social Hall. The editors at the *Deseret News* described the event:

> None went from the hospitable board dissatisfied; the tea and the coffee were excellent, there was plenty of sugar to sweeten with, and no draining of cream jugs, for there seemed to be a perfect flow of milk and, not honey, but good tea and coffee.[9]

Even with the demonstrated popularity of coffee in these early days, the beverage had its detractors as well. Herbalist and folk physician Priddy Meeks practiced his craft in Parowan, Utah, in the 1860s. In his very intriguing diary Meeks recounts a celestial vision or flood of revelation wherein he was told that coffee can be providential for an older person whose "system is weak and feeble, and blood weak and languid and below a natural action." But he was warned that younger people may be harmed by drinking coffee, as their constitution is already in an agitated state. Even so, gentle readers, I offer this preparation here. You have been warned.

Coffee

It requires a tea-spoonful of ground coffee, to every cup of tincture. Take six tea-spoonsful of ground coffee, add the white of an egg, mix it well together with a small quantity of cold water, pour on it six or seven tea-cupsful of boiling water; stir it well, let it boil ten minutes; then let it stand by the fire, without boiling, ten minutes. It will then be ready to pour off.   —*The Great Western Cookbook*, 1857[10]

To brew coffee, begin with green beans. Using a skillet over an open flame, shake the green beans in the pan as you would popcorn. Mrs. Beeton, the English household guru of the day, recommended the French method of adding "a piece of butter the size of a nut" and an equal amount of powdered sugar.[11] Stir from time to time to help roast the beans thoroughly. Roast to your preferred shade: a darker bean makes a darker coffee. However, Mrs. Collins warns, "Coffee should never be roasted too much; a light brown is sufficient; when it is suffered to become black, it loses its flavor, and is bitter and disagreeable."[12] Roast and grind only what you will use in a few days. Many coffee aficionados advise against boiling coffee. Yet Osborne Russell, a fur trapper in early days, camped near present-day Ogden, Utah, and noted that for his Christmas dinner of 1840 his party drank coffee in which the grounds were boiled with sugar.[13] When cooking over a fire, boiling is the simplest method. If you choose to boil, do so gently for ten minutes. Some use isinglass, eggshells, or a splash of cold water in the pot to settle the grounds.

Tea

British converts represented more than half of the foreign Mormon migration from Europe. Hence tea also figured prominently on the trail. A descendant from these handcart fathers once displayed for me his family heirlooms from the handcart experience. Four artifacts were passed carefully over five generations: a candle mould, a pistol-style flint and steel tinderbox, a teapot, and a colander. With their handcarts loaded down with 500 pounds of flour, pioneers often carried such personal items by hand over the thousand-mile journey. Handcart trekker Mary Ann Jones observed: "One old sister carried a teapot and colander on her apron string all the way to Salt Lake. Another carried a hat box full of things, but she died on the way."[14] Tea was just that important.

In Salt Lake City dry goods merchants advertised a wide variety of teas for sale. Holliday and Warner offered "Imperial, Gun Powder, Young Hyson, and Black tea" in 1851. Every fresh shipment of goods and groceries was heralded in the newspaper with fanfare. Another retailer announced: "Tea! Tea! Tea! Wm. S. Godbe has just received a fine lot of good teas, which he is selling at the unparalleled low price of one dollar and a half per pound."[15] Though grown on the other side of the globe, teas in variety hit the markets of Mormon Utah with force.

Although tea culture had been practiced in Asia for more than a thousand years, its introduction to Western civilization came in the seventeenth century. Trade with China supplied green tea varieties such as oolong. Ceylon tea, however, was not commercially available until the 1870s.[16] Black variants such as India's Darjeeling tea came in the early nineteenth century as Britain's colonization expanded around the world and the British East India Company became a powerhouse of global trade. At this early date it was not understood that the difference between black and green tea was primarily due to processing methods; instead they were supposed to be entirely different plants.[17] The heavy bricks of compressed black tea (such as Hunan tea) from the eighteenth century, while still available, conceded market share to loose leaf and powdered teas as shipping costs came down and consumer appetites shifted. Tea leaves were sold loose as well as in compressed blocks. Tea blocks made sense for Mormon emigrants, because they took a concentrated form and required little space. To prepare this, the cook had only to scrape a few crumbs from the block into the kettle to steep and then strain them out through a small colander as the tea was poured into each cup.

Gunpowder tea also utilizes compression for its preservation; each tea leaf is individually rolled by hand into a small pellet and then dried, giving the appearance of cannon powder. Oolong teas from China often took this form. When steeped in hot water, the pellets unroll into long whole leaves. Like compressed tea bricks, gunpowder teas can be stored for years if kept dry.

The black tea with hints of citrus has been known as Earl Grey since the 1830s. Various legends ascribe its discovery or invention to a charitable act by the second Earl Grey toward either a Chinese mandarin or an Indian rajah, who then repaid him with this tea. It is more likely that an enterprising merchant used the earl's name without permission to promote a new variety. Traditionally black tea was used, though in modern times some green varieties have been passed off under this moniker. In the nineteenth century the tea was seasoned with bergamot oil, from a southern Italian citrus fruit.[18] In our modern era, synthesized chemical bouquets achieve the same effect. Reflective of all that is British, Earl Grey tea would have had broad appeal to the thousands of British immigrants in Utah's early Mormon settlements.

Other Teas

Particular note should be made of two other herbal teas important to Mormon settlers. Many Mormons today refer to "Mormon tea" or "Brigham tea" as *the* essential tea for early pioneers. The tea is supposed to have come from a native ephedra variety common to the deserts of the Southwest, and many attribute its use to Brigham Young. His frugal Yankee sensibility promoted the local ephedra as an alternative to Asian imports. The only hitch is that we have yet to discover a diary or other early document from the period that refers to this herb during Brigham Young's lifetime. The earliest references to the use of this herb seem to coincide with the expansion of Mormon settlements into Arizona and Mexico during the last decade of the nineteenth century. The plant is rather common there, while it has no indigenous claim on northern Utah. Nevertheless, this tea continues to hold a prominent place in Mormon folklore.

In contrast, it is well documented that Brigham Young and many others used a tea composed primarily of cayenne pepper with other herbs and spices to balance it out. Brigham's composition tea found some popular acceptance. Priddy Meeks noted the tea in his herbal pharmacopeia, with a possible nod to Thompsonian origins.[20] Meeks's recipe calls for bayberry bark, ginger, hemlock bark, cayenne, and cloves, ground to a fine powder.[21] Elizabeth Kane also observed settlers in the upper echelons of Mormon society using the tea in Utah's southern settlements. She described this tea as being composed of ginger, cayenne pepper, cloves, and bayberries, sweetened and mixed with cream in boiling water. She also noted that it was sometimes drunk cold.[22] One unsuspecting friend of Brigham consumed the tea to excess and found himself the worse for wear. Thereafter he called this tonic the "Mormon Highball."

While traveling through Utah with Brigham Young, Elizabeth Kane made other observations about the beverages that Mormons consumed. Mrs. Mary Steerforth of Nephi related that in the early days settlers had little food and were constantly hungry. But, she observed, "With a little milk we could make cambric tea, which was found to be one of the best remedies for hunger—taken hot, and with a little spice or aromatic herbs to flavor it."[23] Cambric tea is usually prepared with a bit of sugar in a teacup, to which is added hot milk and sometimes a shot of well-brewed black tea. Though this tea was the traditional choice for children's tea parties and for older persons of delicate constitution, it also had more nutritive value for starving pioneers than traditional black tea. Mrs. Steerforth doesn't mention sugar, as molasses was the common sweetener of this era. The likely spice for her cambric was nutmeg, which was more common than cinnamon at the time.

> **Brigham's Tea**
> Here is Father's own recipe for it: 4 oz. each of ground bayberry, poplar bark, and hemlock; 2 oz. each of ground ginger, cloves and cinnamon; and 1 oz. of cayenne pepper . . . take a small bit on the end of a spoon, fill the cup with hot water, and use plenty of cream and sugar.[19]   —from Brigham Young's daughter Clarissa

Milk

Following established lists of requisite provisions, many immigrants also brought fresh dairy cows on the trail. Martha Heywood noted her husband's fatigue at having to milk two cows as well as drive the oxen each day. Likewise, Emily Stewart Barnes remembered her father's milk cow on the Mormon pioneer trail:

> Say, what a fuss my father made about milking the cow as he had never milked one before! At last when done he would bring the milk and put it in a little tin pail and hang it up in the top of the wagon where the shaking as we were traveling along would churn a little butter.[24]

Fresh cows likely contributed cream for tea and coffee as well as butter for cooking. Sour milk, soured cream, and buttermilk are often referenced as an ingredient in cakes. Hot milk served over toast or biscuit shows up as well. In these instances, milk (and its products) functions more as a food item than as a beverage.

Mary Ann Hafen remembered that her first meal after leaving the ship that brought her to America was "sweet milk and bread."[25] Pioneer Caroline Barnes Crosby recalled a daily trail meal of "nothing but milk to eat": once she arrived in Salt Lake City she was disinclined toward milk for the rest of her life.[26] In both of these instances, however, the milk was eaten with bread as a sort of cold porridge. Andrew Israelson, a Danish immigrant, wrote of eating bread in milk as a breakfast dish.[27]

> **Milk Toast**
> Boil a pint of rich milk, and then take it off, and stir into it a quarter of a pound of fresh butter, mixed with a small table-spoonful of flour. Then let it again come to a boil. Have ready two deep plates with a half a dozen slices of toast in each. Pour the milk over them hot, and keep them covered till they go to table. Milk toast is generally eaten at breakfast.   —*Directions for Cookery*, 1853[28]

Reports of drinking milk as a beverage are much less frequent but not nonexistent. Elizabeth Kane noted creamy whole milk served as a beverage with meals in Provo.[29] Legend has it that during the days of wine production in St. George three pitchers accompanied good meals: one of water, one of milk, and one of wine.[30] Ruth Page Rogers, however, used skimmed milk to fatten her pigs: the economic value of lard ranked higher than the dietary value of skimmed milk for drinking.[31] I must agree.

Alcohol

Though Joseph Smith began promoting the prohibition of alcohol in the Word of Wisdom in 1833, Mormons as a whole didn't pay much attention for a century after its introduction.[32] From the Nauvoo House to the Lion House, alcohol had a place at the Mormon table and bar. These patterns followed the Mormon pioneers across the plains to Utah. Soon after settling in at Winter Quarters, Wilford Woodruff wrote: "We commenced getting juice out of the grape. We got out about 20 gallons of juice for wine."[33] Patty Sessions also made wine and brewed beer that season at Winter Quarters. This theme emerges again in the Utah Territory.

Author Del Vance opined that Porter Rockwell's Point-of-the-Mountain brewery (established in 1856) was the first in the territory and the only operational brewery during this era,[34] but there are competing claims. Over the winter of 1849–50 hundreds of miners headed for California stayed in the Mormon settlements. Seeing a demand that they could supply, some settlers commenced the sale of a locally brewed whiskey for $6 a gallon as well as "a very light and wholesome beer." Historian Leonard Arrington noted a proliferation of "grog shops" to serve the flow of Forty-niners.[35]

This early note marks the beginning of what was to become known as Valley Tan. The term was first applied to leather goods processed entirely in the valley but was soon applied to whiskey produced in the territory. Popular folklore often holds that Brigham Young held a monopoly on distillation via legislative fiat, but the broad and common availability of Valley Tan liquor argues to the contrary. Captain Albert Tracy noted Mormon sutlers who plied the Camp Floyd soldiers with Valley Tan liquor. Sir Richard Burton recorded another Mr. Burton in Utah selling Valley Tan in his store. And Arthur Jones donated gallon kegs of "Moon's very best Valley Tan" to assist the church emigration efforts, particularly hoping to warm travelers who were chilled from crossing creeks along the trail. Valley Tan, though perhaps not a particularly refined or pleasing product, served for common whiskey in territorial Utah.[36] Even so, beer might have been the more common beverage for many.

The David Day brewery showed up for sale in the *Deseret* News in 1859, but the advertiser noted that it had formerly been owned and operated by Mr. B. Dallow.[37] Local restaurants continued thereafter to offer "Day Beer" for sale with a meal. W. H. Hockings expanded his "eating room" in 1859 to include a brewery. In 1860 he expanded the operation again by "having engaged a Dutch Brewer who has had long experience in Philadelphia and other large cities as a malt master and brewer. He can now offer to the public first rate articles of LAGER BEER AND ALE wholesale or retail." Hockings also offered services and supplies for home brewers: "Facilities are hereby offered for malting and grinding, which have been heretofore unknown in

The Exchange Saloon, one of Salt Lake City's earliest beverage emporia.

Utah, giving families an opportunity of brewing for themselves, and thereby ensuring a good and pure article."[38] In the twenty-first century a handful of brew shops supply the same ingredients and services for home brewers that continue the tradition.

Home Brewing

As already discussed in relation to bread, brewing activities depend on yeast. Bakers and brewers seem to go hand in hand as they work with the same commodities of grain and yeast in fermentation. Anna Madsen Bench left this account of the beer making of her mother (Mette Andersen Madsen, 1834–1896) and noted that the yeast was at least as important a product as the alcohol:

> For beer making, mother first made the malt. This was done in the summer time. Clean grain was selected, put into a wooden tub that was used only for that purpose, and soaked until it would hold no more water. Then drained and put up in an attic on a scrubbed platform, heaped in a pile, well covered, to make it heat and sprout. When it was well sprouted and matted together it was spread out gradually and thoroughly dried. Then taken to the mill and crushed or ground. A wooden tub with a hole in the bottom near the edge was used in which to brew the beer. Clean straw was scalded, twisted and put in the hole, this served to strain the beer. A stick the size of the opening and as high as the tub was forced into the hole. A portion of the malt was placed in the tub, and boiling water poured over it, in proportion to the malt. When the strength of the malt was well absorbed by the water, the stop was

loosened a little, so the beer could filter through the straw. This dripped into another wooden tub and while at blood heat yeast saved from the last batch was added. A little flour was sprinkled over the top, the vessel well covered, and the liquid allowed to ferment. When well worked and settled it was put into jugs, stored in a cool place, was then ready for use. The yeast which had settled in the bottom was carefully stored for bread-making and for the next batch of beer. Sometimes for the sake of variation part of the malt was put in the oven and slightly browned to make the beer a darker color and some-times the hops were boiled and the liquid added to give it a bitter tang. Beer was made as much to obtain fresh yeast as for the drink.[39]

Brewing Made Simple

1. Get some malt, which comes from barley grain. The maltster soaks the grain and then lets the grain begin to sprout. Sprouting causes an enzymatic conversion of starch to sugar. The sprout is then halted by heating and drying before all starch is consumed in the growth of the new sprout.
2. Convert sugar to a fermentable liquid. If you are using whole grain malt, this is done by grinding the grain then extracting the sugars in a thick soup. Careful temperature regulation causes further enzyme conversion to sugar. Some use malt extract in liquid or powder form, eliminating this step.
3. After straining or "sparging" the grain from the soup (this liquid sugar base is called wort: see the glossary), boil it with hops for nearly an hour. Boiling homogenizes the sugars as well as extracts the essential oils from the hops.
4. After cooling the wort to room temperature, yeast is added. This is done in a closed fermenting vessel with an air lock to prevent vinegar bacteria from spoil-ing the wort. The yeast begins to ferment the sugar, resulting in alcohol ranging between 3 and 12 percent.
5. After fermentation has subsided, the new beer is drawn off the yeast bed, which has settled to the bottom of the fermentation vessel. The beer is then stored in a new clean vessel or bottled, to age for a month or more.

Visit your home brew store for more information.

A skilled brewer might notice several process flaws in Anna's description of her mother's brewing activities. Even so, she illustrates quite nicely the state of the art for her time. While some references illustrate the complexity of historic brewing opera-tions, brewing and wine making are really quite simple. Priddy Meeks, while waiting out the winter before beginning his trek to Utah, described his production of elder-berry wine in Missouri:

> The Bluffs here was lined with any amount of Chickasaw plums and was just getting ripe and a large amount of elderberries in right order for making wine, and we turned in and made eighty (80) gallons of wine. We put a hundred and fifty pounds of sugar in it, which made it splendid.[40]

A barley field, harvested and shocked. Barley grain was malted to create a sweet base and brewed to make beer or distilled to make whiskey.

Elder Wine

To every gallon of picked ripe berries, allow 1 gallon of water, and let them stand 24 hours, often stirring them; then put them into a copper, and boil well for half an hour, when draw the whole off, and strain it through a sieve; put the juice into the copper a second time, and to each gallon add 3½ lbs. of moist sugar; boil it for half an hour, and, within the last 5 minutes, add, tied in muslin, bruised ginger and all-spice, of each 4 ounces to every 10 gallons; then take out the spice, and, when cool, set the must to work, with some good yeast upon a toast. When it ceases to ferment put it into a cask, bung down closely, let it stand 3 or 4 months, and bottle it, though it may remain in the wood if more convenient. The addition of a few damsons, sloes, or any rough plum, to the elder-berries, will give this wine the roughness of port. It will likewise be improved by the addition of crude tartar, before the wine is set to ferment.

A superior elder wine may be made by using, instead of moist sugar, 4 pounds of loaf sugar to every gallon of mixed juice and water.

—*The Ladies' New Book of Cookery*, 1852[41]

Alcohol production is just that simple: prepare a naturally sweet liquid concoction (from barley malt, wheat malt, fruit juice, or honey dissolved in water). To increase alcohol content, Priddy added more sugar. Then add yeast. Wait anywhere from a week to a month, depending on the fermentation cycle—and enjoy.

Once Mormon pioneers settled in Utah, they continued making "wine" from a variety of plants, both native and domestic. Anything that could be fermented was, including potatoes, watermelon, loganberries, grapes, apples, and sorghum molasses. Before the end of the century settlers fermented pomegranate and casaba melons as well. Rhubarb, that pioneer standby from the garden, showed up in puddings, in pies, and of course in wine as well. Joseph Ellis Johnson, a supplier of garden seeds, also worked as a newspaperman from his home in Spring Lake Villa (now called Springville, Utah). His newspaper, the *Farmer's Oracle*, often published directions for different kinds of brewing processes, including one for wine.

Rhubarb Wine

A very good beverage can be made of the juice of the common pie-plant [rhubarb]; it is not strictly a wine, as that dainty can only come of ripened fruit. Dr. Marsh gives the following receipt for making rhubarb wine, which he says is the best remedy for dysentery and diarrheas yet known. —Peel and slice the leaf-stock as for pies; put a very small quantity of water in the vessel, only just enough to cover the bottom; cover the vessel and gradually bring to a slight boil, then strain, pressing out all the liquid; to this liquid add an equal quantity of water; to each gallon (after mixed) add four to six pounds of sweetening, set aside, ferment and skim like currant wine; put it in a cask and leave it in bulk as long as possible.[42]   —*The Farmer's Oracle*, 1863

Note: Such divergent and homegrown recipes continue to circulate in Utah's Sanpete Valley. A strikingly similar version was recently collected from a wine maker in Ephraim, Utah.

Wine-Making Traditions

Under Brigham Young's direction, wine making took a more thoughtful approach in the 1860s. In the October 1860 General Conference of the LDS Church, Young called several families to undertake a mission to settle on the Virgin River. Specifically, these pioneering settlers were called to explore the cultivation of cotton, sugar, grapes, tobacco, figs, and olives. The previous prophet, Joseph Smith, had directed that Mormons should not rely on outsiders for wine, which should be of their own making. To this end, Brigham Young anticipated that Utah's Dixie would allow the communion sacrament to change from water back to wine.

Settlement efforts in Dixie initially focused on cotton production. In the fall of 1860 Brigham Young called thirty families to "become permanent settlers in the Southern Region." These families, headed by Swiss convert Daniel Bonelli, were to "cheerfully contribute their efforts to supply the Territory with cotton, sugar, grapes, tobacco, figs, almonds, olive oil and other such articles."[43] As the Civil War ravaged agricultural production in the Southern states, Mormons found ready markets for their cotton crop. With the end of the war, however, textile markets returned to normal. Dixie farmers found themselves searching for a different cash crop. Brigham answered their need by calling John Naegle to Dixie. Raised in Bavaria and apprenticed in the wine-making trade, Naegle tackled the problem head on. Constructing immense stone cellars and a winery in Toquerville, he quickly taught local growers the tricks of the trade. Leaning primarily on Old Mission or Isabella grape varieties, Dixie produced thousands of gallons of wine annually. Naegle's winery still stands as the last building in Toquerville as the road winds out toward Zion National Park.[44]

Naegle's process for making wine was simple. Young boys picked clusters of grapes from the vines and tossed them into a wagon that followed them through the vineyard. The wagons hauled these loads to the winery, where young men pitchforked the bunches into crushing barrels. Naegle used a crushing mechanism that ground the grapes using a hand-cranked apparatus. Other wine makers in Dixie trod the grapes by foot. Dixie girls were said to have the whitest legs in the territory.[45] These barrels were made with gaps between the staves so that as the grapes were crushed the juice would readily run out to catch basins below. Most Dixie vintners then allowed the skins and stems to soak in the juice. At this point the juice became infused with natural yeasts from the dusty skins of the grapes. Left to stand for a few days, the yeasts began gobbling the sugary juice, resulting in alcohol. When the roiling fermentation ceased and the grape pulp rose to sit on the surface, the wine was said to be finished.[46]

To Make Seven Gallons of Good Grape Wine.—Take 4½ gallons of water, and 5 gallons of ripe grapes; crush the fruit, and soak it in the water for a week; then add 18 pounds of good loaf-sugar, ferment, and put into a 7 gallon cask. Wine made as above may be kept good for 10 years.

* The *use* of wine is permitted, we may add *encouraged*, by Scripture authority; and, though the *abuse* of this privilege, when extended to intoxicating drinks in general, has led to such dreadful results of crime and misery, as to induce many Christians to abstain entirely from *wines*, as well as from *distilled liquors*, yet that the former may be considered, under proper restrictions, a suitable and beneficial beverage, is certain— because the Word of God sanctions their use. Therefore, a few receipts for the manufacture of these domestic wines, in which not a drop of distilled spirit is admitted, are necessary to the wise household economy we advocate, that provides for every taste and enjoyment compatible with health, humanity, and virtue.

—*The Ladies' New Book of Cookery*, 1852[48]

While sacramental wine may have been the stated original goal, tithing houses quickly found surpluses spilling from the region. Functioning as a medium of exchange (similar to wheat in the northern settlements), wine held universal value and could be readily shipped. Excess wine was shipped to northern Utah tithing houses by the thousands of gallons. Even so, production exceeded the local markets. Mormons sold wine to the mining camps, but the bottomless cup still flowed over. Fearing a society of wine bibbers, church leaders implemented market restrictions on the purchase of small bottles of wine. Only five-gallon quantities were allowed. Upon meeting one Brother drunken in the street, Brigham received the explanation: "it is utterly impossible to drink five gallons of wine and stay sober!"[47] Brigham loosened restrictions on wine consumption for local congregations through the 1870s, but some consumers were unable to maintain the moderation advised by the Word of Wisdom. Church leaders eventually curtailed wine making as the regional economic engine. Washington County became just another desert incapable of sustaining viable agriculture. Though some isolated local families continue their ancestral wine-making traditions, institutional culture has abandoned the practice.

Much ballyhoo surrounds wine and its production. A visit to a modern commercial winery may leave the impression that wine making is sophisticated beyond reach of the average housewife, but historical records show otherwise. Production of wine and beer was a part of every household economy.

Reduced to an even simpler form, we can describe the process thus:

1. Get some juice. Juice intended for wine is called must. You might try using a frozen grape juice concentrate from the grocery store, or you could crush your own grapes stolen from the neighbor's fence. If you use your neighbor's grapes, don't wash them first: the skins will have a lovely coating of yeast that we desire. Simply crush the grapes, skins and all, in as large a container as is practical. Letting the crushed grapes sit in the must within a closed container will contribute to a better wine. Naturally, the character of the grapes and must will determine the quality of the wine; juice from frozen concentrate may not produce impressive results. A higher-quality must is also available for purchase from a wine-making shop.
2. Put the must in a sanitized container (glass preferred). Don't fill the jar more than two-thirds full. Add yeast to the juice. Wine-making yeast is specially cultivated to live in the high-alcohol environment, while bread-making yeast has other properties. You might try a tablespoon of dry active baker's yeast. Or you can purchase yeast from the wine maker's supply store.
3. Maintain a closed environment at a constant temperature. Allowing open-air contamination is the greatest danger for spoilage at this point. Old-time pioneers would put the must in a barrel and cork the bung loosely so that gasses could escape. You might use a gallon glass cider jug with screw-on threads,

A newly planted grape vineyard in the new Mormon settlements of southern Utah. These vines became the lifeblood of Dixie's wine culture.

The Hurricane Fruit Festival displayed the pride of Mormon farmers in southern Utah. Peaches, apples, and grapes were all turned to alcohol, but grapes especially.

leaving the lid set on loosely. Or you can buy an air lock at the wine maker's supply for about $2. The air lock is a much safer bet.

4. Wait. Fermentation should begin within 12–24 hours. You will know when fermentation begins because the must will begin to foam and roil inside the jar. This is a good thing. Yeasts are busy converting sugar to alcohol and CO_2. This process should complete in five days. If you are using an air lock, watch for it to stop bubbling.

5. Carefully strain the wine from the yeast that has settled on the bottom of the jar. Siphon or pour it into a clean jug or bottle. You might use it immediately or let it sit in the cellar for a month first—it's your choice. Wine that has rested for a few weeks after fermentation has a more mellow and well-blended flavor. If you decide to cellar your wine before using it, you should be absolutely certain that the fermentation has ceased completely before corking the bottles. The bottles could explode if fermentation continues, sending glass in dangerous directions.

Pioneers in Utah's southern settlements used this wine for many different purposes. From the outset church leaders emphasized that the production of wine should be "for the Holy Sacrament, for medicine, and for sale to outsiders."[49] Naturally, the sacrament used wine for its holy purposes, as directed by Mormon scripture. John Stucki, a Swiss immigrant and vintner, had the privilege of supplying the first wine for a Mormon sacrament in southern Utah.[50] Wine was also consumed with meals: pitchers of water, wine, and milk marked a well-set table. Wine figured prominently in the medical remedies of folk-healer Priddy Meeks.[51] And wine was

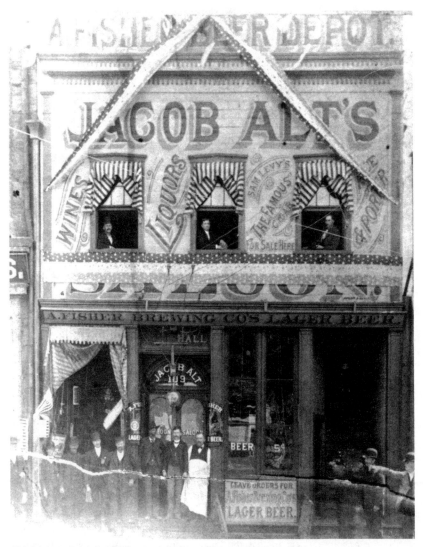

Alt's Saloon in Salt Lake City featured the best of German brewing traditions.

consumed casually as a social lubricant. When the community called for a dance, a barrel of wine accompanied the occasion. Peter Anderson, a Dane living in Toquerville, preferred his wine in eggnog. This concoction required one well-beaten egg, to which he added wine. The acidic nature of the wine curdled the egg. He soaked this mixture up with a slice of bread and considered it quite a delicacy.[52]

From cold water to whiskey, from herbal tea to wine, Mormon settlers consumed a wide variety of beverages. Pioneers drank diverse beverages with meals. They consumed all sorts of liquids for social leisure and recreation, from carbonated sodas to beer, wine, and liquor. Mormons drank medicinal compositions and drank for survival in the desert.

In the intervening years Mormon attitudes have shifted dramatically regarding beverage consumption. Larger social and political movements in the United States (such as enactment and repeal of Prohibition) have affected Mormon observation of the Word of Wisdom. Furthermore, Mormons have followed the larger population of the United States in their embrace of sugary caffeinated soda beverages. Religious belief continues to influence beverage choice in dynamic ways.

The beverages of early Mormon settlers reflect the diversity of their heritage and culture. The beverages of modern Mormons define their religious observance. Who knows what Mormons might drink tomorrow?

CHAPTER 12

To Nuts

A CONCLUSION

Our food was plain but wholesome.
—Eliza Brockbank Hales

Upon arriving in Utah from Denmark, Andrew Christian Nielsen recorded the diet of his West Jordan neighbors with horror: "Their grub was mostly rabbit for breakfast, hare for dinner, and sorghum for supper with a little burnt molasses and cornmeal mush or cooked wheat." In contrast, Eliza Brockbank Hales summed up her pioneer diet in Spanish Fork: "Our food was plain but wholesome. We had milk, home-made bread, vegetables, dried fruit, and meat. Our home-cured hams were tops. We also had a barrel of corned beef and a good root cellar for potatoes, apples, vegetables, and so on."[1] Even within the narrow restrictions laid out at the beginning of this study, pioneer foodways have proven to be diverse.

Published cookbooks from the eastern United States demonstrate that many of the foods that Mormon pioneers ate were also typical for their eastern contemporaries. Coming from a common geographical and cultural experience before their exodus, Mormons shared many food traditions with mainstream America in the mid-nineteenth century. Food studies of the Oregon Trail, mining camps, and military life also illuminate patterns in common with the Mormon experience. But make no mistake: Mormon pioneer food had its own unique dimensions as well.

Mormon pioneer foodways are distinguished from other contemporary American food patterns in three fundamental ways: geographical isolation, poverty, and ethnic tradition. As time passed, the importance of each of these factors declined. In the early years of settlement Utah Mormons found the isolation that Brigham Young had hoped for, but at a cost. They were completely on their own for their survival, with no safety net. Overland shipping costs made outside food sources prohibitively expensive. Mormon settlers operated on a fixed income; the limited pool of cash available in the isolated communities couldn't increase. Instead, it seemed to dwindle constantly as settlers spent their limited cash to purchase imported essentials. Their trade deficit perpetuated poverty. As new converts arrived from Europe and the eastern states, ethnic cultures were kept alive through concentrated ethnic settlements.

These effects were slowly ameliorated over time. As Salt Lake City and nearby settlements found their footing, settlers expanded their safety nets to form a broader community. Expanded farm acreage eventually allowed early settlers to rise above poverty. Trade routes to other Rocky Mountain communities developed over time, decreasing economic and social isolation. Likewise, the passage of time diminished some of the cultural attributes that originally distinguished settlers from each other as they merged to form a common Mormon identity, rather than being Yankees, Brits, or Danes.

Even as these changes were occurring for these older settlers, new converts arrived and began carving out new settlements farther from the Salt Lake City core. Although Salt Lake City had plenty of wealth, new waves of immigrants had to pay their dues through blood, sweat, and tears, establishing new settlements in the spirit of the first pioneers of 1847. Even new arrivals to the Salt Lake Valley in the 1860s experienced hunger as they worked to scratch out a living from their new farms, while their older established neighbors dined comfortably. New farms and communities in Saint George in the 1860s (and the Arizona Strip in the 1880s) experienced many hardships in common with those seen in the Great Salt Lake Valley more than a decade earlier. Uncertain crops, hostilities with Indians, and economic and social isolation impacted younger communities in similar ways.

Utah farmers eventually found outside markets for some of their crops. Neighboring communities in the Rocky Mountains experienced the same growth curve as the Mormon communities. Mormon farms had a ten-year head start. They shipped their first wagon train of food supplies to Denver in 1859.[2] Markets in other mining communities soon followed in Idaho, Montana, and Nevada.[3] Some sharing of food items (and the economy) occurred between Mormons and their neighbors in the West. Still, situated on the eastern slope of the Rockies, Denver was much closer to the farmlands of Kansas, without the obstacle of mountains to negotiate. Likewise, from San Francisco's early beginnings during the gold rush of 1849, its Pacific Ocean port facilitated trade that Utah could only dream of. The Montana market for Mormon produce lasted only until Montana farmers managed to grow local wheat a few years later.

Furthermore, the economic policies Brigham Young established for his followers discouraged commerce with outside sources. Most notorious of these was the "Gentile Boycott," in which Brigham endorsed a loose cooperative of Mormon retailers and mandated that observant Mormons do business only with them. Brigham also made efforts to limit exchange with providers outside of Utah. "We do not intend to have any trade or commerce with the gentile world," he contended. "For so long as we buy of them, we are in a degree dependent on them. The kingdom of God cannot rise independent of the gentile nations until we produce, manufacture and make every article of use, convenience or necessity among our own people."[4] The actual effect of the boycott was limited, however. Mormon farmers and manufacturers simply were not self-sufficient. While Brigham Young tried to keep a positive trade balance, retaining Mormon cash in Utah proved nearly impossible. Even as Brigham condemned purchase from outsiders, he realized the necessity of selling to them. Wine makers in Saint George, Utah, targeted the nearby mining community of Silver Reef to sell off their excess product.[5] The theoretical boycott was a one-way street. The net result was that Mormon communities remained cash poor even after their crops found stability. New communities in remote areas experienced the same effects.

As a result of these ongoing geographical, social, and economic factors, Mormons often relied on wild sources for foodstuffs (particularly in the early years of settlement). All manner of wild berries, roots, vegetables, and meat played a part in the Mormon diet. Likewise, Mormon settlers carried on direct relations with Native Americans for food in their early years of settlement, though often with a threat of force. Incorporation of wild foods frequently came with an interpretation of divine providence:

> The place where the weeds were gathered was down on the south side of the [Manti] stone quarry where the Mormons first camped. After each day a-gathering, there was none left for the next day. But like the food miraculously supplied to the Israelites in the wilderness, each day, just so the Lord provided for this supply of pig weed each day.[6]

In addition to these factors, religion had its effects on the diet of Mormon settlers. Mormon religious prohibitions against coffee, tea, and alcohol seem to have had little effect on day-to-day food patterns. But a New England puritan influence pervaded many meals, emphasizing simple wholesome food, with a limited acceptance of gluttony when food was plentiful. After all, surplus food is a sign of God's blessing. In retrospect, anecdotes about pioneer privations and food shortages have been interpreted as religious observances and as a manifestation of piety and devotion. Even the seasonality of food patterns has been reinterpreted as reflecting a religious theme: LDS scripture promotes balance and moderation in seasonal consumption.

The trail experience in Mormon history has a profound effect on our view of pioneer history. For example, the Daughters of Utah Pioneers only claim those immigrants who walked across the plains before the arrival of the transcontinental railroad in 1869. A settler born in Utah in 1850 does not have the same mythical status, lacking the trail experience. Likewise, the trail experience defines a significant portion of Mormon foodways, even though this was a relatively small portion of the overall food experience of the Mormon pioneers. As shown here, most pioneers crossed the trail comfortably with plenty of food. Yet the privations and hardships of the trail experience hold a more prominent position in our collective psyche. I could point to cake with peach sauce on the trail, but most prefer to remember a soda biscuit served with bone soup instead. With trail food in particular, we often make a selective focus on privations, creating a distorted sense of what actually happened.

As we have seen, Mormon pioneer food experiences were often determined by the Mormon settlement pattern. Settlers came west with very little. They often made a new life in Utah entirely divorced from the place where they originated. This required resourceful efforts to acquire the physical necessities to establish a new home and hearth. As a result, the food patterns of early settlement stood in stark contrast with those of later years. Early settlers often reported eating wild-gathered foods such as pigweed or lamb's quarter, in the absence of more cultivated crops. As settlements matured over time, food supplies became more stable and abundant. In the early 1860s a bumper crop of Mormon wheat pushed prices down all over the West.

Food patterns in these settlements followed a similar course over time. With empty pantries and lean meals in early years, settlers looked forward to better crops as they dug new irrigation ditches. They made do with rough commodities such as bran flour and blackstrap molasses. White sugar and white flour came only with time. The Mormon settlement pattern also dictated a slow adaptation to newer technology. Prohibitive freight costs limited access to newer farming implements and cast-iron stoves. Mormon industry and production within the state failed to meet the market for newer technology. Mormon farmers and cooks remained behind the times as a result of geographic and economic factors.

Utah settlements differed from others in the West as a result of higher levels of foreign immigration. By 1870 nearly half of Brigham City's population was foreign-born or of European descent. Of foreign-born settlers over thirty years old, more than half were Scandinavian.[7] Other states and territories in the West also experienced the effects of foreign immigrants. These communities generally were composed of immigrants from multiple source countries, who settled in intermingled patterns. San Francisco's Chinese population remains a notable exception. Just as San Francisco is home to the largest Chinese population outside of China, Utah became home to the largest population of Scandinavians outside their homeland by the end of the nineteenth century. These ethnic communities settled in homogeneous blocks, maintaining cultural identity with their homelands.

As a result of Utah's foreign immigration, food patterns in Mormon communities demonstrated a consistent ethnic flavor over generations. In the non-Mormon West immigrants often assimilated into a larger American culture within a generation. In Utah's ethnic communities we see some assimilation into larger Mormon culture. Still, settlers maintained their native languages and ethnic foodways as part of their transplanted cultural identity over three or more generations. These food patterns continue into the present generation, with German-Swiss, Danish, and British food traditions playing out in contemporary Mormon families.

Some elements of pioneer food patterns have changed or disappeared completely as food culture in America evolved. Pioneer chefs worked largely from memory. This survey failed to discover an intact manuscript recipe collection from the pioneer era, primarily because of the Mormon rote tradition. Likewise, the local archival sources consulted failed to yield any published cookery books from Utah's pioneer period. But several sources noted the twentieth-century transcription of recipes that had been passed down orally for three generations.[8] The early Mormon approach using rote memory for preparation avoided exact measurements of ingredients. In contrast, modern Mormon cooks circulate manuscript recipes, publish their own cookbooks, and rely on exact measurements for success. In this regard, modern Mormon cooks have assimilated into mainstream cooking patterns of broader American culture.

The ingredients and tools used by contemporary Mormon chefs also have evolved away from their historical counterparts. Early Mormon settlers utilized whole foods, manual tools, and microbiological processes. Modern Mormon cooks rely on heavily processed prepared foods and power tools in the kitchen. Microbial cultures are rarely employed. The heirloom open pollinated seeds used by Mormon pioneers have been replaced by hybrids and genetically modified crops, if a garden is grown at all. The intimate relationship between farmers and their food has been replaced by a distanced relationship wherein food consumers are removed and isolated from food producers.

Not all elements of Mormon pioneer foodways have disappeared, however. Pioneers leaned heavily on wild-gathered food items, particularly in the early years of settlement. Hunting and fishing played an important role in Mormon foodways then and now. In the 1850s fishing in Utah Lake supplied food for settlers throughout the Utah Territory. Berry picking supplied sweets for the table, and some modern Utah Mormons (as well as non-Mormons and Indians) continue to utilize this resource today. Most Mormons today have never tasted a sego bulb. Through the late twentieth century Utah schools were dismissed for the fall deer hunt. And though many modern Mormons are more socially isolated from their Indian neighbors, Mormon-Indian relations are friendlier today.

Through the course of this study I discovered that one of the most significant elements in defining historic Mormon foodways is food preservation. Settlers lacked the technological aid of refrigeration and the benefits of the modern food-preservation industry. Mormon pioneers carried their own burden of putting food by for the winter. As a result, many of the dishes they prepared using dried and pickled foods came with distinctive flavors and textures that seem foreign to the modern Mormon consumer. Though Mormon pioneers lacked technology and industry, they compensated with a sophisticated skill at using microbial cultures for food preservation. The relative absence of bacteria in modern Mormon foodways marks a swing of 180 degrees away from the foods of our ancestors.

Likewise, the strict contemporary enforcement of prohibitions on coffee, tea, and alcohol is antithetical to the beverage consumption of pioneers. Early Mormons exercised liberty in consuming beer, wine, and spirits as well as milk, cider, soda water, coffee, and various black, green, and herbal teas. Beyond these consumption habits, this flexibility speaks directly to a moderate approach to religious identity, defined more through community association than through personal practice and habit. Contemporary pious Mormons, in contrast, are more socially isolated than their historical counterparts but find more religious identity in following the prohibitions of the Word of Wisdom.

Our stereotypes of pioneer diet have focused on privation. Early settlers certainly experienced hunger due to failed crops, pests, and an unfamiliar climate. Once established in the West, however, Mormon settlers had access to a great variety of exotic food items and delicacies. Out-of-town observers at the Pioneer Day feast of 1849 remarked that a greater abundance and variety of foods would not have been found in Boston. Although locally produced agriculture may have provided a narrow range of traditionally American food items, those foods were often abundant. Moreover, many upper-class and wealthy Mormon pioneers indulged in food delicacies with flair. The sheer girth of men like Heber Kimball and Brigham Young is testimony to the epicurean indulgences allowed in elite pioneer Mormon society.

Through the course of this study I have traced foodways patterns back over the course of generations. These patterns show integrity to the original source, while also manifesting minor adaptations over time. Oral and written transmission continues to keep these traditions alive today. Some appear to be losing ground in the face of mass-produced food, and it is uncertain whether these pioneer traditions will be received by another generation.

In his sweeping epic history titled *Utah: The Right Place* Thomas Alexander presented a version of history that focused on politics and elections, military campaigns, religious power structures, and wealth from industry. Certainly he makes a strong argument in using those well-worn themes. I have taken a different angle here: the story of pioneer Utah can be told in a compelling fashion by using food as our main theme. Descendants of pioneers point to the plowing of a furrow as the first momentous act of pioneers in the Salt Lake Valley. Mormon-Indian relations centered on negotiations for food. Settlers spent the overwhelming bulk of their energies and time in the pursuit of growing and preparing food—not in pursuit of military campaigns or mining claims. European immigrants to Utah clung tenaciously to ethnic food items and consciously passed these on to succeeding generations as a way of preserving identity. Mormons have used food as their primary vehicle for celebration and defining identity for more than 150 years. The story of Utah's Mormon settlers is a story about food.

This food-centered story may be told through citations from pioneer diaries. When we read Isabella Rogers's directions for making hominy, we hear the distant voice of one player in the story. When we move from the words on a page to fingers sifting through an actual bowl of hominy grits, however, the story comes to life in a dramatic fashion. We will never reclaim the past—it is gone. But if we want to understand the past in new and vibrant ways, we might try re-creating some of the dishes presented here.

Bon appétit!

Clabber: a biological process by which enzymes in milk or cream cause it to thicken. Also used to describe a dessert similar to crème fraiche.

Cooper: an artisan who constructs wooden barrels using staves bound together with hoops. Also a verb used to describe that process.

Curing: a preservation process for long-term storage of food. Most often this involves infusing potassium nitrate into meat products.

Dutch oven: a particular type of cooking vessel, usually with three short spiked legs, a flat bottom, and a fitted lid with a rim for holding live coals on the lid. Also called a bake oven, bake kettle, or camp kettle.

Folklore: traditions or practices passed on orally to reinforce membership in a particular group or community, often serving to convey values. In pejorative uses the term often implies an amateurish, nonscholarly approach to historical topics without adequate documentation.

Foodways: the study of food processes and their cultural context, including but not limited to gardening, harvests, butchering, cookery, dining, festivals, and ethnic celebrations.

Foolscap: a printer's paper sometimes used in historical baking, similar to parchment paper in modern baking.

Gill (or jill): a unit of liquid measure equal to one-fourth pint.

Hearth: the stone or brick area near a fire where live coals are used to cook food. In architectural usage it is the masonry area directly outside the firebox of a fireplace. The interior floor of a brick oven is also called a hearth.

Heirloom: seeds that reproduce true to type, kind from kind. In other words, they are not hybrid and not genetically modified. The term also refers to older, less specialized breeds of animals not widely used in modern industrial agriculture.

Hops: a flowering vine indigenous to many areas of North America. The green feathery flowers have astringent properties and a bitter flavor. Hops are used in culturing yeast and in making beer.

Hybrid: a crossing of two varieties of plant or animal, intended to produce vigor in the second generation but usually resulting in sterility.

Isinglass: a pure, transparent form of gelatin, obtained from the air bladders of certain fish, especially the sturgeon. It is used in glue and jellies and as a clarifying agent.

Larding: the practice of inserting slivers of suet, fat, or lard into incisions to keep the meat from becoming dry while cooking.

Lye: a caustic agent, historically obtained by leeching water through hardwood ashes. It is used in some food processes (such as making hominy) to break down fibers.

Must: the juice obtained from grapes or apples intended for fermentation into wine or cider.

Pearlash: a food-grade form of potassium carbonate, used like baking soda to leaven bread. Historically it was obtained from either seaweed or hardwood ashes. Pearlash usually predates other chemical leavens such as artificial saleratus and baking powder.

Pommace: the pulpy fruit crushed to make wine or cider.

Quartern: a less-than-specific measure, dry or liquid, indicating a fourth-part of a larger unit, such as a gallon or pound.

Rennet: traditionally the inner lining of the stomach of a calf, lamb, or goat that has not eaten solid food. The lining contains enzymes that cause milk to set a curd, used in cheese making. In modern practice rennet can be purchased as vegetable-based tablets.

Saleratus: from the Latin *sal aeratus*, meaning aerated salt. The term usually indicates a naturally occurring alkaline or carbonate mineral. Early settlers gathered saleratus for use as a chemical leavening agent in bread.

Saltpeter (or saltpetre): potassium nitrate or potassium nitrite (or both), used in curing hams, bacon, and corned beef.

Scion: a pruning from a tree used to graft onto root stock. This practice perpetuates the original DNA of the first tree. All true Red Delicious apples can be traced through scion prunings back to a single original tree.

Sieve: a flour sifter. Sometimes a specific sieve was used as a measure, though measurements differed from sieve to sieve.

Sourdough: a culture composed of bacteria and wild yeast, regenerated through feedings of flour and water (and sometimes other ingredients such as milk or sugar), used as the leaven for sourdough bread. It is also called start, mother, barm, or *levain* (French).

Spider: a frying pan with legs used for hearth cooking over live coals; also a long-legged trivet with a handle used for the same purpose.

Sweetbreads: usually offal such as brains, heart, or kidneys.

Word of Wisdom: the Mormon dietary commandment found in Doctrine and Covenants (Section 89) that dictates, among other things, abstinence from hot drinks, strong (alcoholic) beverages, and tobacco. Though the text specifically allows mild beverages made from barley (beer) in contrast to strong alcoholic drinks, modern Mormonism prohibits these. Conversely, though the text forbids all hot beverages, modern Mormonism usually proscribes only tea and coffee, allowing hot cocoa and other hot drinks.

Wort: the sweet soup made with a base of malted barley, intended for fermentation to become beer.

Yeast or yeast foam: any of various single-celled organisms associated with the genus *Saccharomyces*. The organism consumes sugars and in turn produces carbon dioxide and alcohol, a process known as fermentation. Traditionally yeast was cultured at home or purchased from bakers or brewers who cultured it as part of their enterprise. Home-cultured yeast was usually heavily adulterated with flour and hops to help perpetuate and feed the culture. Often historical recipes call for a large volume of yeast, allowing for the additional flour contained in the culture beyond the active yeast cells.

NOTES

Preface

1. For one example, see LeRoy R. Hafen, "Utah Food Supplies Sold to the Pioneer Settlers of Colorado."
2. Lorraine Hammond, "Var Sa God." Hammond (a vernacular Mormon chef working from oral tradition over three generations) notes the difference between historical process dishes and those requiring precise formulas for success.
3. Susan Stauffer Cheney, interview. If Ulrich used sweetening on his mush, it was certainly not white sugar. Molasses would have been more common. See the discussion of sweetening in chapter 3.
4. *Catalogue of the Utah Territorial Library.*
5. Kate B. Carter Collection, Pioneer Resource Files.
6. William Montell, *The Saga of Coe Ridge: A Study in Oral History.*
7. See Doctrine and Covenants, Section 89, as an example.
8. Mary Ellen Snodgrass, *Encyclopedia of Kitchen History*, 226.
9. Rae Thorup, Ruth Thorup, and Marne Thorup, "Danish Cooking School Recipes: Grenaa, Denmark, about 1847," describe the process of transcribing their mother's rote formulas.

Chapter 1   From Soup: An Introduction

1. *New West Magazine* (July 1918): 39.
2. Parley P. Pratt, *Autobiography*, 325.
3. Andrew Jackson Allen, "Diary," August 8, 1848.
4. Louisa Barnes Pratt, *The History of Louisa Barnes Pratt: Being the Autobiography of a Mormon Missionary Widow and Pioneer*, 101.
5. Caroline Barnes Crosby, *No Place to Call Home: The 1807–1857 Life Writings of Caroline Barnes Crosby, Chronicler of Outlying Mormon Communities*, 89–90.
6. See Doctrine and Covenants, Section 89 (usually known as the Word of Wisdom), which enumerates Mormonism's dietary prohibitions. Even so, alcohol became part of Mormon celebrations in later years. Orson Huntsman, a settler in southern Utah, commented in his journal: "July 24, 1899. Monday. We celebrate Pioneer Day. But some must get drunk before they can get the spirit of the day and have what they think is a good time, which is hell for the rest of us" (cited in Daughters of Utah Pioneers, *Heart Throbs of the West*, 7:125). More recently the town of Hagerman, Idaho, ceased its Pioneer Day celebration due to drunken non-Mormon celebrants, who outnumbered the Mormons.

7. Pratt, *Autobiography*, 325.
8. William Morley Black, "Journal."
9. *Deseret News*, June 24, 1936, recounts the history of Utah's Old Folk's Day tradition from its beginning.
10. Carol Edison, "The Role of Food at Two Utah Homecoming Celebrations," 138–39.
11. Providence History Committee, *Providence and Her People: A History of Providence, Utah, 1857–1974*, 93–95, 152–53. See also Paige Lewis, "From Germany with Love."
12. Henriette Davidis, *Henriette Davidis' Practical Cook Book Compiled for the United States from the Thirty-fifth German Edition*, 99–100.
13. Providence History Committee, *Providence and Her People*. See also Lewis, "From Germany with Love."
14. Daughters of Utah Pioneers, *Heart Throbs of the West*, 11:375. Cecilia Ence Tobler (b. 1885) was the daughter of Swiss emigrants to Utah's southern wine region.
15. Ken Braegger, interview.
16. Ibid.
17. Daughters of Utah Pioneers, *Heart Throbs of the West*, 11:349.
18. Elizabeth Bott, "Life History of Elizabeth Bott."
19. Daughters of Utah Pioneers, *Heart Throbs of the West*, 11:345.
20. Jay Anderson, interview.
21. Mary Douglass, "Decyphering a Meal," 250.
22. Braegger, interview.

Chapter 2   Setting the Table: Tools and Artifacts

1. Andrew Israelson, *Utah Pioneering*, 22 (Utah State History Archives). Artifacts in the DUP Memorial Museum suggest that this would have been silver plated, stamped from sheet, and in a "fiddle" pattern.
2. Shane A. Baker, *At Rest in Zion: The Archaeology of Salt Lake City's First Pioneer Cemetery*. The archaeological report is thorough in its documentation of artifacts and skeletal remains. The overwhelming majority of cultural artifacts from the excavation date from 1880 to 1920, however, occurring primarily as secondary refuse, and as such are not directly relevant to the current study.
3. Dale L. Berge, "Lower Goshen: Archaeology of a Mormon Pioneer Town."
4. Ibid., 88.
5. Daughters of Utah Pioneers, *Heart Throbs of the West*, 11:337.
6. William Clayton, *William Clayton's Journal: A Daily Record of the Journey of the Original Company of "Mormon" Pioneers from Nauvoo, Illinois, to the Valley of the Great Salt Lake*, 90.
7. "Interviews with Living Pioneers: Copied by the BYU Library, 1939," 42.
8. Sarah Josepha Buell Hale, *The Ladies' New Book of Cookery*, 74–75.
9. Jay Anderson documented a patriarchal rather than matriarchal Dutch oven culture. He theorized that the symbology of Mormon pioneers required oversight by a male priesthood, especially when paired with open fire cooking, similar to the commonly male domain of the barbeque grill. Fife Folklore Conference, Utah State University, Logan, 1992; interview.
10. Patty Bartlett Sessions, *Mormon Midwife: The 1846–1888 Diaries of Patty Bartlett Sessions*, June 16, 1846.
11. Claude Teancum Barnes, *The Grim Years, or, The Life of Emily Stewart Barnes*, 32.
12. Ibid.

13. Elizabeth Dennistoun Wood Kane, *Twelve Mormon Homes Visited in Succession on a Journey through Utah to Arizona*, 118 and 127, respectively.
14. Allen, "Diary," 4 (all odd spellings in the original).
15. "Interviews with Living Pioneers," 18.
16. Vincent Foley, "Salt Lake City Social Hall Summary."
17. Clarissa Wilhelm, "Diary," 5.
18. *Deseret News*, May 28, 1856.
19. *Deseret News*, November 19, 1862.
20. *Deseret News*, June 9, 1869.
21. Lorena Washburn Larsen, *Autobiography of Lorena Washburn Larsen, Printed for Her Children*, 19.
22. "Interviews with Living Pioneers," 18.
23. Sessions, *Mormon Midwife*, August 19, 1854.
24. Barnes, *The Grim Years*, 44.
25. Elizabeth Fries Ellet, *The Practical Housekeeper: A Cyclopaedia of Domestic Economy*, 118.
26. Daughters of Utah Pioneers, *Heart Throbs of the West*, 11:340.
27. *Deseret News*, November 29, 1851.
28. Timothy James Scarlett, "Potting in Zion," 10.
29. Ibid., 253, 291.
30. *Deseret News*, September 6, 1865 (capitalization in the original).
31. Berge, "Lower Goshen," 87. The Blue Willow pattern, with its distinctive Chinese scene of two birds flying over a pagoda and bridge, originated in the eighteenth century in England and is still in production today.
32. Mark Thomas, "Grafts from a Lost Orchard."
33. Braegger, interview.

Chapter 3   Pasture, Garden, Pantry, and Cellar: Ingredients

1. Sessions, *Mormon Midwife*, October 29, 1854.
2. Clayton, *William Clayton's Journal*, July 31, 1847. Apples being heterozygous from seed, the resulting fruit could have been tart, sweet, or even inedible.
3. Mary Ann Stuki Hafen, *Reflections of a Handcart Pioneer of 1860*, 34.
4. Daniel Tyler, *A Concise History of the Mormon Battalion in the Mexican War, 1846–1848*, 318. This all-Mormon muster became the longest march in U.S. military history, beginning at Winter Quarters, Iowa, and continuing to California, before a return to Utah after being dismissed.
5. Utah Cooperative Extension Service, *Old West Heritage Recipes*, 20. Some say that St. Jacob is the patron saint of travelers and pilgrims, which would make this an appropriate name for the soup, given the context.
6. Michael Pollan, *The Botany of Desire*, 51.
7. Wilford Woodruff, *Wilford Woodruff's Journal, 1833–1898*, May 14, 1857.
8. *Deseret News*, December 31, 1856.
9. T. W. Ellerbeck, Great Salt Lake City, in *Deseret News*, April 4, 1862.
10. Craig Allen Lindquist, "Garnet Chili Potatoes."
11. J. E. Johnson, "Seed List."
12. Edward Sayers, 12th Ward, in *Deseret News*, February 19, 1853.
13. Patience Loader Archer, *Recollections of Past Days: The Autobiography of Patience Loader Rozsa Archer*, 102.

14. Woodruff, *Wilford Woodruff's Journal*, May 14, 1857. See also Thomas, "Grafts from a Lost Orchard."
15. Barnes, *The Grim Years*, 21.
16. Ibid., 45.
17. *Deseret News*, August 19, 1851.
18. Kate B. Carter, *The Chase Mill, 1852*, 7.
19. "Interviews with Living Pioneers," 42.
20. Sessions, *Mormon Midwife*, June 12, 1847, and August 7, 1847.
21. Daughters of Utah Pioneers, *Heart Throbs of the West*, 11:367.
22. Henry Ballard, "Journal of Henry Ballard," 36.
23. Woodruff, *Wilford Woodruff's Journal*.
24. Deseret Agricultural and Manufacturing Society, "Report for 1863," 56.
25. Ibid., April 3, 1866.
26. Leonard Arrington, *Great Basin Kingdom: An Economic History of the Latter-Day Saints, 1830–1900*, 120.
27. The notable exception is modern "white" vinegar, which is simply water with food-grade acid added.
28. Barnes, *The Grim Years*, 50.
29. Levi Savage, "Diary," October 1, 1877.
30. Alvin Wood Chase, *Dr. Chase's Recipes, or Information for Everybody*, 33–34.
31. *Journal of Discourses, by Brigham Young, President of the Church of Jesus Christ of Latter-Day Saints, His Two Counselors, the Twelve Apostles, and Others*, 12:211 and 11:142.
32. Sessions, *Mormon Midwife*, September 16, 1846.
33. John D. Lee, *Journals of John D. Lee, 1846–47 and 1859*, 227.
34. Robert G. Stone and David M. Hinkley (The Fat Little Pudding Boys), *The Pudding Book: Authentic American and English Pudding Recipes from 1782–1882 with Instructions for the Modern Kitchen*, 6.

Chapter 4   Four Ounces of Flour: Food on the Trail

1. Diane Wheeler, "Life History of Harriet Amelia Folsom Young." Harriet's anecdotes were recorded by her granddaughters from her oral transmission. The DUP museum also exhibits a sample of quail feathers that Amelia saved from this experience.
2. Wil Bagley, "One Long Funeral March: A Revisionist History of the Mormon Handcart Disasters," 114.
3. *Mormon Pioneer National Historic Trail: Historic Resource Study*.
4. John D. Unruh, *The Plains Across: The Overland Emigrants and the Trans-Mississippi West, 1840–1860*, 408; Lynn Arave, "Some Myths Accompany Stories of Pioneers' Arrival"; Federal Writers' Project, *The Oregon Trail* (New York, 1939), 32, cited in Unruh, *The Plains Across*, 516 n. 74.
5. *Nauvoo Neighbor*, October 29, 1845, cited in William Slaughter and Michael Landon, *Trail of Hope*, 24.
6. Howard L. Eagan, *Pioneering the West*, 24.
7. Caroline Hopkins Clark, "Diary of Caroline Hopkins Clark and Letters to England." For a thoroughly British recipe for "nice potatoe pies," see chapter 8.
8. Many PEF immigrants were limited to "a bundle," while others were allowed up to 50 pounds. Still, I'm a little puzzled by John Bond, a Hodgett company handcarter, who describes his mother bringing the No. 8 Charter Oak cookstove on her handcart: John Bond, "Handcarts West in '56."

9. Peder Madsen, "Journal," June 27, 1857.

10. Stella Jaques Bell, *Life History and Writings of John Jaques*, 142.

11. Andrew Jenson, *Autobiography of Andrew Jenson*, 21. Jenson went on to become historian of the LDS Church.

12. Arrington, *Great Basin Kingdom*, 105.

13. *Millennial Star* (Liverpool, England), 18 (1856), 811–12.

14. Diary of Twiss Bermingham," cited in LeRoy R. Hafen, *Handcarts to Zion*, 74–75.

15. Bell, *Life History and Writings of John Jaques*, 142.

16. John Fairbanks, "Diary," 35.

17. Woodruff, *Wilford Woodruff's Journal*, June 8, 1847.

18. Bell, *Life History and Writings of John Jaques*, 134.

19. Eliza Leslie, *Directions for Cookery, in Its Various Branches*, 300.

20. Lorenzo Young, "Diary of Lorenzo Dow Young," 141.

21. Archer, *Recollections of Past Days*, 73.

22. Annie Taylor Dee, *Memories of a Pioneer*, 17. "Freshened" refers to cows that have started giving milk after calving.

23. Hale, *The Ladies' New Book of Cookery*, 83.

24. "Willie Company Journal," October 14, 1857, cited in Paul D. Lyman, *The Willie Handcart Company*, 143.

25. Clark, "Diary of Caroline Hopkins Clark and Letters to England."

26. Ibid., 6.

27. Angelina Maria Collins, *The Great Western Cookbook, or Table Receipts, Adapted to Western Housewifery*, 59.

28. Eliza Maria Partridge Lyman, *Eliza Maria Partridge Journal*, May 13, 1846.

29. Ellet, *The Practical Housekeeper*, 470. Ellet's "pint of yeast" was not a pure article but rather fresh yeast adulterated in a starchy medium like mashed potatoes to extend its life. See chapter 5 for more information on yeast cultures.

30. Jacqueline Williams, *Wagon Wheel Kitchens: Food on the Oregon Trail*, 5–8.

31. Pratt, *The History of Louisa Barnes Pratt*, 80.

32. Hale, *The Ladies' New Book of Cookery*, 374–75 (emphasis in the original).

33. Jenson, *Autobiography of Andrew Jenson*, 16.

34. *Deseret News*, March 20, 1852.

35. *Told by the Pioneers*, 72.

36. Anna Jewel Rowley, "Life History."

37. Alice Strong, "Autobiographical Sketch" in Josiah Rogerson Papers, fd. 2, LDS Archives; Archer, *Recollections of Past Days*, 73.

38. Elijah Nicholas Wilson, *Among the Shoshones*, 13.

39. Courtesy Kate B. Carter Collection, International Society of Daughters of Utah Pioneers, Salt Lake City, Utah.

40. Utah Cooperative Extension Service, *Old West Heritage Recipes*, 15.

41. Bond, "Handcarts West in '56," 23.

42. J. M. Sanderson, *The Complete Cook*, 153.

43. Hale, *The Ladies' New Book of Cookery*, 303.

44. Lyman, *Eliza Maria Partridge Journal*, April 17, 1846.

45. Clark, "Diary of Caroline Hopkins Clark and Letters to England," 6.

46. Hale, *The Ladies' New Book of Cookery*, 276.

47. Bell, *Life History and Writings of John Jaques*, 141.

48. Hans Jensen Hals, "Life Writings of Hans Jensen Hals," 7.

49. Sessions, *Mormon Midwife*, May 11, 1847.

50. Barnes, *The Grim Years*, 16.
51. See chapter 6 for another historical description of making jerky.
52. John Chislett, "Narrative," October 23, 1857, cited in Loleta Dixon, "Life History of William James."
53. Hale, *The Ladies' New Book of Cookery*, 186. "Larding" refers to a process of stuffing slivers of fat into the meat so that the lard will keep the meat moist as it cooks.
54. Bell, *Life History and Writings of John Jaques*, 147; Sydney Alvarus Hanks and Ephraim K. Hanks, *Scouting for the Mormons on the Great Frontier*.
55. Lewis H. Garrard, *Wah-To-Yah and the Taos Trail*, 28–29.
56. Allen, "Diary," October 11, 1857, 13.
57. Daniel Webster Jones, *Forty Years among the Indians*, 81–82.
58. Ibid., 91–92.
59. Ibid., 93.
60. Archer, *Recollections of Past Days*, 79.

Chapter 5   The Staff of Life: Bread and Leaven

1. Lori F. Tigner-Wise, "Skeletal Analysis of a Mormon Pioneer Population from Salt Lake Valley, Utah," 1, 5.
2. Ibid., 88–90.
3. For a thorough discussion of the demographics of territorial Utah, see Wayne L. Wahlquist, "Settlement Processes in the Mormon Core Area, 1847–1890."
4. "Journal History of the Church of Jesus Christ of Latter Day Saints," September 30, 1848, Salt Lake City: LDS Archives. Also see Arringon, *Great Basin Kingdom*, 49–51. Surprisingly, the Deseret Manufacturing and Agricultural Society recorded very little information about what was grown.
5. Williams, *Wagon Wheel Kitchens*, 11–12. See chapter 4 for a discussion of saleratus.
6. Hubert Howe Bancroft, *The Works of Hubert Howe Bancroft: vol. 26: History of Utah*, 437. Even so, it seems preposterous to believe that housewives in the eastern states understood how to culture yeast but that this understanding failed to make the trek to Utah with Mormon pioneers. Because Utah cooks demonstrated their ability to culture yeast shortly after arriving in Utah, it would seem that Bancroft's assertions may be partly in error.
7. Livy Olsen, "Reminiscences," 4.
8. Barnes, *The Grim Years*, 24.
9. Collins, *The Great Western Cookbook*, 55.
10. *Deseret News*, February 19, 1853, and November 2, 1859.
11. James Bryant Conant, *Pasteur's and Tyndall's Study of Spontaneous Generation*, 26.
12. Hale, *The Ladies' New Book of Cookery*, 404–5 (emphasis in the original).
13. Collins, *The Great Western Cookbook*, 56. The purpose of hops in the recipe is to serve as an antibacterial agent, protecting the culture against contaminants. The modern *Deseret Recipes* contains very similar directions for maintaining a live yeast culture, though omitting hops.
14. *Deseret News*, November 30, 1854.
15. Daughters of Utah Pioneers, *Heart Throbs of the West*, 11:340.
16. Floss Cate and Nellie Child, "History of Bread Making." Kate B. Carter Collection, Salt Lake: DUP Archives. Other early Mormon yeast keepers include Sarah Johnson Carter and Mary McDonald Rider.
17. *Deseret News*, February 19, 1853, and April 18, 1860.

18. Daughters of Utah Pioneers, *Heart Throbs of the West*, 11:343.
19. Esther Howland, *The New England Economical Housekeeper, and Family Receipt Book*, 19. The inclusion of salt is counterintuitive. Salt kills all manner of bacteria, including yeast.
20. Daniel Leader and Judith Blahnik, *Bread Alone: Bold Fresh Loaves from Your Own Hands*, 119. This book is a good beginner's source for learning to bake traditional bread from the hearth.
21. For a complete and authoritative discussion of sourdough basics, see Ed Wood, *Classic Sourdoughs: A Home Baker's Handbook*.
22. http://findarticles.com/p/articles/mi_m0EIN/is_1999_August_26/ai_55565713/.
23. Mary Lois Walker Morris, *Before the Manifesto: The Life Writings of Mary Lois Walker Morris*, 103.
24. Sanderson, *The Complete Cook*, 132.
25. Donald Duke, "Sourdough: Yeast of the American West." Lydia is possibly the wife of Francis Titus, 1835–1917.
26. *Kitchen Treasures, 1830–1980: Roy 13th Ward Sesquicentennial* (pages not numbered).
27. *Deseret News*, September 7, 1864.
28. Ellet, *The Practical Housekeeper*, 465.
29. Clark, "Diary of Caroline Hopkins Clark and Letters to England," 6.
30. By telegraph from Raleigh, North Carolina, in *Deseret News*, February 6, 1856. This volume of yeast is not pure fresh baker's yeast; "well risen" indicates home-cultured yeast that contains a large amount of flour to feed the culture. A much smaller volume of dry active yeast would suffice.
31. Sanderson, *The Complete Cook*, 158.
32. *Pioneer Recipes*, 159.
33. Jenson, *Autobiography of Andrew Jenson*, 16.
34. Eleanor Parkinson, *The Complete Confectioner, Pastry-Cook, and Baker*, 150.
35. From the *Germantown Telegraph*, in *Deseret News*, January 19, 1859.

Chapter 6   Berries, Bulbs, and Beasts: Wild-Gathered Food

1. Barnes, *The Grim Years*, 73.
2. Hubert Howe Bancroft, *History of California*, 7 vols. (San Francisco, 1886–90), 6:56.
3. Newman Buckley, "Diary," 78. Sego lily: *Calochortus nuttallii*; stinging nettle: *Urtica dioica*.
4. "George Washington Brown—Frontiersman," 496.
5. For a thorough discussion of Brigham Young's policies on Mormon/Indian relations, see Howard Christy, "Open Hand and Mailed Fist: Mormon-Indian Relations in Utah, 1847–1852," *Utah Historical Quarterly* 46:3 (1978): 216–35. Christy describes a rapid transition in policies: from isolationist, to fair dealing, to preemptive violence, to extermination, to cultural assimilation. See also Floyd A. O'Neil and Stanford J. Layton, "Of Pride and Politics: Brigham Young as Indian Superintendent," in the same issue. In spite of his explicit extermination order in 1850, Brigham later stated: "I have uniformly pursued a friendly course toward them, feeling convinced that independent of the question of exercising humanity towards so degraded and ignorant a race of people, it was manifestly more economical and less expensive, to feed and clothe, than fight them"; cited in B. H. Roberts, *A Comprehensive History of the Church of Jesus Christ of Latter-Day Saints*, 6 vols. (Salt Lake City: Deseret News Press, 1930), 4:51.
6. Heber Robert McBride, "Autobiography," 17.
7. Allen, "Diary," 4. Wild onion: *Allium*.
8. Barnes, *The Grim Years*, 53. Pigweed: *Amaranthus retroflexus*.

9. Hafen, *Reflections of a Handcart Pioneer of 1860*, 34. Lamb's quarter: *Chenopodium album*. Of pigweed, John Hyrum Barton (1868–1944) said, "We considered pigweed greens a des[s]ert."

10. Mary O. White, "A History of William and Ann Greenwood by Their Daughter Mary O. White," 4. Though I found no berry by this colloquial name, one possibility is the serviceberry: *Amelanchier alnifolia*.

11. Priddy Meeks, *Journal of Priddy Meeks*, 17.

12. Ibid., 18–19.

13. Catherine Ellen Camp Greer, "Reminiscences" (no pagination).

14. Sanderson, *The Complete Cook*, 273.

15. Allen, "Diary," 4 (misspellings in the original).

16. Anson Call, "Journal," 37.

17. John Treat Irving Jr., *Indian Sketches*, 197.

18. Garrard, *Wah-To-Yah and the Taos Trail*, 95.

19. "Digger" as a cultural identifier was often used in a pejorative sense. Anglo-American culture allowed romantic affinity for the "noble savage" who rode a horse and hunted megafauna. But gatherers (as well as agrarians) who subsisted by digging for roots received Anglo disdain. See Catherine S. Fowler and Don D. Fowler, "Notes on the History of Southern Paiutes and Western Shoshonis," *Utah Historical Quarterly* 39 (1971): 96–113. Many of our cultural values are rooted in our perceptions of food.

20. Larsen, *Autobiography of Lorena Washburn Larsen*, 16.

21. Barnes, *The Grim Years*, 43.

22. Aroet L. Hale, "Diary [Autobiography] of Aroet L. Hale," 20.

23. Barnes, *The Grim Years*, 73.

24. Daughters of Utah Pioneers, *Heart Throbs of the West*, 11:337.

25. Olsen, "Reminiscences," 6.

26. "Three Important Manuscripts," 279, 303–6.

27. Sanderson, *The Complete Cook*, 82.

28. Woodruff, *Wilford Woodruff's Journal*, April 4, 1851.

29. For a thorough social history of Utah Lake, see D. Robert Carter's thesis, "A History of Commercial Fishing on Utah Lake" (Provo: Brigham Young University, 1969).

30. Peter Madsen, "The Grasshopper Famine—The Mullet and the Trout, Part I," 516–21.

31. Barnes, *The Grim Years*, 69.

32. Cecil Alter, "The Utah War Journal of Albert Tracy, 1858–1860," 28.

33. Kane, *Twelve Mormon Homes Visited in Succession*, 9.

34. *Salt Lake Tribune*, June 17, 1923.

35. Eliza Leslie, *The Lady's Receipt Book*, 23–24.

36. Woodruff, *Wilford Woodruff's Journal*, May 27, 1851.

37. Catharine Esther Beecher, *Miss Beecher's Domestic Receipt Book: Designed as a Supplement to Her Treatise on Domestic Economy*, 62.

38. Woodruff, *Wilford Woodruff's Journal*, September 16, 1867.

39. Ibid., May 12, 1859, and May 19, 1859.

40. Beecher, *Miss Beecher's Domestic Receipt Book*, 47.

41. Allen, "Diary," 16.

42. Collins, *The Great Western Cookbook*, 70.

43. Woodruff, *Wilford Woodruff's Journal*, December 11, 1867.

44. Collins, *The Great Western Cookbook*, 76.

45. Richard F. Burton, *City of the Saints*, 256.

Chapter 7   Put By for Winter: Preserved Foods

1. Larsen, *Autobiography of Lorena Washburn Larsen*, 15.
2. Ibid., 10. Brigham Young's daughter Clarissa also remembered a separate cellar in the garden for potatoes and hard cider. See chapter 9.
3. Conant, *Pasteur's and Tyndall's Study of Spontaneous Generation*, 26.
4. Sessions, *Mormon Midwife*, September 16, 1846.
5. "Interviews with Living Pioneers," 43 (Alice Langston Dalton, born February 5, 1865).
6. Daughters of Utah Pioneers, *Heart Throbs of the West*, 11:356.
7. Archer, *Recollections of Past Days*, 147.
8. Larsen, *Autobiography of Lorena Washburn Larsen*, 15.
9. "Interviews with Living Pioneers," 42.
10. Arrington, *Great Basin Kingdom*, 204–5.
11. Larsen, *Autobiography of Lorena Washburn Larsen*, 15.
12. "Interviews with Living Pioneers," 22.
13. Daughters of Utah Pioneers, *Heart Throbs of the West*, 11:338.
14. Ibid., 11:366. See chapter 10 for a roly-poly recipe. Hattie Thornton Snow (1875–1963) was the daughter of Mary Whittaker Thornton, an English immigrant to southern Utah. The boiled molasses approach combined with the roly-poly pudding reference suggests a mid-nineteenth century approach to preserves.
15. Clarissa Young Spencer, *Brigham Young at Home*, 59. Clarissa likely remembers sugar because she was living in the Brigham Young home. Other Mormon homes would have used molasses more commonly, as indicated here.
16. Barnes, *The Grim Years*, 32.
17. Leslie, *Directions for Cookery*, 288.
18. Larsen, *Autobiography of Lorena Washburn Larsen*, 14.
19. J. M. Tanner, "Biographical Sketch of James Jensen," 49.
20. Beecher, *Miss Beecher's Domestic Receipt Book*, 161.
21. *Deseret News*, December 13, 1851.
22. Edith Madsen Powell, "History of Bishop Peter Madsen."
23. George W. Brimhall, *The Workers of Utah*, 30. Brimhall describes salting fish on the shores of Utah Lake in 1856. See chapter 6 for more detail on this episode in history.
24. Elizabeth Baxter, "Personal History," 3.
25. Hale, *The Ladies' New Book of Cookery*, 36.
26. Lemuel Redd (1836–1910) settled initially in Spanish Fork, Utah, but then relocated to a farm in New Harmony, formerly the home of John D. Lee, in about 1862. These butchering recollections come from the New Harmony farm, though probably in the 1870s.
27. Daughters of Utah Pioneers, *Heart Throbs of the West*, 11:348. This citation also makes reference to the use of saltpeter but misrepresents its application.
28. Ibid., 11:347 (from Luella McAllister).
29. Eliza Brockbank Hales, "Reminiscences of a Pioneer Childhood."
30. Daughters of Utah Pioneers, *Heart Throbs of the West*, 11:348. Harriet Robinson Jones was the daughter of Mary Taylor, an English convert and member of the 1857 Martin handcart company. Harriet likewise married a second-generation son of English converts, demonstrating the English cultural traditions that were perpetuated over generations.
31. Mette Johanna Andersen (1834–96) was born in Saal, Denmark. She married Ole Madsen in 1863, and they settled in the Sanpete Valley with other Danish immigrants.
32. Daughters of Utah Pioneers, *Heart Throbs of the West*, 11:314.

33. Ibid., 11:348.

34. *An Enduring Legacy*, 12:267.

35. Daughters of Utah Pioneers, *Heart Throbs of the West*, 11:338. Leah's mother was Rachel Elizabeth Pyne (1870–1933), an immigrant from Norfolk, England, who settled in Provo, Utah. Though she postdates our era, her foodway approaches hold fast to pioneer-era processes of cellaring, salting, and simple chemical treatments. This approach to pickles is strongly reminiscent of sauerkraut preparation and fermentation.

36. Beecher, *Miss Beecher's Domestic Receipt Book*, 154. Brandied peaches were likely used to prepare the peach sauce served to Brigham Young on the Wyoming plains in the fall of 1847.

37. Savage, "Diary," October 1, 1877.

38. Barnes, *The Grim Years*, 50. See also the discussion of vinegar in chapter 3.

39. In fact, Gustava Lundstrom Capson (1836–1914) and her husband, Nils, were Swedish. Cornelia's paternal lines and her husband's lines are all Danish, however. We selectively shape our cultural affiliations.

40. Daughters of Utah Pioneers, *Heart Throbs of the West*, 11:371. The use of sealed bottles indicates a later period than when Gustava first immigrated to Utah. Still, the process would work well in a sealed keg or even a crock.

41. John Lindquist, "Sauerkraut Fermentation."

42. Kate B. Carter Collection, Salt Lake City: DUP Library. Mary was an immigrant from Strausberg, Germany, and married into a German family from Pennsylvania and Ohio.

43. A "freshened" cow is one that has recently had a calf and is being actively milked. Cows, like other mammals, produce milk only to feed their young. The cow will eventually go dry when the calf is weaned. Emily's neighbors likely coordinated the breeding and freshening of their cows, allowing them to share excess milk and cheese-making tools communally.

44. Barnes, *The Grim Years*, 44.

45. Ibid.

Chapter 8   Brit, Dane, and Swiss: Immigrant Food

1. Hans Christensen, "Memoirs." Also cited in William Mulder, *Homeward to Zion: The Mormon Migration from Scandinavia*, 205. Mulder's work remains the definitive text regarding Scandinavian immigration and settlement in Utah.

2. For a thorough survey of Utah pioneer settlement patterns, including demographics of origin, see Wayne L. Wahlquist, "Settlement Processes in the Mormon Core Area, 1847–1890." See also Douglas D. Alder, "The German-speaking Immigration to Utah, 1850–1950" (M.A. thesis, University of Utah, 1959).

3. Wahlquist, "Settlement Processes in the Mormon Core Area," 113, 118.

4. Ibid., 131.

5. U.S. Eighth Census, Schedule I, "Free Inhabitants in 2nd Ward Great Salt Lake City in the County of Salt Lake, Territory of Utah," 125–30; cited in Mulder, *Homeward to Zion*, 340 n. 18.

6. Charles L. Walker, "Journal," October 20, 1859, and October 21, 1860.

7. *Der Darsteller* 1 (October 1856): 71; cited in Alder, "The German-Speaking Immigration to Utah," 49.

8. William Ajax, "Journal," October 5, 1862.

9. Mount Pleasant Pioneer Relic Home Blog: http://mtpleasantpioneer.blogspot.com, July 12, 2009.

10. "Life History of Ole Poulson," 8; and Mulder, *Homeward to Zion*, 257.

11. Mulder, *Homeward to Zion*, 257.

12. Daughters of Utah Pioneers, *Heart Throbs of the West*, 2:313.

13. *Deseret News*, March 20, 1852.

14. Daughters of Utah Pioneers, *Heart Throbs of the West*, 11:337.

15. See Pearl Wannacott, "Life History of Annie Underwood"; and Elizabeth Bott, "Life History of Elizabeth Bott."

16. See "Family History Journal of John S. Stucki, Handcart Pioneer of 1860," cited in Douglas D. Alder and Karl F. Brooks, *A History of Washington County*, 157. Stucki notes that his family was sent to the Swiss Colony in southern Utah for the purpose of making wine for the LDS sacrament.

17. Ibid. The "paddle" she references is a long-handled baker's peel with a broad, flat surface. Bakers use it to insert loaves into the depths of the hot oven.

18. Daughters of Utah Pioneers, *Heart Throbs of the West*, 11:375 (from her mother, Lena Knecht Ence, 1842–1917). Both the Tobler and Ence families come from a Swiss background with the early immigration and settlement of Santa Clara as a wine-making region. Cecilia may not have known that her grandmother would have called this dish *Zwiebelkuchen*. Note that Rosina Beacham called it a "cake," which correlates with the German *Kuchen*.

19. Anders Thomsen, "History of Anders Thomsen, by Himself," 3.

20. Tanner, *Biographical Sketch of James Jensen*, 49.

21. Cited in Mulder, *Homeward to Zion*, 201.

22. Daughters of Utah Pioneers, *Heart Throbs of the West*, 11:373.

23. Ibid., 11:337.

24. Ibid.

25. Thorup, Thorup, and Thorup, "Danish Cooking School Recipes."

26. Author's collection. The original recipe is for volumes three times greater than given here; they are usually served for a large group, as a demonstration of heritage.

27. Adapted from Ken Braegger. Special thanks for permission to reprint this recipe.

28. "Three Important Manuscripts," 279. Maren Kirstine Nielsen also mentions "black pot mush which was a mixture of flour, salt and water" (303).

29. Ibid., 303–6.

30. Thorup, Thorup, and Thorup, "Danish Cooking School Recipes."

31. Hammond, "Var Sa God."

32. Thorup, Thorup, and Thorup, "Danish Cooking School Recipes" (no page). Possible greens include parsley, green onions, celery, beet greens, shredded spinach, chard, young grape leaves, fresh sage, rosemary, and other herbs.

33. Ibid. An identical recipe comes through Metta Hansen Peterson circa 1860 (author's collection).

34. Daughters of Utah Pioneers, *Heart Throbs of the West*, 11:351. Sarah Elizabeth Caroline Scott married Matthew McCune, a surgeon and commissioned officer in the British royal army, in 1835. Shortly after their marriage, Dr. McCune was stationed near Calcutta, India. There they joined the Mormon Church. They immigrated to Utah in the 1850s as British colonial rule began to destabilize. For more exotic recipes from Caroline's time in India, see chapter 9.

35. Hammond, "Var Sa God," 51.

36. Twelfth Census of the United States, 1900, "Schedule no. 1, Population," Santa Clara Precinct, Washington County, Utah.

37. Daughters of Utah Pioneers, *Heart Throbs of the West*, 11:375. Sadly, little other information about Cecilia is publicly available. In this regard she is quite representative of thousands of Mormon pioneer women whose lives are largely lost to history.

38. Mulder, *Homeward to Zion*, 214.

Chapter 9   Uncommon Fare: Notable and Exotic Meals

1. Andrew Jenson, *The Building of Utah and Her Neighbors*.
2. Sanderson, *The Complete Cook*, 82 (emphasis in the original).
3. Selected pages from the minutes of the Deseret Agricultural and Manufacturing Society reveal some of the international trade to Utah. A note for April 3, 1864, records agricultural specimens received from Japan: "Extra sized chesnuts [*sic*]: Beans: Peas: squash: curious nuts: Highland Rice: Chesnuts" (Salt Lake City: TITP Archives).
4. This refers to glass windows set in frames over wooden boxes to make a miniature greenhouse. If the boxes contained just soil, they would be called "cold frames"; if they contained composted manure mixed with soil, the box could generate temperatures in excess of 120°F even in winter and would be called "hot frames."
5. Spencer, *Brigham Young at Home*, 17.
6. Ibid., 49.
7. Ibid., 59–60.
8. Leslie, *Directions for Cookery*, 396.
9. Spencer, *Brigham Young at Home*, 17.
10. "Brigham Young's Doughnuts," *Ensign* (Salt Lake City: LDS Church), February 1976, 62 (via Emily's granddaughter Naomi Young Schettler). This seems to be the earliest and most direct incarnation of this recipe.
11. Spencer, *Brigham Young at Home*, 54.
12. Sanderson, *The Complete Cook*, 83.
13. Daughters of Utah Pioneers, *Heart Throbs of the West*, 11:351–52. While the published *Heart Throbs* citation attributes the recipe to Mary Smart, the drafts in the DUP Archives show Mary Smart's attribution to her grandmother, Harriet Thorn. Such attributions confirm the transgenerational transfer of foodways. See chapter 7 for directions on reconstituting salt cod, which is still available at the grocery store today.
14. Orson F. Whitney, *History of Utah*, 1:359.
15. Howland, *The New England Economical Housekeeper*, 63.
16. Ann Allen, *The Housekeeper's Assistant, Composed upon Temperance Principles*, 15.
17. Kane, *Twelve Mormon Homes Visited in Succession*, 9 (emphasis in the original). Kane's note about pies drawn from the oven after grace makes satiric reference to an earlier observation that covers were removed from dishes before saying grace to allow the food to be exposed to the prayer. In like manner, some Mormons today humorously open their mouths during the saying of grace if they have begun eating prematurely.
18. Daughters of Utah Pioneers, *Heart Throbs of the West*, 11:373. The recipe itself appears to have been modernized somewhat. "1 pkg. raisins" would have been "a pound" in the original. Likewise, the cup of sugar would have been molasses in common homes. No doubt a feast for Brigham would use white sugar if it was available. See chapter 10 for a more traditional English plum pudding.
19. Beecher, *Miss Beecher's Domestic Receipt Book*, 129.
20. Kane, *Twelve Mormon Homes Visited in Succession*, 127.
21. Woodruff, *Wilford Woodruff's Journal*, September 13, 1857.

22. Ibid., September 11, 1859.
23. Ibid., May 4, 1857, and May 10, 1859.
24. Ibid., January 1, 1866.
25. Brigham Young, *Diary of Brigham Young, 1857*, 15. Brigham discusses his financial backing for the business. The Globe was one of the earliest upscale restaurants in the city and flourished through the pioneer era.
26. Spencer, *Brigham Young at Home*, 52.
27. Daughters of Utah Pioneers, *Heart Throbs of the West*, 11:363.
28. Woodruff, *Wilford Woodruff's Journal*, January 6, 1857.
29. *Deseret News*, February 12, 1868. Also see January 22, 1868, "Home Items," 3.
30. Sam'l P. Arnold, *Eating Up the Santa Fe Trail*, 8.
31. Allen, *The Housekeeper's Assistant*, 131.
32. Woodruff, *Wilford Woodruff's Journal*, December 25, 1840.
33. Archer, *Recollections of Past Days*, 93–94.
34. See chapters 3 and 10 for more detail on molasses as a sweetener in Utah.
35. Woodruff, *Wilford Woodruff's Journal*, February 25, 1859.
36. Collins, *The Great Western Cookbook*, 119–20. Such fruity and richly spiced cakes seem to be typical for nineteenth-century wedding cakes.
37. Burton, *City of the Saints*, 232.
38. Leslie, *The Lady's Receipt Book*, 149.
39. Daughters of Utah Pioneers, *Heart Throbs of the West*, 11:367. See chapter 3 for Mrs. Rogers's instruction on making hominy.
40. Sarah Elizabeth Caroline Scott McCune, "Life History."
41. Ibid.
42. *Pioneer Recipes*, 33.
43. Ibid., 333. Though the basic recipe certainly hails from the McCunes' time in India, the process of using sealed bottles marks a later date.
44. Spencer, *Brigham Young at Home*, 34.

Chapter 10   The Complete Confectioner: Sweets and Treats

1. Larsen, *Autobiography of Lorena Washburn Larsen*, 16.
2. Woodruff, *Wilford Woodruff's Journal*, November 14, 1857.
3. Hales, "Reminiscences of a Pioneer Childhood."
4. "Interviews with Living Pioneers," 22.
5. Collins, *The Great Western Cookbook*, 128.
6. Arrington, *Great Basin Kingdom*, 120.
7. Leslie, *The Lady's Receipt Book*, 193–94 (emphasis in the original). The DUP Memorial Museum in Salt Lake City exhibits an egg-beating artifact like the one Leslie describes, made of twigs.
8. Barnes, *The Grim Years*, 32.
9. Daughters of Utah Pioneers, *Heart Throbs of the West*, 11:357. The Pack home served as the precursor to what would become the University of Utah, and Ruth hosted numerous social occasions. Use one cup of brewed coffee, *not* one cup of coffee grounds.
10. Spencer, *Brigham Young at Home*, 59.
11. Leslie, *The Lady's Receipt Book*, 198 (emphasis in the original).
12. Daughters of Utah Pioneers, *Heart Throbs of the West*, 11:358. Although Christiana Thompson grew up eating the pioneer dishes described here, this recipe likely debuted

in the 1870s. The use of baking powder and cake tins indicates a later era, working on a cookstove. Even so, this recipe is likely a "modernized" version of one that her mother prepared using stiffly beaten eggs as leaven.

13. Charles Dickens, *A Christmas Carol* (New York: Scholastic, 1999), 69.
14. For a thorough overview of historical puddings, see Stone and Hinkley, *The Pudding Book*, 6.
15. Daughters of Utah Pioneers, *Heart Throbs of the West*, 11:361.
16. Kane, *Twelve Mormon Homes Visited in Succession*, 9.
17. Nathan Hale Gardner, *Alma Helaman Hale: History and Genealogy*, 90.
18. Pottawatamie plum is an indigenous wild plum frequently referenced by early settlers.
19. Daughters of Utah Pioneers, *Heart Throbs of the West*, 11:361. See also a peach filling made with molasses in chapter 7.
20. Ibid., 11:360.
21. Ibid., 11:362.
22. Ibid., 11:376.
23. Sessions, *Mormon Midwife*, September 26, 1846.
24. Daughters of Utah Pioneers, *Heart Throbs of the West*, 11:359.
25. Ibid., 11:337.

Chapter 11   Wetting the Whistle: Beverages Hot and Cold

1. *Deseret News*, May 14, 1856 (capitalization in the original).
2. Chase, *Dr. Chase's Recipes*, 56–57 (capitalization and emphasis in the original).
3. Bond, "Handcarts West in '56," 23.
4. Beecher, *Miss Beecher's Domestic Receipt Book*, 292.
5. Crosby, *No Place to Call Home*, 83.
6. Jones, *Forty Years among the Indians*, 91–92.
7. Johnson, "Seed List."
8. Captain James Cook had already established the value of fruits and vegetables in warding off scurvy and promoting a healthy diet. Patty Sessions made a note in her diary each year to record her first consumption of fresh vegetables after winter's end.
9. *Deseret News*, November 29, 1855.
10. Collins, *The Great Western Cookbook*, 142.
11. Mrs. Beeton, *Beeton's Book of Household Management*, 876.
12. Collins, *The Great Western Cookbook*, 142.
13. Osborne Russell, *Journal of a Trapper*, 114.
14. Hafen, *Handcarts to Zion*, 59.
15. *Deseret News*, December 13, 1851, and August 17, 1859.
16. John Griffiths, *Tea: The Drink That Changed the World* (London: Andre Deutsch, 2007), 50.
17. Ibid., 33.
18. Ibid., 252.
19. Spencer, *Brigham Young at Home*, 78. The hemlock noted here is not the kind that killed Socrates but a kinder herbal commonly used even today.
20. Thompsonian medicine, a school of quackery favored by early LDS Church leaders, emphasized vomiting and purging through the use of lobelia's toxic qualities, paired with steam baths known as hydrotherapy.
21. Meeks, *Journal of Priddy Meeks*, 69.
22. Kane, *Twelve Mormon Homes Visited in Succession*, 73.
23. Ibid., 30.
24. Barnes, *The Grim Years*, 16.

25. Hafen, *Reflections of a Handcart Pioneer of 1860*, 20.
26. Crosby, *No Place to Call Home*, 81.
27. Israelson, *Utah Pioneering*, 22.
28. Leslie, *Directions for Cookery*, 446.
29. Kane, *Twelve Mormon Homes Visited in Succession*, 9.
30. Dennis Lancaster, "Dixie Wine," 72, referencing the pioneer home of Thomas Cottam.
31. Ruth Page Rogers, "Diary of Ruth Page Rogers," 22.
32. Thomas Alexander, *Utah: The Right Place*, 258–59, discusses opposition to the 18th Amendment prohibiting alcohol by LDS Church president Joseph F. Smith.
33. Woodruff, *Wilford Woodruff's Journal*, October 7, 1846.
34. Del Vance, *Beer in the Beehive: A History of Brewing in Utah*.
35. Jules Remy and Julius Brenchley, *A Journey to Great-Salt-Lake-City*, 2:269.
36. Alter, "The Utah War Journal of Albert Tracy," 41–42; Burton, *City of the Saints*, 170; and Arrington, *Great Basin Kingdom*. 208.
37. *Deseret News*, August 17, 1859. *Deseret News*, April 18, 1860, also notes that Day's Beer was sold at the Globe Saloon.
38. *Deseret News,* April 18, 1860 (capitalization in the original).
39. Daughters of Utah Pioneers, *Heart Throbs of the West*, 2:311.
40. Meeks, *Journal of Priddy Meeks*, 11.
41. Hale, *The Ladies' New Book of Cookery*, 407–8.
42. *Farmer's Oracle*, August 14, 1863.
43. "History of Brigham Young," 440–41.
44. Lancaster, "Dixie Wine," 31–33.
45. Ibid., 59.
46. Ibid., 53–54.
47. Reed Farnsworth, M.D., "Wine Making in Southern Utah" (unpublished manuscript), cited in ibid., 99.
48. Hale, *The Ladies' New Book of Cookery*, 405 (emphasis in the original).
49. *Deseret News*, October 1, 1862.
50. Ivan Barrett, *History of the Cotton Mission and Cotton Culture in Utah*, 117; cited in Lancaster, "Dixie Wine," 30.
51. Farnsworth, "Wine Making in Southern Utah"; cited in Lancaster, "Dixie Wine," 81.
52. Lancaster, "Dixie Wine," 74.

Chapter 12   To Nuts: A Conclusion

1. "Three Important Manuscripts," 279; Hales, "Reminiscences of a Pioneer Childhood."
2. Hafen, "Utah Food Supplies Sold to the Pioneer Settlers of Colorado," 446; *Rocky Mountain News* (Denver), October 5, 1860.
3. Betty M. Madsen and Brigham D. Madsen, *North to Montana: Jehus, Bullwhackers and Mule Skinners on the Montana Trail*.
4. Dale Morgan, *The Great Salt Lake*, 202.
5. Lancaster, "Dixie Wine," 86.
6. Barbara Lee Hargis, "A Folk History of the Manti Temple: A Study of the Folklore and Traditions Connected with the Settlement of Manti, Utah, and the Building of the Temple," 25.
7. Wahlquist, "Settlement Processes in the Mormon Core Area," 117.
8. See Hammond, "Var Sa God"; and Thorup, Thorup, and Thorup, "Danish Cooking School Recipes."

WORKS CITED

Alder, Douglas D. "The German-speaking Immigration to Utah, 1850–1950." MA thesis, University of Utah, 1959.
Alder, Douglas D., and Karl F. Brooks. *A History of Washington County*. Salt Lake City: Utah State Historical Society, 1996.
Ajax, William. "Journal." MS 4401 (microfilm). Salt Lake City: LDS Church History Archives.
Alexander, Thomas. *Utah: The Right Place*. Salt Lake City: Gibbs Smith, 2003.
Allen, Andrew Jackson. "Diary." Logan: Utah State University Special Collections.
Allen, Ann. *The Housekeeper's Assistant, Composed upon Temperance Principles*. Boston: J. Munroe, 1845.
Alter, Cecil. "The Utah War Journal of Albert Tracy, 1858–1860." *Utah Historical Quarterly* 13 (1945).
Anderson, Jay. Interview. Providence, Utah, September 18, 2006.
Arave, Lynn. "Some Myths Accompany Stories of Pioneers' Arrival." *Deseret News*, July 24, 2008 ("Mormon Times" section).
Archer, Patience Loader. *Recollections of Past Days: The Autobiography of Patience Loader Rozsa Archer*. Ed. Sandra Ailey Petree. Logan: Utah State University Press, 2006.
Arnold, Sam'l P. *Eating Up the Santa Fe Trail*. Niwot: University Press of Colorado, 1990.
Arrington, Leonard. *Great Basin Kingdom: An Economic History of the Latter-Day Saints, 1830–1900*. Cambridge, Mass: Harvard University Press, 1958.
Bagley, Will. "One Long Funeral March: A Revisionist History of the Mormon Handcart Disasters." *Journal of Mormon History* 35:1 (Winter 2009).
Baker, Shane A. *At Rest in Zion: The Archaeology of Salt Lake City's First Pioneer Cemetery*. Occasional Paper No. 14. Provo: Brigham Young University Museum of Peoples and Cultures, 2010.
Ballard, Henry. "Journal of Henry Ballard." Logan: Utah State University, Library Special Collections.
Bancroft, Hubert Howe. *History of California*. 7 vols. San Francisco: A. L. Bancroft & Co., 1886–90.
———. *The Works of Hubert Howe Bancroft, vol. 26: History of Utah*. San Francisco: A. L. Bancroft & Co., 1890.
Barnes, Claude Teancum. *The Grim Years, or, The Life of Emily Stewart Barnes*. Kaysville, Utah: Inland Printing, 1964.
Baxter, Elizabeth. "Personal History." WPA Oral History Project. Salt Lake City: Utah State History Archives.
Beecher, Catharine Esther. *Miss Beecher's Domestic Receipt Book: Designed as a Supplement to Her Treatise on Domestic Economy*. New York: Harper & Brothers, 1850.

Beeton, Mrs. [Isabella Maria]. *Beeton's Book of Household Management*. London: S. O. Beeton, 1861.

Bell, Stella Jaques. *Life History and Writings of John Jaques*. Rexburg, Idaho: Ricks College Press, 1978.

Berge, Dale L. "Lower Goshen: Archaeology of a Mormon Pioneer Town." *Brigham Young University Studies* 30:2 (1990).

Black, William Morley. "Journal." Typescript. M270, M82, vol. 11. Provo, Utah: Brigham Young University Special Collections.

Bond, John. "Handcarts West in '56." Typescript. Salt Lake City: LDS Archives.

Bott, Elizabeth. "Life History of Elizabeth Bott." Salt Lake City: Daughters of Utah Pioneers Memorial Museum.

Braegger, Ken. Interview. Providence, Utah, July 9, 2009.

Brimhall, George W. *The Workers of Utah*. Provo, Utah: Enquirer Company, 1889.

Buckley, Newman. "Diary." In *Treasures of Pioneer History*, ed. Kate B. Carter, vol. 4. 6 vols. Salt Lake City: Daughters of Utah Pioneers Memorial Museum, 1952–57.

Burton, Richard F. *City of the Saints* (1862). Ed. Fawn Brodie. New York: Knopf, 1963.

Call, Anson. "Journal." Ogden, Utah: Weber State University Library Special Collections.

Carter, D. Robert. "A History of Commercial Fishing on Utah Lake." MA thesis, Brigham Young University, 1969.

Carter, Kate B. *The Chase Mill, 1852*. Salt Lake City: Utah Printing Company, 1957.

———. Kate B. Carter Collection. Salt Lake City: Daughters of Utah Pioneers Memorial Museum.

Catalogue of the Utah Territorial Library. Great Salt Lake City, Utah: Brigham H. Young, Printer, 1852. Facsimile copy courtesy of Stephen A. Shepherd, 2007.

Chase, Alvin Wood. *Dr. Chase's Recipes, or Information for Everybody*. Ann Arbor, Mich.: Chase, 1864.

Cheney, Susan Stauffer. Interview. Bountiful, Utah, June 10, 2009.

Christensen, Hans. "Memoirs." Salt Lake City: Utah State History Archives.

Clark, Caroline Hopkins. "Diary of Caroline Hopkins Clark and Letters to England." MSS 114, Box 6, Fd4. Logan: Utah State University, Library Special Collections.

Clayton, William. *The Latter-Day Saints' Emigrants' Guide*. St. Louis: Chambers & Knapp, 1848.

———. *William Clayton's Journal: A Daily Record of the Journey of the Original Company of "Mormon" Pioneers from Nauvoo, Illinois, to the Valley of the Great Salt Lake*. Salt Lake City: Deseret News, 1921.

Collins, Angelina Maria. *The Great Western Cookbook, or Table Receipts, Adapted to Western Housewifery*. New York: A. S. Barnes & Co., 1857.

Conant, James Bryant, ed. *Pasteur's and Tyndall's Study of Spontaneous Generation*. Harvard Case Histories in Experimental Science. Cambridge, Mass.: Harvard University Press, 1959.

Crosby, Caroline Barnes. *No Place to Call Home: The 1807–1857 Life Writings of Caroline Barnes Crosby, Chronicler of Outlying Mormon Communities*. Ed. Edward Lyman et al. Logan: Utah State University Press, 2005.

Daughters of Utah Pioneers. *Heart Throbs of the West*. Ed. Kate B. Carter. 12 vols. Salt Lake City: Daughters of Utah Pioneers, 1939–1951.

Davidis, Henriette. *Henriette Davidis' Practical Cook Book Compiled for the United States from the Thirty-fifth German Edition*. Milwaukee, Wis.: C. N. Caspar, Book Emporium, and H. H. Zahn & Co., Printers & Publishers, 1896.

Dee, Annie Taylor. *Memories of a Pioneer*. [Salt Lake City?: n.p., 1931?] Ogden, Utah: Weber State University Library Special Collections.

Deseret Agricultural and Manufacturing Society. "Report for 1863." Salt Lake City: This Is the Place Heritage Park Archives.

Deseret Recipes. Salt Lake City: Church of Jesus Christ of Latter-Day Saints, 1981.

Dixon, Loleta. "Life History of William James." Typescript. Salt Lake City: Daughters of Utah Pioneers Memorial Museum.

Douglass, Mary. "Deciphering a Meal." In *Implicit Meanings: Essays in Anthropology*. Boston: Routledge & Kegan Paul, 1975.

Duke, Donald. "Sourdough: Yeast of the American West." *Branding Iron* 153 (December 1983). Los Angeles: Westerners Corral.

Eagan, Howard L. *Pioneering the West*. Richmond, Utah: Eagan Estate, 1917.

Edison, Carol. "The Role of Food at Two Utah Homecoming Celebrations." In *We Gather Together: Food and Festival in American Life*, ed. Theodore C. Humphrey and Lin T. Humphrey. Ann Arbor: University of Michigan Research Press, 1988.

Ellet, Elizabeth Fries. *The Practical Housekeeper: A Cyclopaedia of Domestic Economy*. New York: Stringer & Townsend, 1857.

An Enduring Legacy. Ed. Kate B. Carter. 12 vols. Salt Lake City: Daughters of Utah Pioneers, 1978–89.

Evans, Oliver. *The Young Mill-wright and Miller's Guide*. Philadelphia, 1795.

Fairbanks, John. "Diary." Salt Lake City: University of Utah Special Collections.

Farmer's Oracle. Ed. Joseph Ellis Johnson. Spring Lake Villa, Utah. Salt Lake City: University of Utah Special Collections.

Foley, Vincent. "Salt Lake City Social Hall Summary." N.p., n.d. M282.2, s678, 1978–80. Salt Lake City: LDS Archives.

Gardner, Nathan Hale. *Alma Helaman Hale: History and Genealogy*. 2nd ed. Vol. 1. Centerville, Utah: Published by the author, 2001.

Garrard, Lewis H. *Wah-To-Yah and the Taos Trail*. Norman: University of Oklahoma Press, 1955.

"George Washington Brown—Frontiersman." In *Our Pioneer Heritage*, comp. Kate B. Carter, vol. 2. 20 vols. Salt Lake City: Daughters of Utah Pioneers, 1958–77.

Greer, Catherine Ellen Camp. "Reminiscences." Unpublished manuscript. Salt Lake City: LDS Archives.

Griffiths, John. *Tea: The Drink That Changed the World*. London: Andrew Deutsch, 2007.

Hafen, LeRoy R. *Handcarts to Zion*. Glendale, Calif.: A. H. Clark Co., 1960.

———. "Utah Food Supplies Sold to the Pioneer Settlers of Colorado." *Utah Historical Quarterly* 4:2 (1931): 2.

Hafen, Mary Ann Stuki. *Reflections of a Handcart Pioneer of 1860*. Denver, Colo.: Privately published, 1938. Ogden, Utah: Weber State University Library Special Collections.

Hale, Aroet L. "Diary [Autobiography] of Aroet L. Hale." Typescript. Provo, Utah: Brigham Young University, Harold B. Lee Library Special Collections.

Hale, Sarah Josepha Buell. *The Ladies' New Book of Cookery*. New York: H. Long & Brother, 1852.

Hales, Eliza Brockbank. "Reminiscences of a Pioneer Childhood." Logan: Utah State University, Library Special Collections.

Hals, Hans Jensen, "Life Writings of Hans Jensen Hals." Trans. William Mulder. Typescript. Salt Lake City: Utah State History Archives.

Hammond, Lorraine. "Var Sa God." Logan: Utah State University, Library Special Collections.

Hanks, Sydney Alvarus, and Ephraim K. Hanks. *Scouting for the Mormons on the Great Frontier*. Salt Lake City: Deseret News Press, 1948.

Hargis, Barbara Lee. "A Folk History of the Manti Temple: A Study of the Folklore and Traditions Connected with the Settlement of Manti, Utah, and the Building of the Temple." Master's thesis. Provo, Utah: Brigham Young University, 1968.

Heywood, Martha Spence. *Not by Bread Alone: The Journal of Martha Spence Heywood, 1850–1856*. Ed. Juanita Brooks. Salt Lake City: Utah State Historical Society, 1978.

"History of Brigham Young." Manuscript. Salt Lake City: LDS Archives.

Howland, Esther. *The New England Economical Housekeeper, and Family Receipt Book*. Cincinnati: H. W. Derby, 1845.

"Interviews with Living Pioneers: Copied by the BYU Library, 1939." Provo, Utah: Brigham Young University Special Collections.

Irving, John Treat, Jr. *Indian Sketches*. Ed. J. F. McDermott. Norman: University of Oklahoma Press, 1955.

Israelson, Andrew. *Utah Pioneering*. Salt Lake City: Deseret News Press, 1938.

Jenson, Andrew. *Autobiography of Andrew Jenson*. Salt Lake City: Deseret News Press, 1938.

———. *The Building of Utah and Her Neighbors*. No. 95. Salt Lake City: Deseret News Press [n.d.]. Ogden, Utah: Weber State University Library Special Collections.

Johnson, J. E. "Seed List." Salt Lake City: LDS Church Archives.

Jones, Daniel Webster. *Forty Years among the Indians*. Salt Lake City: Juvenile Instructor Office, 1890. Ogden, Utah: Weber State University Library Special Collections.

Journal of Discourses, by Brigham Young, President of the Church of Jesus Christ of Latter-Day Saints, His Two Counselors, the Twelve Apostles, and Others. 26 vols. Liverpool: Franklin D. Richards, 1854–89.

Kalcik, Susan. "Ethnic Foodways in America: Symbol and the Performance of Identity." In *Ethnic and Regional Foodways in the United States: The Performance of Group Identity*, ed. Linda Keller Brown and Kay Mussell. Knoxville: University of Tennessee Press, 1984.

Kane, Elizabeth Dennistoun Wood. *Twelve Mormon Homes Visited in Succession on a Journey through Utah to Arizona*. Salt Lake City: Tanner Trust Fund, University of Utah Library [1974].

Kitchen Treasures, 1830–1980: Roy 13th Ward Sesquicentennial. Ogden, Utah: n.p., 1980. Ogden, Utah: Weber State University Library Special Collections.

Lancaster, Dennis. "Dixie Wine." Master's thesis. Provo, Utah: Brigham Young University, 1972.

Larsen, Lorena Washburn. *Autobiography of Lorena Washburn Larsen, Printed for Her Children*. Provo, Utah: Brigham Young University Press, n.d. Salt Lake City: LDS Church Archives.

Leader, Daniel, and Judith Blahnik. *Bread Alone: Bold Fresh Loaves from Your Own Hands*. New York: William Morrow & Company, 1993.

Lee, John D. *Journals of John D. Lee, 1846–47 and 1859*. Ed. Charles Kelly. Salt Lake City: University of Utah Press, 1984.

Leslie, Eliza. *Directions for Cookery, in Its Various Branches*. Philadelphia: E. L. Carey & Hart, 1853.

———. *The Lady's Receipt Book: A Useful Companion for Large or Small Families*. Philadelphia: Carey & Hart, 1847.

Lewis, Paige. "From Germany with Love." Folk Coll 8 Grad: Box 18, 92-002. Collected by Paige Lewis. Fife Folklore Archives, Special Collections and Archives. Logan: Utah State University.

"Life History of Ole Poulson." Typescript (n.d.). Brigham City, Utah: Brigham City Library.

Lindquist, Craig Allen. "Garnet Chili Potatoes." *Vegetables of Interest* [online resource] (Sonoma County, California). Hosted online at http://vegetablesofinterest.typepad.com/vegetablesofinterest/2007/08/garnet-chili-po.html.

Lindquist, John. "Sauerkraut Fermentation." In *Laboratory Manual for Food Microbiology Laboratory*. Madison: University of Wisconsin, 1998. Hosted online at http://www.jlindquist.net/generalmicro/324sauerkraut.html.

Lyman, Eliza Maria Partridge. *Eliza Maria Partridge Journal*. Ed. Scott Partridge. Provo, Utah: Grandin Book Co., 2003.

Lyman, Paul D. *The Willie Handcart Company: Their Day-by-Day Experiences, Including Trail Maps and Driving Directions*. Provo, Utah: Brigham Young University Studies, 2006.

Madsen, Betty M., and Brigham D. Madsen. *North to Montana: Jehus, Bullwhackers and Mule Skinners on the Montana Trail*. Salt Lake City: University of Utah Press, 1980.

Madsen, Peder. "Journal." Provo, Utah: Brigham Young University Special Collections.

Madsen, Peter. "The Grasshopper Famine—The Mullet and the Trout, Part I." In *The Improvement Era*, vol. 13 (1910). Salt Lake City: Church of Jesus Christ of Latter-Day Saints.

McBride, Heber Robert. "Autobiography." MSS 501. Provo, Utah: Brigham Young University.

McCune, Sarah Elizabeth Caroline Scott. "Life History." Typescript. Salt Lake City: Daughters of Utah Pioneers Memorial Museum.

Meeks, Priddy. *Journal of Priddy Meeks*. N.p., n.d. [1900s]. Ogden, Utah: Weber State University Library Special Collections.

Montell, William. *The Saga of Coe Ridge: A Study in Oral History*. Knoxville: University of Tennessee Press, 1970.

Morgan, Dale. *The Great Salt Lake*. New York: Bobbs-Merrill, 1947.

Mormon Pioneer National Historic Trail: Historic Resource Study. National Parks Service. http://www.nps.gov/history/history/online_books/mopi/hrs5.htm.

Morris, Mary Lois Walker. *Before the Manifesto: The Life Writings of Mary Lois Walker Morris*. Ed. Melissa Lambert Milewski. Logan: Utah State University, 2007.

Mulder, William. *Homeward to Zion: The Mormon Migration from Scandinavia*. Minneapolis: University of Minnesota Press, 2000.

Olsen, Livy. "Reminiscences." WPA Oral History. Box 8, MSS B289. Salt Lake City: Utah State History Archives.

Our Pioneer Heritage. Ed. Kate B. Carter. 20 vols. Salt Lake City: Daughters of Utah Pioneers, 1958–77.

Parkinson, Eleanor. *The Complete Confectioner, Pastry-Cook, and Baker*. Philadelphia: J. B. Lippincott & Co., 1864.

Piercy, Frederick. *Route from Liverpool to Great Salt Lake Valley*. Liverpool: Franklin D. Richards, 1855.

Pioneer Recipes. Salt Lake City: Deseret News Press, 1950.

Pollan, Michael. *The Botany of Desire*. New York: Random House, 2001.

Powell, Edith Madsen. "History of Bishop Peter Madsen." WPA Oral History, 1941. Salt Lake City: Utah State History Archives.

Pratt, Louisa Barnes. *The History of Louisa Barnes Pratt: Being the Autobiography of a Mormon Missionary Widow and Pioneer*. Ed. S. George Ellsworth. Logan: Utah State University Press, 1998.

Pratt, Parley P. *Autobiography*. Arlington, Va.: Stratford Books, 2005.

Providence History Committee. *Providence and Her People: A History of Providence, Utah, 1857–1974*. Providence, Utah: K. W. Watkins & Sons, 1974.

Remy, Jules, and Julius Brenchley. *A Journey to Great-Salt-Lake-City*. London: W. Jeffs, 1861.

Rogers, Ruth Page. "Diary of Ruth Page Rogers." Typescript. Logan: Utah State University Special Collections.

Rowley, Anna Jewel. "Life History." Salt Lake City: Daughters of Utah Pioneers Memorial Museum.

Russell, Osborne. *Journal of a Trapper*. Lincoln: University of Nebraska Press, 1965.

Sanderson, J. M. *The Complete Cook*. Philadelphia: J. B. Lippincott, 1864.

Savage, Levi. "Diary." Typescript. Salt Lake City: Utah State History Archives.

Scarlett, Timothy James. "Potting in Zion." Ph.D. dissertation. University of Nevada, Reno, 2002.

Sessions, Patty Bartlett. *Mormon Midwife: The 1846–1888 Diaries of Patty Bartlett Sessions*. Ed. Donna Toland Smart. Logan: Utah State University Press, 1997.

Slaughter, William, and Michael Landon. *Trail of Hope*. Salt Lake City: Shadow Mountain Press, 1997.

Snodgrass, Mary Ellen. *Encyclopedia of Kitchen History*. New York: Taylor & Francis Books, 2004.

Spencer, Clarissa Young. *Brigham Young at Home*. Salt Lake City: Deseret Book, 1940.

Stone, Robert G., and David M. Hinkley (The Fat Little Pudding Boys). *The Pudding Book: Authentic American and English Pudding Recipes from 1782–1882 with Instructions for the Modern Kitchen*. Lee's Summit, Mo.: Fat Little Pudding Boys Press, 1996.

Tanner, J. M. *Biographical Sketch of James Jensen*. Salt Lake City: Deseret News Press, 1911. Salt Lake City: Utah State History Archives.

Thomas, Mark. "Grafts from a Lost Orchard." *Utah Historical Quarterly* 74:3 (2006): 231–40.

Thomsen, Anders. "History of Anders Thomsen, by Himself." Salt Lake City: Utah State History Archives.

Thorup, Rae, Ruth Thorup, and Marne Thorup. "Danish Cooking School Recipes: Grenaa, Denmark, about 1847." Salt Lake City: Utah State History Archives, 1978.

"Three Important Manuscripts." In *Our Pioneer Heritage*, ed. Kate B. Carter, 11:269–332. 20 vols. Salt Lake City: Daughters of Utah Pioneers, 1958–77.

Tigner-Wise, Lori F. "Skeletal Analysis of a Mormon Pioneer Population from Salt Lake Valley, Utah." M.S. thesis. Laramie: University of Wyoming, 1989.

Told by the Pioneers. Vol. 2. Olympia, Wash.: WPA, 1937.

Tyler, Daniel. *A Concise History of the Mormon Battalion in the Mexican War, 1846–1848*. Glorieta, NM: Rio Grande Press, 1980.

Unruh, John D. *The Plains Across: The Overland Emigrants and the Trans-Mississippi West, 1840–1860*. Chicago: University of Illinois Press, 1979.

Utah Cooperative Extension Service. *Old West Heritage Recipes*. New Circular Series, no. 374. Logan: Utah Cooperative Extension Service, n.d. [1976?].

Vance, Del. *Beer in the Beehive: A History of Brewing in Utah*. Salt Lake City: Dream Garden Press, 2008.

Wahlquist, Wayne L. "Settlement Processes in the Mormon Core Area, 1847–1890." Ph.D. dissertation. Lincoln: University of Nebraska, 1974.

Walker, Charles. "Journal." Typescript. Salt Lake City: Utah State History Archives.

Wannacott, Pearl. "Life History of Annie Underwood." Salt Lake City: Daughters of Utah Pioneers Memorial Museum.

Wheeler, Diane. "Life History of Harriet Amelia Folsom Young." Salt Lake City: Daughters of Utah Pioneers Memorial Museum.

White, Mary O. "A History of William and Ann Greenwood by Their Daughter Mary O. White." MSS 114, Box 6, Fd 6. Logan: Utah State University, Library Special Collections.

Whitney, Orson F. *History of Utah*. 4 vols. Salt Lake City: G. Q. Cannon, 1892–1904.

Wilhelm, Clarissa. "Diary." Typescript. Logan: Utah State University Special Collections.

Williams, Jacqueline. *Wagon Wheel Kitchens: Food on the Oregon Trail*. Lawrence: University Press of Kansas, 1993.

Wilson, Elijah Nicholas. *Among the Shoshones*. Salt Lake City: Skelton Publishing Company, 1910.

Wood, Ed. *Classic Sourdoughs: A Home Baker's Handbook*. Berkeley: Ten Speed Press, 2001.

Woodruff, Wilford. *Wilford Woodruff's Journal, 1833–1898*. Ed. Scott G. Kenny. Salt Lake City: Signature Books, 1983.

Young, Brigham. *Diary of Brigham Young, 1857*. Ed. Everett Cooley. Salt Lake City: Tanner Trust Fund, University of Utah Library, 1980.

Young, Lorenzo. "Diary of Lorenzo Dow Young." *Utah Historical Quarterly* 14 (1946).

INDEX

wolf, and eating of, 80–81

Wonnacott, Pearl, 14

Woodruff, Wilford: breakfast on trail, 46; Christmas dinner, 136; eats oysters, 135; fishing, 86, 88; and fruit varieties, 29, 134; and grape roots, 134; makes molasses, 38; makes wine, 160; shares cake, 137; shoots ducks, 88–89;

Word of Wisdom, 113, 153, 155, 169, 174, 178, 181n6 (chapter 1)

yeast, 63–66, 161–62, 179; gathering, 65

Yorkshire Pudding, 116

Young, Amelia. *See* Folsom, Harriet Amelia.

Young, Brigham: favorite foods, 129; and feasting, 1–3, 132–34; and household foods, 129; and fruit trees, 27; and Pioneer Day, 1–2; portrait of, 136; and shortcakes, 145; and squab, 129–30; and tea, 158; and wine mission, 164–65

Young, Clarissa. *See* Spencer, Clarissa Young

Young, Emily Partridge, 129

Young, Feramorz, 134

Young, Lorenzo, 47

Young, Lucy, 145

Young, Richard, 134

Zwiebelcuchen (**Onion Cobbler**), 115